T0192221

Communications
in Computer and Information Science   1669

More information about this series at https://link.springer.com/bookseries/7899

Maosong Sun · Guilin Qi · Kang Liu ·
Jiadong Ren · Bin Xu · Yansong Feng ·
Yongbin Liu · Yubo Chen (Eds.)

Knowledge Graph and Semantic Computing: Knowledge Graph Empowers the Digital Economy

7th China Conference, CCKS 2022
Qinhuangdao, China, August 24–27, 2022
Revised Selected Papers

Springer

Editors

Maosong Sun
Tsinghua University
Beijing, China

Guilin Qi
Southeast University
Nanjing, China

Kang Liu
Institute of Automation
Beijing, China

Jiadong Ren
Yanshan University
Qinhuangdao, China

Bin Xu
Tsinghua University
Beijing, China

Yansong Feng
Peking University
Beijing, China

Yongbin Liu
University of South China
Hunan, China

Yubo Chen
Institute of Automation
Beijing, China

ISSN 1865-0929   ISSN 1865-0937 (electronic)
Communications in Computer and Information Science
ISBN 978-981-19-7595-0   ISBN 978-981-19-7596-7 (eBook)
https://doi.org/10.1007/978-981-19-7596-7

This Springer imprint is published by the registered company Springer Nature Singapore Pte Ltd.
The registered company address is: 152 Beach Road, #21-01/04 Gateway East, Singapore 189721, Singapore

Preface

This volume contains the papers presented at CCKS 2022: the China Conference on Knowledge Graph and Semantic Computing held during August 24–27, 2022, in Qinhuangdao.

CCKS is organized by the Technical Committee on Language and Knowledge Computing of the Chinese Information Processing Society. CCKS is the merger of two previously-held relevant forums, i.e., the Chinese Knowledge Graph Symposium (CKGS) and the Chinese Semantic Web and Web Science Conference (CSWS). CKGS was previously held in Beijing (2013), Nanjing (2014), and Yichang (2015). CSWS was first held in Beijing in 2006 and has been the main forum for research on Semantic (Web) technologies in China for a decade. Since 2016, CCKS brings together researchers from both forums and covers wider fields, including knowledge graphs, Semantic Web, linked data, natural language processing, knowledge representation, graph databases, information retrieval, and knowledge aware machine learning. It aims to become the top forum on knowledge graph and Semantic technologies for Chinese researchers and practitioners from academia, industry, and government.

The theme of this year was "Knowledge Graph Empowers the Digital Economy". Enclosing this theme, the conference scheduled various activities, including keynotes, academic workshops, industrial forums, evaluation and competition, knowledge graph summit reviews, academic paper presentations, etc. The conference invited Maosong Sun (Full Professor of the Department of Computer Science and Technology, Tsinghua University), Hong-Gee Kim (the CIO of Seoul National University), and Mark Steedman (Professor of Cognitive Science in the School of Informatics at the University of Edinburgh) to present the latest progress and development trends in natural language processing, data-centric university and inference in question answering, respectively. The conference also invited industrial practitioners to share their experiences and promote industry-university-research cooperation.

As for peer-reviewed papers, 100 submissions were received in the following six areas:

- Knowledge Representation and Reasoning
- Knowledge Acquisition and Knowledge Base Construction
- Linked Data, Knowledge Fusion, and Knowledge Graph Management
- Natural Language Understanding and Semantic Computing
- Knowledge Graph Applications
- Knowledge Graph Open Resources

During the double-blind reviewing process, each submission was assigned to at least three Program Committee members. The committee decided to accept 37 full papers (17 papers in English). The CCIS volume contains revised versions of the 17 English full papers.

The hard work and close collaboration of a number of people have contributed to the success of this conference. We would like to thank the Organizing Committee and Program Committee members for their support, and the authors and participants who are the primary reason for the success of this conference. We also thank Springer for their trust and for publishing the proceedings of CCKS 2022.

Finally, we appreciate the sponsorships from EpiK Tech and Meituan as chief sponsors, Tencent Technology and Haizhi Xingtu Technology as diamond sponsors, Global Tone Communication Technology, Oppo, and Haiyizhi Information Technology as platinum sponsors, Ant Group, Xiaomi, Baidu, TOP KG, Vesoft, Yidu Cloud, Huawei, IFLYTEK, and 360 Artificial Intelligence Institute as gold sponsors, Zhipu.ai, Yunfu Technology, and Magic Data as silver sponsors, and OneConnect Technology as evaluation sponsors.

August 2022

Maosong Sun
Guilin Qi
Kang Liu
Jiadong Ren
Bin Xu
Yansong Feng
Yongbin Liu
Yubo Chen

Organization

CCKS 2022 was organized by the Technical Committee on Language and Knowledge Computing of the Chinese Information Processing Society.

Honorary General Chair

Maosong Sun — Tsinghua University, China

General Chair

Guilin Qi — Southeast University, China
Kang Liu — Institute of Automation, Chinese Academy of Sciences, China
Jiadong Ren — Yanshan University, China

Program Committee Chairs

Bin Xu — Tsinghua University, China
Yansong Feng — Peking University, China

Local Chairs

Yuefeng Qi — Yanshan University, China
Changwu Wang — Yanshan University, China
Peiliang Wu — Yanshan University, China
Jianzhou Feng — Yanshan University, China

Publicity Chairs

Jianfeng Du — Guangdong University of Foreign Studies, China
Hai Wan — Sun Yat-sen University, China

Publication Chairs

Yongbin Liu — University of South China, China
Yubo Chen — Institute of Automation, Chinese Academy of Sciences, China

Tutorial Chairs

Qili Zhu   Shanghai Jiao Tong University, China
Ming Liu   Harbin Institute of Technology, China

Evaluation Chairs

Meng Wang   Southeast University, China
Ningyu Zhang   Zhejiang University, China

Top Conference Reviewing Chairs

Jing Zhang   Renmin University of China, China
Quan Wang   Beijing University of Posts and
                                     Telecommunications, China

Young Scholar Forum Chairs

Zhichun Wang   Beijing Normal University, China
Wen Zhang   Zhejiang University, China

Poster/Demo Chairs

Lin Wang   Yanshan University, China
Jibing Gong   Yanshan University, China

Sponsorship Chairs

Junyu Lin   Institute of Information Engineering, Chinese
                                     Academy of Sciences, China
Lei Hou   Tsinghua University, China

Industry Track Chairs

Zuopeng Liu   Suning, China
Zhixu Li   Fudan University, China

Website Chair

Yuanzhe Zhang   Institute of Automation, Chinese Academy of
                                     Sciences, China

Best Paper Award Committee

Houfeng Wang	Peking University, China
Xianpei Han	Institute of Software, Chinese Academy of Sciences, China
Gong Cheng	Nanjing University, China
Xianling Mao	Beijing Institute of Technology, China
Nan Duan	Microsoft Research, China
Shujian Huang	Nanjing University, China

Area Chairs

Knowledge Graph Representation and Reasoning

Xiang Zhao	National University of Defense Technology, China
Yankai Lin	WeChat, Tencent, China

Knowledge Acquisition and Knowledge Graph Construction

Liang Hong	Wuhan University, China
Xiao Ding	Harbin Institute of Technology, China

Linked Data, Knowledge Integration, and Knowledge Graph Storage Management

Youhuan Li	Hunan University, China
Bo Xu	Donghua University, China

Natural Language Understanding and Semantic Computing

Chongyang Tao	Microsoft Software Technology Center Asia, China
Richong Zhang	Beihang University, China

Knowledge Graph Applications (Semantic Search, Question Answering, Dialogue, Decision Support, and Recommendation)

Xin Zhao	Renmin University of China, China
Zhen Jia	Southwest Jiaotong University, China

Knowledge Graph Open Resources

Jie Bao	Memory Connected, China
Tianxing Wu	Southeast University, China

Program Committee

Bi, Sheng	Southeast University, China
Bibo, Cai	Harbin Institute of Technology, China
Bingfeng, Luo	Bytedance, China
Bo, Xu	Donghua University, China
Bowen, Chen	Harbin Insititute of Technology, China
Can, Xu	Microsoft Software Technology Center Asia, China
Chang, Liu	Peking University, China
Chengzhi, Zhang	Nanjing University of Science and Technology, China
Chongyang, Tao	Microsoft Corporation, China
Chuan, Shi	Beijing University of Posts and Telecommunications, China
Cuijuan, Xia	Shanghai Library, China
Cuiyun, Gao	The Chinese University of Hong Kong, China
Deming, Ye	Tsinghua University, China
Dongfang, Li	Harbin Institute of Technology, Shenzhen, China
Gang, Wu	Northeastern University, China
Gerhard, Weikum	Max Planck Institute for Informatics, Germany
Gong, Cheng	Nanjing University, China
Guoqiang, Li	Shanghai Jiao Tong University, China
Hai, Wan	Sun Yat-sen University, China
Haiyun, Jiang	Tencent, China
Han, Yang	Peking University, China
Hongyu, Wang	Wuhan University of Technology, China
Huaiyu, Wan	Beijing Jiaotong University, China
Huiying, Li	Southeast University, China
Jia, Li	Peking University, China
Jia-Chen, Gu	University of Science and Technology of China, China
Jiaqi, Li	Harbin Institute of Technology, China
Jiaqing, Liang	Fudan University, China
Jiazhan, Feng	Peking University, China
Jie, Bao	Memory Connected, China
Jie, Hu	Southwest Jiaotong University, China
Jihao, Shi	Harbin Institute of Technology, China

Jing, Zhang	Renmin University of China, China
Jinglong, Gao	Harbin Institute of Technology, China
Jingping, Liu	East China University of Science and Technology, China
Jinming, Zhao	Renmin University of China, China
Jiwei, Ding	Nanjing University, China
Jixin, Zhang	Hubei University of Technology, China
Jun, Pang	Wuhan University of Science and Technology, China
Junfan, Chen	Beihang University, China
Junshen, Huang	PingCAP, China
Junshuang, Wu	Beihang University, China
Junwen, Duan	Central South University, China
Junyi, Li	Renmin University of China, China
Kai, Zhang	Zhejiang University City College, China
Kai, Xiong	Harbin Institute of Techonology, China
Kang, Xu	Nanjing University of Posts and Telecommunications, China
Kun, Zhou	Peking University, China
Le, Wu	Hefei University of Technology, China
Li, Li	Chongqing University, China
Li, Du	Harbin Institute of Technology, China
Liang, Hong	Wuhan University, China
Liang, Pang	Institute of Computing Technology, Chinese Academy of Sciences, China
Lijun, Lan	Tencent, China
Lili, Yao	Peking University, China
Meng, Wang	Southeast University, China
Ming, Zhong	Wuhan University, China
Ming, Liu	Harbin Institute of Technology, China
Ningyu, Zhang	Zhejiang University, China
Peng, Peng	Hunan University, China
Peng, Peng	Wuhan University, China
Philipp, Christmann	Max Planck Institute for Informatics, Germany
Qi, Dai	Southwest Jiaotong University, China
Qiannan, Zhu	Renmin University of China, China
Qing, Liu	CSIRO, Australia
Qingfu, Zhu	Harbin Institute of Technology, China
Qiyu, Wu	Peking University, China
Quan, Lu	Wuhan University, China
Richong, Zhang	Beihang University, China
Ruifang, He	Tianjin University, China

Ruijian, Xu	Peking University, China
Ruijie, Wang	University of Zurich, Switzerland
Shen, Gao	Peking University, China
Shengrong, Gong	Changshu Institute of Technology, China
Shuqing, Bian	Renmin University of China, China
Tao, Peng	University of Illinois Urbana-Champaign, USA
Tao, Shen	Microsoft, China
Tianxing, Wu	Southeast University, China
Tianyang, Shao	National University of Defense Technology, China
Tingting, Wu	Harbin Institute of Technology, China
Tongtong, Wu	Southeast University, China
Wei, Hu	Nanjing University, China
Wei, Shen	Nankai University, China
Weiguo, Zheng	Fudan University, China
Weixin, Zeng	National University of Defense Technology, China
Weizhuo, Li	Nanjing University of Posts and Telecommunications, China
Wen, Zhang	Zhejiang University, China
Wen, Hua	University of Queensland, China
Wenpeng, Lu	Qilu University of Technology, China
Wenqiang, Liu	Tencent, China
Xiang, Zhao	National University of Defense Technology, China
Xiang, Zhang	Southeast University, China
Xiao, Ding	Harbin Institute of Technology, China
Xiaobo, Zhang	Southwest Jiaotong University, China
Xiaohui, Han	Shandong Computer Science Center, China
Xiaosen, Li	Tencent, China
Xiaowang, Zhang	Tianjin University, China
Xiaozhi, Wang	Tsinghua University, China
Xin, Zhao	Renmin University of China, China
Xinhuan, Chen	Tencent, China
Xiuying, Chen	Peking University, China
Xu, Lei	Wuhan University, China
Xue-Feng, Xi	Suzhou University of Science and Technology, China
Xueliang, Zhao	Peking University, China
Xusheng, Luo	Alibaba Group, China
Xutao, Li	Harbin Institute of Technology, China
Yang, Li	Northeast Forestry University, China

Yang, Liu	Wuhan University, China
Yankai, Lin	WeChat, Tencent, China
Yanxia, Qin	Donghua University, China
Yaojie, Lu	Institute of Software, Chinese Academy of Sciences, China
Yinglong, Ma	North China Electric Power University, China
Yixin, Cao	Singapore Management University, Singapore
Yongbin, Liu	University of South China, China
Yongpan, Sheng	Chongqing University, China
Youhuan, Li	Hunan University, China
Yuan, Yao	Tsinghua University, China
Yuanyuan, Zhu	Wuhan University, China
Yubo, Chen	Institute of Automation, Chinese Academy of Sciences, China
Yufei, Wang	Macquarie University, Australia
Yuxia, Geng	Zhejiang University, China
Yuxiang, Wang	Hangzhou Dianzi University, China
Yuxiang, Wu	University College London, UK
Zequn, Sun	Nanjing University, China
Zhen, Jia	Southwest Jiaotong University, China
Zhixu, Li	Fudan University, China
Zhiyi, Luo	Zhejiang Sci-Tech University, China
Zhongyang, Li	Harbin Institute of Technology, China
Zhuosheng, Zhang	Shanghai Jiao Tong University, China
Ziyang, Chen	National University of Defense Technology, China
Kai, Sun	Beihang University, China
Hui, Song	Donghua University, China
Yi, Zheng	Huawei Cloud, China

Sponsors

Chief Sponsor

Diamond Sponsors

Platinum Sponsors

Gold Sponsors

Silver Sponsors

Evaluation Track Sponsor

Contents

Natural Language Understanding and Semantic Computing

Knowledge Graph Applications

Knowledge Graph Open Resources

Knowledge Representation
and Reasoning

Investigating the Parallel Tractability of Knowledge Graph Reasoning via Boolean Circuits

Zhangquan Zhou[✉], Jun Liu, and Shijiao Tang

School of Information Science and Engineering, Nanjing Audit University Jinshen College, Nanjing, China
`quanzz1129@gmail.com`

Abstract. Symbolic based logic reasoning is always an important service for correctness sensitive applications built on knowledge graphs. To make reasoning efficient in practice, current research focuses on designing parallel reasoning algorithms or employing high-performance computing architectures, like neural networks. No matter what architecture we choose, the computational complexity of reasoning is upper-bounded by the PTime-completeness or higher ones that are not parallelly tractable. This means that the task of reasoning can be inherently sequential in the worst cases. In this paper, we investigate the parallel tractability of knowledge graph reasoning from the theoretical perspective. We focus on datalog rewritable knowledge graphs and work to identify the classes of datalog programs, for which, reasoning complies with the NC complexity that is parallelly tractable. To this end, we utilize the tool of *Boolean circuit* to obtain all the theoretical results given in this paper. One can utilize our results to check the parallel tractability of a given knowledge graph. Further, the Boolean circuits proposed in this paper can also be used to construct neural networks to perform knowledge graph reasoning.

1 Introduction

Knowledge graph reasoning plays an important role in downstream applications built on knowledge graphs (KGs) [7], such as query answering [15] and recommendation [27]. One line of studying knowledge graph reasoning proposes to embed knowledge graphs into vector space, and to perform reasoning by the means of vector operations [6,26] or tensor decompositions [20,28]. Although this line is further enhanced by deep neural networks [8,24] and symbolic methods [13,14], the issues of inaccuracy and weak interpretability of reasoning results remain unsolved [16]. Symbolic based logic reasoning, as the second line, is still the main choice for many correctness sensitive fields, e.g. medicine [29] and finance [10]. The accuracy and interpretability of logic reasoning can also be ensured in theory.

To make logic reasoning sufficiently efficient and scalable in practice, current works mainly employs parallel techniques. Several state-of-the-art parallel reasoning systems have been proposed, like RDFox [19] and OWLim [17], which

M. Sun et al. (Eds.): CCKS 2022, CCIS 1669, pp. 3–15, 2022.
https://doi.org/10.1007/978-981-19-7596-7_1

are designed for reasoning on KGs modeled by ontology languages [3]. Recently, deep neural networks have also been introduced to improve the efficiency of logic reasoning [4,9,23] (usually quoted by *logic neural networks*), since they naturally process data, i.e. vectors or tensors, in parallel. From the theoretic perspective, no matter what parallel architecture we choose, the task of reasoning has to comply with its inner computational complexity. According to [11], even for KGs modeled by lightweight logic languages, like RDFS [22] and datalog rewritable ontology languages [12], the PTIME-completeness or higher complexities can be reached. This indicates that reasoning on such KGs is not *parallelly tractable* [11], i.e., reasoning may be inherently sequential even on a parallel implementation. More precisely, the lack of parallel tractability may lead to uncontrolled time cost or distent sizes of neural networks. Thus, it is meaningful to illustrate, under what conditions, reasoning on KGs is parallelly tractable. The theoretical results can further guide engineers in creating large-scale KGs or constructing logic neural networks for which parallel tractability can be guaranteed for knowledge graph reasoning.

In this paper, we investigate the parallel tractability of knowledge graph reasoning from the theoretical perspective. We focus on datalog rewritable KGs for two reasons. Firstly, most KGs can be directly mapped to datalog predicates [5]. Specifically, a triple $\langle h, r, t \rangle$ (resp., the attribute A of entity e) in a KG can be translated to a 2-ary predicate in the form of $r(h, t)$ (resp., a unary predicate of the form $A(e)$) in a datalog program. In this way, user-defined datalog rules can be easily applied on KGs to compute new facts. The second reason is that datalog, as a fragment of first-order logic, enjoys strict definitions and has been comprehensively studied for data management [1]. We utilize the idea of the work [30] and specify the parallel tractability by the parallel complexity NC. That is, we aim to identify the class of datalog rewritable KGs such that reasoning is upper bounded by the complexity NC. The differences of our work to that of [30] lie in the following aspects.

- The work of [30] is restricted in *description logics*, i.e. DL-lite and $\mathcal{EL}^+$, while the results in this paper apply to general KGs that can be handled by datalog programs.
- The proofs given in [30] are built on irregular NC algorithms, which can hardly convince the readers to some extent. Since the NC complexity is formally defined on *NC circuits* that are the restricted versions of *Boolean circuits* [11], we strictly follow its definition and give all the proofs based on Boolean circuits.
- The results in this paper have wider range of usage compared to that of [30]. One can use our results to create parallel tractable KGs. On the other hand, the models of Boolean circuits given in this work can be used to transform knowledge graph reasoning to the computation of logic neural networks by applying the method given in [23].

The rest of the paper is organized as follows. In Sect. 2, we introduce some basic notions. We then define the NC circuits for reasoning on datalog programs in Sect. 3. We identify the parallelly tractable classes in Sect. 4. We discuss the usability of our theoretical results in Sect. 5 and conclude in Sect. 6. The technical report can be found at this address[1].

2   Background Knowledge

In this section, we introduce some notions that are used in this paper.

2.1   Datalog

In datalog [1], a *term* is a variable or a constant. An *atom* A is defined by $A \equiv p(t_1, ..., t_n)$ where p is a *predicate* (or *relational*) name, $t_1, ..., t_n$ are terms, and n is the arity of p. If all the terms in an atom A are constants, then A is called a *ground atom*. A datalog *rule* is of the following form[2]:

$$`B_1, ..., B_n \to H.'$$

where H is referred to the *head atom* and $B_1, ..., B_n$ the *body atoms*. A datalog program P consists of rules and facts. For an atom A, if each variable x in A is assigned by a constant in P, then A is called a *ground atom*. A *ground instantiation* of a rule is just defined on ground atoms. The ground instantiation of P, denoted by P^*, consists of all ground instantiations of rules in P. Furthermore we use N_P to denote the set of all possible ground atoms with respect to the constants occurring in P.

Knowledge graph reasoning can be transformed to the reasoning of datalog programs. Specifically, given a datalog program $\langle R, \mathbf{I} \rangle$, where R is a set of user-defined datalog rules and $\mathbf{I}$ contains all unary and 2-ary ground atoms mapped from a given KG. Let $T_R(\mathbf{I}) = \{H | \forall B_1, ..., B_k \to H \in R, B_i \in \mathbf{I}(1 \leq i \leq k)\}$, where $B_1, ..., B_k \to H$ is a ground instantiation of rule R; further let $T_R^0(\mathbf{I}) = \mathbf{I}$ and $T_R^i(\mathbf{I}) = T_R^{i-1}(\mathbf{I}) \cup T_R(T_R^{i-1}(\mathbf{I}))$ for each $i > 0$. The smallest integer n such that $T_R^n(\mathbf{I}) = T_R^{n+1}(\mathbf{I})$ is called *stage*, and the reasoning task refers to the computation of $T_R^n(\mathbf{I})$ with respect to R and $\mathbf{I}$. $T_R^n(\mathbf{I})$ is also called the *fixpoint* and denoted by $T_R^\omega(\mathbf{I})$. For any ground atom H, if $H \in T_R^\omega(\mathbf{I})$, we say that H is *derivable*. Further, for two ground atoms B and H, if the derivability of B implies the derivability of H, we say that H *derivably-depends* on B; we also say that there is a *derivability dependence* between H and B.

2.2   Boolean Circuit and the NC Complexity

A *Boolean Circuit* (circuit for short) is a computation model that has been widely used in the area of computational complexity due to its mathematical simplicity [2]. The circuits used in this paper are defined as follows.

---

[1] https://gitlab.com/p9324/CCKS2022.
[2] In datalog rules, a comma represents a Boolean conjunction '$\wedge$'.

Definition 1 *(Boolean Circuit).* A circuit $\mathcal{C}$ is a directed acyclic graph where all nodes are called *gates* and are labeled with $\vee$, $\wedge$ (i.e., the logical operations OR, AND)[3]. Each gate in $\mathcal{C}$ has several incoming edges and a unique outgoing edge.

For the *signals* or *variables* with only outgoing (resp., incoming) edges for any gate in a circuit $\mathcal{C}$, we call them *source variables* (resp., *sink variables*); for each gate, the incoming edges (resp., the outgoing edges) are called the *input variables* or *inputs* (resp., the *output variables* or *outputs*). The evaluation of $\mathcal{C}$ is initialized by assigning each source variable a truth value 1 (TRUE) or 0 (FALSE). Then, the evaluation of each variable x in $\mathcal{C}$, denoted by $\mathcal{C}(x)$, is then defined in the natural way by easily performing the Boolean operations. The *size* of $\mathcal{C}$, denoted by $|\mathcal{C}|$, is the number of gates in it. The *depth* of $\mathcal{C}$, denoted by $\mathtt{depth}(\mathcal{C})$, is the length of the longest directed path from a source variable to a sink variable. In the following, we also use the symbols $\mathcal{C}$ to denote a circuit.

The parallel complexity class NC, known as Nick's Class [11], is studied by theorists as a class of decision problems that can be efficiently solved in parallel (or says *parallelly tractable*). The NC complexity is defined based on circuits. Formally, each decision problem in NC can be decided by a family of circuits $\mathbb{C}$ where each circuit $\mathcal{C}_I \in \mathbb{C}$ is a LOGSPACE *uniform* circuit of polynomial size and poly-logarithmic depth (such a circuit is also called an *NC circuit*), and decides this problem on the input I. The key issues that influence parallel computation can be analyzed using LOGSPACE uniform circuits; developers can also construct an efficient parallel algorithm by referring to a LOGSPACE uniform circuit [11].

3 Performing Reasoning via Circuits

Our target is to identify a class of KGs (or the corresponding datalog programs) for which reasoning falls in the NC complexity. However reasoning of datalog programs is in data complexity PTIME-completeness. We actually work on identifying a subclass of general datalog programs for our purpose. On the other hand, since the NC complexity is defined on NC circuits, we should find a kind of circuits that can equivalently perform reasoning. Before discussing the details, we first give the formal definition of parallelly tractable class based on NC circuits as follows.

Definition 2 *(Parallelly Tractable Class).* Given a class $\mathcal{D}$ of datalog programs, we say that $\mathcal{D}$ is a parallelly tractable datalog program (PTD) class if there exists a family of NC circuits $\mathbb{C}$ such that for each datalog program $P \in \mathcal{D}$, an NC circuit $\mathcal{C} \in \mathbb{C}$ performs the reasoning of P. The corresponding class of knowledge graphs of $\mathcal{D}$ is called a parallelly tractable knowledge graph (PTG) class.

Driven by the above definition, we focus on identifying a PTD class $\mathcal{D}_{\mathbb{C}}$ where each datalog program in this class can be handled by some circuit in the NC circuits

---

[3] the logical operation NOT is also allowed in a general Boolean circuit. We do not consider this operation here.

$\mathbb{C}$ in terms of reasoning. In the following, we first give a kind of circuits that handle reasoning of general datalog programs. We then restrict these circuits to NC versions and identify the target PTD class.

We say that, a circuit performing reasoning of a datalog program P is a *reasoning circuit* of P. We use an example to illustrate how to simulate reasoning of datalog programs by evaluating circuits, and then derive a kind of reasoning circuits.

Example 1. Given a KG $\mathcal{G}_{ex_1}$ that contains two facts $A(b)$ and $R(a, b)$ where a, b are the two entities; A is the property of b and R is a binary relation between a and b. A user-defined datalog rule $R(x, y), A(y) \rightarrow A(x)$ is also given. The corresponding datalog program of this KG is $P_{ex_1} = \langle R, I \rangle$ where $\mathbf{I}$ contains all facts in $\mathcal{G}_{ex_1}$ and R contains the rule '$R(x, y), A(y) \rightarrow A(x)$'.

By performing reasoning on P_{ex_1}, one can get a new ground atom $A(a)$ through the rule instantiation '$r : R(a, b), A(b) \rightarrow A(a)$'. If we use a circuit to simulate the rule application of r, we can map r to an AND gate, denoted by AND_r; the body atoms $R(a, b)$ and $A(b)$ of r are mapped to the input variables $x_{R(a,b)}$ and $x_{A(b)}$ of AND_r respectively; the head atom $A(a)$ is mapped to the output variable $x_{A(a)}$ of AND_r. Further, we require that $x_{A(a)}$ is evaluated with 1 from the gate AND_r if $A(a)$ is derived from r. On the other hand, there may exist several rule instantiations with the same atom being as their heads. For example, if P_{ex_1} also contains two ground atoms $R(a, c)$ and $A(c)$, then $A(a)$ can also be derived through the rule instantiation '$r' : R(a, c), A(c) \rightarrow A(a)$'. Similar to AND_r, we can map r' to a new AND gate $\text{AND}_{r'}$ with $x_{R(a,c)}$ and $x_{A(c)}$ being as its input variables and $x_{A(a)}$ being as its output variable. To describe in a circuit that $A(a)$ can be derived in different ways, we introduce an OR gate corresponding to $A(a)$ (denoted by $\text{OR}_{A(a)}$); let the variable $x_{A(a)}$ be the output of $\text{OR}_{A(a)}$; let the outputs of AND_r and $\text{AND}_{r'}$ be the inputs of $\text{OR}_{A(a)}$. In this way, whenever r or r' is applied to derive $A(a)$, $x_{A(a)}$ has to be evaluated with 1.

The above discussion guides us to give the following definition of reasoning circuits.

Definition 3. *(Basic Reasoning Circuits)* Given a datalog program P and a function f whose input is the size of P, denote by $|P|$, and the output is a non-negative integer. A basic reasoning circuit $\mathcal{B}_P^f$ with respect to P and f is a circuit containing $f(|P|)$ layers and is built as follows:

1. For each ground atom $H \in N_P$, $\mathcal{B}_P^f$ contains a source variable x_H^0, and a sink variable $x_H^{f(|P|)}$;
2. In the ith layer of $\mathcal{B}_P^f$ where $1 \leq i \leq f(|P|)$, there are OR gates of the number $|N_P|$. Each OR gate is uniquely corresponding to a ground atom $H \in N_P$, denoted by OR_H^i. The output of OR_H^i is the variable x_H^i. The inputs of OR_H^i include the following variables: (a) for each rule instantiation '$B_1, ..., B_n \rightarrow H$', an AND gate is contained in $\mathcal{B}_P^f$ with $x_{B_1}^{i-1}, ..., x_{B_n}^{i-1}$ being as its inputs and the output is an input of the gate OR_H^i; (b) x_H^{i-1} is an input of OR_H^i.

In what follows, we use the symbol $\mathcal{B}$ to specially denote a basic reasoning circuit. For a datalog program P, one of its basic reasoning circuits consists of several layers where each layer has the same structure: each OR gate corresponds to an atom in N_P and each AND gate corresponds to a rule instantiation in P^*. The function f in the above definition is used to bound the number of layers of a basic reasoning circuit. Since the depth of each layer is at most 2 (an OR gate and an AND gate), the depth of the whole circuit is thus at most $2f(|P|)$. We call such a function f a *depth function*. Further, if a path between two variables only contains OR gates, we call it an *OR path*. OR paths ensure that the variable x_H^i has to be evaluated with 1 whenever x_H^j is evaluated with 1 where $0 \leq j < i$.

To this point, we can illustrate how to transform reasoning on a datalog program $P = \langle R, \mathbf{I} \rangle$ to valuation of its corresponding basic reasoning circuit $\mathcal{B}_P^f$. Firstly, all the source variables x_A are assigned 1 where $A \in \mathbf{I}$ and the rest source variables are assigned 0 (we call this initial assignment the *valid assignment*). Then, the rest variables in the circuit are evaluated accordingly. A variable is called a *valid variable* if it is finally evaluated with 1 under the valid assignment; a gate is valid if its output is valid. We also say that checking whether a variable is valid is *deciding its validity*. In addition, a variable x is evaluated in n *evaluation steps* (short by *E-steps*) if it is evaluated with 1 (resp., 0) through the shortest (resp., longest) path that is starting from a source variable and ending at x and n gates are involved in this path.

The correctness of evaluating a basic reasoning circuits is ensured by its valid assignment. That is, if $\mathcal{B}_P^f(x_H) = 1$ for some variable x_H, then H can be derived from P; otherwise, H is not a consequence of P. We say that a reasoning circuit $\mathcal{C}$ is a *valid reasoning circuit* if $\mathcal{C}$ is initialized with a valid assignment and satisfies: for any ground atoms H and H', (completeness) $H \in T_R^\omega(\mathbf{I})$ if there exists an integer $0 \leq i \leq f(|P|)$ such that $\mathcal{C}(x_H^i) = 1$; (correctness) $H' \notin T_R^\omega(\mathbf{I})$ iff for all integers $0 \leq j \leq f(|P|)$ such that $\mathcal{C}(x_{H'}^j) = 0$. We next give a basic reasoning circuit of the datalog program P_{ex_1} in Example 2.

Example 2. Consider the datalog program P_{ex_1} in Example 1 again. Since P_{ex_1} contains two entities (a and b) and two predicates (R and A), there are six ground atoms, i.e., $A(a), A(b), R(a,b), R(b,a), R(a,a)$ and $R(b,b)$ in $N_{P_{ex_1}}$. According to Definition 3, we give the basic reasoning circuit $\mathcal{B}_{ex_1}$ of P_{ex_1} in Fig. 1 based on a constant depth function $f(|P_{ex_1}|) = 1$. The OR gates in $\mathcal{B}_{ex_1}$ are labeled by '$\vee$'; the AND gates are labeled by '$\wedge$'. The size of $\mathcal{B}_{ex_1}$ is the number of nodes, that is 10. The depth of $\mathcal{B}_{ex_1}$ is 2.

To perform reasoning of P_{ex_1} via $\mathcal{B}_{ex_1}$, $\mathcal{B}_{ex_1}$ is firstly initialized with the valid assignment, i.e., the two source variables $x_{R(a,b)}^0$ and $x_{A(b)}^0$ are assigned by 1, while other source variables are assigned by 0. Then the Boolean operations of all gates are performed until all variables in $\mathcal{B}_{ex_1}$ are evaluated. We use the bold edges in $\mathcal{B}_{ex_1}$ to represent valid variables. The variable $x_{A(a)}^1$ is evaluated in 2 E-steps, while $x_{A(b)}^1$ is evaluated in 1 E-step since there is an OR path between $x_{A(b)}^1$ and $x_{A(b)}^0$. All the other variables in the first layer are evaluated in 1 E-step. Since $A(a)$ is the unique consequence of P_{ex_1}, $\mathcal{B}_{ex_1}$ is a valid reasoning circuit.

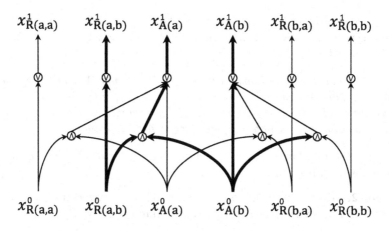

Fig. 1. A basic reasoning circuit.

Further, we use the following theorem to show the correctness of performing reasoning via a basic reasoning circuit.

Theorem 1. [4]Given a datalog program $P = \langle R, \mathbf{I} \rangle$, there exists a polynomially bounded function f_p such that for the basic reasoning circuit $\mathcal{B}_P^{f_p}$, we have,

1. $\mathcal{B}_P^{f_p}$ is a valid reasoning circuit of P;
2. $\mathcal{B}_P^{f_p}$ is LOGSPACE uniform.

4   Parallelly Tractable Classes Captured by NC Circuits

We now discuss how to restrict a basic reasoning circuit $\mathcal{B}_P^f$ to an NC circuit. (I) Each layer of $\mathcal{B}_P^f$ has a depth of at most 2. Thus, if the depth function f is poly-logarithmically bounded, the depth of $\mathcal{B}_P^f$ is also poly-logarithmically bounded. (II) In each layer of $\mathcal{B}_P^f$ the number of OR gates is $|N_P|$; the number of AND gates is $|P^*|$. Since the number of predicate arities and the number of rule body atoms are constants, $|N_P|$ and $|P^*|$ turn out to be polynomial in the size of P. Thus the number of gates in each layer is also polynomial in the size of P. Further, if the depth function f is poly-logarithmically bounded, then $\mathcal{B}_P^f$ has a polynomial size. (III) $\mathcal{B}_P^f$ is LOGSPACE uniform with f being a polynomial function (see Theorem 1). Based on (I, II, III), if the depth function f is a poly-logarithmic function, then $\mathcal{B}_P^f$ is an NC circuit.

In what follows, we use the symbol ψ to represent a poly-logarithmically bounded depth function. Based on the above analysis, for some poly-logarithmic function ψ, we have a family of basic reasoning circuits whose depth is bounded by ψ. We use $\mathbb{B}^\psi$ to denote this kind of circuit family. Further, we can identify a

---

[4] The proofs of this theorem and other theorems can be found in the technical report.

class of datalog programs, denoted by $\mathcal{D}_{\mathbb{B}^\psi}$, where each datalog program $P \in \mathcal{D}_{\mathbb{B}^\psi}$ has a corresponding valid reasoning circuit in $\mathbb{B}^\psi$. Obviously, $\mathcal{D}_{\mathbb{B}^\psi}$ is a PTD class according to Definition 2.

Example 3. Consider the datalog program P_{ex_1} in Example 1. One can check that $P_{ex_1} \in \mathcal{D}_{\mathbb{B}^\psi}$. This is because the reasoning circuit $\mathcal{B}_{ex_1}$ given in Example 2 is a valid reasoning circuit of P_{ex_1}. Further the depth function of $\mathcal{B}_{ex_1}$ is actually a constant function, obviously being poly-logarithmically bounded.

We give the following theorem to show that $\mathcal{D}_{\mathbb{B}^\psi}$ can also be captured by stages of datalog programs.

Theorem 2. Given a poly-logarithmic function ψ, we have that any datalog program $P \in \mathcal{D}_{\mathbb{B}^\psi}$ iff the stage of P is upper-bounded by $\psi(|P|)$.

Although $\mathcal{D}_{\mathbb{B}^\psi}$ covers a wide range of parallelly tractable datalog programs, it cannot even capture the computation of *transitivity*. Consider a datalog program involving only the rule: '$ancestor(x,y), ancestor(y,z) \rightarrow ancestor(x,z)$', describing the transitivity of the predicate *acncestor*. On can check that its corresponding basic reasoning circuit has the depth polynomially bounded by the number of inputs. However, there indeed exits a kind of reasoning circuits with poly-logarithmically bounded depths. In the following, we give the definition of such a kind of reasoning circuits and call them *efficient reasoning circuits*.

Definition 4 *(Efficient Reasoning Circuits).* Given a datalog program P and a function f; the size of P is denote by $|P|$, and the output is a non-negative integer. An efficient reasoning circuit $\mathcal{E}_P^f$ with respect to P and f is a circuit containing $n = f(|P|)$ layers and $m = \lceil \log(|N_P|) \rceil$ sub-layers in each layer, and is built as follows. For each atom $H \in N_P$, $\mathcal{E}_P^f$ contains a corresponding source variable $x_{(H,H)}^0$, and a sink variable $x_{(H,H)}^n$.

In the ith layer of $\mathcal{E}_P^f$ where $1 \leq i \leq f(|P|)$, for each ground atom $H \in N_P$, there is an OR gate, denoted by $\mathrm{OR}_{(H,H)}^i$, whose output is $x_{(H,H)}^i$; there is a spacial OR gate (called *fast OR gate*), denoted by $\mathrm{FOR}_{(H,H)}^{i-1}$. The inputs of $\mathrm{FOR}_{(H,H)}^{i-1}$ are $x_{(H,H)}^j$ for $0 \leq j \leq i-1$ and the output is $y_{(H,H)}^{i-1}$. In the kth sub-layer of the ith layer for $1 \leq k \leq m$, for each atom pair $(B,H) \in N_P \times N_P$, there is an OR gate denoted by $\mathrm{OR}_{(B,H)}^{i,k}$. The output of $\mathrm{OR}_{(B,H)}^{i,k}$ for $1 \leq k \leq m$ is the variable $x_{(B,H)}^{i,k}$. The inputs of $\mathrm{OR}_{(B,H)}^{i,k}$ for $1 \leq k \leq m$ and the inputs of $\mathrm{OR}_{(H,H)}^i$ involve the following variables:

1. For any atom H, let $y_{(H,H)}^{i-1}$ be an input of $\mathrm{OR}_{(H,H)}^i$.
2. For each rule instantiation '$B \rightarrow H$', (a) an AND gate is contained with $y_{(B,B)}^{i-1}$ being as the input and its output is an input of the gate $\mathrm{OR}_{(H,H)}^i$. (b) let 1 (TRUE) be an input of $\mathrm{OR}_{(B,H)}^{i,0}$.
3. For each rule instantiation '$B_1, B_2 \rightarrow H$', (a) an AND gate is contained with $y_{(B_1,B_1)}^{i-1}, y_{(B_2,B_2)}^{i-1}$ being as inputs and its output is an input of the gate

$\text{OR}^i_{(H,H)}$. (b) let $y^{i-1}_{(B_1,B_1)}$ be an input of $\text{OR}^{i,0}_{(B_2,H)}$; let $y^{i-1}_{(B_2,B_2)}$ be an input of $\text{OR}^{i,0}_{(B_1,H)}$.

4. In the kth sub-layer for $1 \le k \le m$, for any three atoms A, B, C (they may be same pairwise), an AND gate is contained with $x^{i,k-1}_{(A,B)}, x^{i,k-1}_{(B,C)}$ being as inputs and its output is an input of the gate $\text{OR}^{i,k}_{(A,C)}$.

5. For each variable of the form $x^{i,m}_{(B,H)}$ in the mth sub-layer, an AND gate is contained with $x^{i,m}_{(B,H)}$ and $y^{i-1}_{(B,B)}$ being as inputs and its output is an input of the gate $\text{OR}^i_{(H,H)}$.   □

We discuss how does an efficient reasoning circuit work by comparing its definition to that of basic reasoning circuits. In each layer of an efficient reasoning circuit, w.l.o.g., for the ith layer and each atom $H \in N_P$, there is an OR gate $\text{OR}^i_{(H,H)}$ that is similar to such a gate OR^i_H in a basic reasoning circuit. For such a variable x^{i-1}_H that is the input of several gates in the ith layer in a basic reasoning circuit, the variable $y^{i-1}_{(H,H)}$ plays a similar role to x^{i-1}_H. Note that $y^{i-1}_{(H,H)}$ is the output of the fast OR gate $\text{FOR}^{i-1}_{(H,H)}$. The item 1 in Definition 4 is similar to the item 2(b) in Definition 3. The item 2 and 3 in Definition 4 handle different rule instantiations according to the number of their body atoms; the item 2(a) and 3(a) in Definition 4 are similar to the item 2(a) in Definition 3. See the item 2(b) in Definition 4, for such a rule instantiation '$B \to H$', the variable $x^i_{(B,H)}$ is always valid. Thus we let the truth value 1 be the input of the OR gate $\text{OR}^{i,0}_{(B,H)}$. In an efficient reasoning circuit, we introduce $\lceil \log(|N_P|) \rceil$ sub-layers and fast OR gates in each layer to accelerate evaluation. Intuitively, a fast OR gate preserves inputs from all previous layers not only its adjacencies.

We use the symbol $\mathcal{E}$ to denote an efficient reasoning circuit. The notions of *valid assignment* and *valid reasoning circuit* should also be modified to adapt to efficient reasoning circuits. Specifically, given a datalog program $P = \langle R, \mathbf{I} \rangle$ and its efficient reasoning circuit $\mathcal{E}^f_P$ for some depth function f, a valid assignment means that all source variables of the form $x^0_{(A,A)}$ are assigned by 1 where $A \in \mathbf{I}$ and other source variables are assigned by 0. We say that $\mathcal{E}^f_P$ is a valid reasoning circuit if $\mathcal{E}^f_P$ is initialized with a valid assignment and satisfies that $H \in T^\omega_R(\mathbf{I})$ iff there exists an integer $0 \le i \le f(|P|)$ s.t. $\mathcal{E}^f_P(x^i_{(H,H)}) = 1$, and $H' \notin T^\omega_R(\mathbf{I})$ iff for all integers $0 \le j \le f(|P|)$ s.t. $\mathcal{E}^f_P(x^j_{(H',H')}) = 0$, for any ground atoms H and H'. We give the following theorem to show the correctness of performing reasoning via an efficient reasoning circuit.

Theorem 3 Given a datalog program $P = \langle R, \mathbf{I} \rangle$, if there exists a polynomially bounded function f_p such that for the efficient reasoning circuit $\mathcal{E}^{f_p}_P$, we have,

1. $\mathcal{E}^{f_p}_P$ is a valid reasoning circuit;
2. $\mathcal{E}^{f_p}_P$ is LOGSPACE uniform.

For an efficient reasoning circuit $\mathcal{E}_P^f$, it can be checked that the number of gates are $2\lceil\log(|N_P|)\rceil \cdot |N_P|^2$ in all sub-layers. Further, the number of gates in a layer is polynomially bounded. On the other hand, since there are $\lceil\log(|N_P|)\rceil$ sub-layers in each layer, the depth of each layer is at most $2(\lceil\log(|N_P|)\rceil + 1)$. Thus, if we restrict that the depth function f is poly-logarithmically bounded, $\mathcal{E}_P^f$ has a polynomial size and a poly-logarithmic depth. Similar to the PTD class $\mathcal{D}_{\mathbb{B}\psi}$, we get a new PTD class $\mathcal{D}_{\mathbb{E}\psi}$ that is captured from efficient reasoning circuits in terms of a poly-logarithmically bounded function ψ.

We can also prove that $\mathcal{D}_{\mathbb{E}\psi}$ is subsumed by $\mathcal{D}_{\mathbb{B}\psi}$.

Corollary 1. For any poly-logarithmic depth function ψ, we have that $\mathcal{D}_{\mathbb{E}\psi} \subseteq \mathcal{D}_{\mathbb{B}\psi}$.

5   Practical Usability of Theoretical Results

The theoretical results given in this work can be used in two ways. One the one hand, one can check the parallel tractability of a given knowledge graph by deciding whether its corresponding datalog program belongs to class $\mathcal{D}_{\mathbb{B}\psi}$ or class $\mathcal{D}_{\mathbb{E}\psi}$. On the other hand, the proposed reasoning circuits can be used to analyze the computational complexities of parallel reasoning algorithms according to [11], or to construct high-performance computing architectures, e.g. logic neural networks by following the methods given in [23].

YAGO. The well-known knowledge graph YAGO[5] is constructed from Wikipedia and WordNet. The version YAGO3 [18] has more than 10 million entities (e.g., persons, organizations, cities, etc.) and contains more than 120 million facts of these entities. In order to balance the expressiveness and computing efficiency, a YAGO-style language, called YAGO *model*, is proposed [25], which allows stating the *transitivity* of a property. In [25], a group of reasoning rules is specified. One can check that all of the rules in YAGO *model* are allowed in the datalog programs that belongs to $\mathcal{D}_{\mathbb{E}\psi}$. Thus, we have that a well-constructed YAGO dataset belongs to $\mathcal{D}_{\mathbb{E}\psi}$.

Ontologies. In the Semantic Web community, different kinds of ontologies are proposed as benchmarks to facilitate the evaluation of ontology-based systems in a standard and systematic way. We investigate several popular ontologies using our results and find that the ontologies used in some benchmarks have simple structured TBoxes that can be expressed in datalog and belong to $\mathcal{D}_{\mathbb{B}\psi}$. These ontologies include SIB[6] (*Social Network Intelligence BenchMark*), BSBM[7] (*Berlin SPARQL Benchmark*) and LODIB[8] (*Linked Open Data Integration Benchmark*). The parallel tractability of the ontology used in IIMB[9] (*The ISLab Instance Matching Benchmark*) is ensured by Theorem 3.

---

[5] https://www.mpi-inf.mpg.de/departments/databases-and-information-systems/research/yago-naga/yago.

[6] https://www.w3.org/wiki/Social_Network_Intelligence_BenchMark.

[7] http://wifo5-03.informatik.uni-mannheim.de/bizer/berlinsparqlbenchmark/.

[8] http://wifo5-03.informatik.uni-mannheim.de/bizer/lodib/.

[9] http://islab.di.unimi.it/iimb/.

Neural Logic Networks. The reasoning circuits given in this paper are basically well-defined Boolean circuits. Thus, one can construct neural networks to evaluate the reasoning circuits by applying the methods proposed in [23]. Briefly, each layer in a reasoning circuit can be mapped to a hidden layer in a network, while all source variables (resp., sink variables) are mapped to input vectors (resp., output vectors). One can also apply the reasoning circuits on the other network architectures for logic reasoning [4,9]. Our theoretical results can further be used to analyze the size of a neural logic network and its computational complexity according to [23]. We further checked that, the two well-known benchmarks *BlockWorld* and *FamilyTree* [21] usually used in these works belong to $\mathcal{D}_{\mathbb{E}\psi}$.

6   Conclusions and Future Work

In this paper, we studied to identify parallelly tractable classes of knowledge graphs that can be rewritten by datalog programs. To this end, we constructed NC circuits such that reasoning can be transformed to the evaluation of circuits. Based on these NC circuits, we identified two parallelly tractable classes $\mathcal{D}_{\mathbb{B}\psi}$ and $\mathcal{D}_{\mathbb{E}\psi}$ such that reasoning on the datalog programs in these classes is in the NC complexity.

In our future work, we will study in detail how to further refine the theoretical results. One idea is to study some expressive symbolic operators for knowledge graphs, like *qualifiers* and *negator*, and investigate their impacts to parallel tractability. The other idea is to use the proposed reasoning circuits to enhance knowledge graph reasoning. That is we can design special parallel reasoning algorithms for knowledge graphs whose corresponding datalog programs belong to $\mathcal{D}_{\mathbb{B}\psi}$ or $\mathcal{D}_{\mathbb{E}\psi}$. We can also study to use the tractable reasoning circuits to construct high-performance logic neural networks.

Acknowledgements. This work was supported by The Natural Science Foundation of the Jiangsu Higher Education Institutions of China under grant 1020221069.

References

1. Abiteboul, S., Hull, R., Vianu, V.: Foundations of Databases. Addison-Wesley, Boston (1995)
2. Arora, S., Barak, B.: Computational Complexity - A Modern Approach. Cambridge University Press, Cambridge (2009)
3. Baader, F., Calvanese, D., McGuinness, D.L., Nardi, D., Patel-Schneider, P.F.: The Description Logic Handbook: Theory. Cambridge University Press, Cambridge, Implementation and Applications (2003)
4. Barceló, P., Kostylev, E., Monet, M., Pérez, J., Reutter, J., Silva, J.-P.: The logical expressiveness of graph neural networks. In: 8th International Conference on Learning Representations (ICLR 2020) (2020)
5. Bellomarini, L., Gottlob, G., Sallinger, E.: The vadalog system: datalog-based reasoning for knowledge graphs. arXiv preprint arXiv:1807.08709 (2018)

6. Bordes, A., Usunier, N., Garcia-Duran, A., Weston, J., Yakhnenko, O.: Translating embeddings for modeling multi-relational data. In: Advances in Neural Information Processing Systems, vol. 26 (2013)

7. Chen, X., Jia, S., Xiang, Y.: A review: knowledge reasoning over knowledge graph. Expert Syst. Appl. **141**, 112948 (2020)

8. Dettmers, T., Minervini, P., Stenetorp, P., Riedel, S.: Convolutional 2D knowledge graph embeddings. In: Proceedings of the AAAI Conference on Artificial Intelligence, vol. 32 (2018)

9. Dong, H., Mao, J., Lin, T., Wang, C., Li, L., Zhou, D.: Neural logic machines. arXiv preprint arXiv:1904.11694 (2019)

10. Gomez-Perez, J.M., Pan, J.Z., Vetere, G., Wu, H.: Enterprise knowledge graph: an introduction. In: Exploiting Linked Data and Knowledge Graphs in Large Organisations, pp. 1–14. Springer, Cham (2017). https://doi.org/10.1007/978-3-319-45654-6_1

11. Greenlaw, R., Hoover, H.J., Ruzzo, W.L.: Limits to Parallel Computation: P-Completeness Theory. Oxford University Press, New York (1995)

12. Grosof, B.N., Horrocks, I., Volz, R., Decker. S.: Description logic programs: combining logic programs with description logic. In Procdings of WWW, pp. 48–57 (2003)

13. Guo, S., Wang, Q., Wang, L., Wang, B., Guo, L.: Jointly embedding knowledge graphs and logical rules. In Proceedings of the 2016 Conference on Empirical Methods in Natural Language Processing, pp. 192–202 (2016)

14. Guo, S., Wang, Q., Wang, L., Wang, B., Guo, L.: Knowledge graph embedding with iterative guidance from soft rules. In Proceedings of the AAAI Conference on Artificial Intelligence, vol. 32 (2018)

15. Huang, X., Zhang, J., Li, D., Li, P.: Knowledge graph embedding based question answering. In: Proceedings of the twelfth ACM International Conference on Web Search and Data Mining, pp. 105–113 (2019)

16. Ji, S., Pan, S., Cambria, E., Marttinen, P., Philip, S.Y.: A survey on knowledge graphs: representation, acquisition, and applications. IEEE Trans. Neural Netw. Learn. Syst. **33**(2), 494–514 (2021)

17. Kiryakov, A., Ognyanov, D., Manov, D.: OWLIM – a pragmatic semantic repository for owl. In: Dean, M., et al. (eds.) WISE 2005. LNCS, vol. 3807, pp. 182–192. Springer, Heidelberg (2005). https://doi.org/10.1007/11581116_19

18. Mahdisoltani, F., Biega, J., Suchanek, F.M.: YAGO3: a knowledge base from multilingual wikipedias. In: Proceedings of CIDR (2015)

19. Motik, B., Nenov, Y., Piro, R., Horrocks, I., Olteanu, D.: Parallel materialisation of datalog programs in centralised, main-memory RDF systems. In Proceedings of AAAI, pp. 129–137 (2014)

20. Nickel, M., Tresp, V., Kriegel, H.-P.: A three-way model for collective learning on multi-relational data. In: ICML (2011)

21. Nilsson, N.J.: Principles of Artificial Intelligence. Springer (1982)

22. Peters, M., Sachweh, S., Zündorf, A.: Large scale rule-based reasoning using a laptop. In Proceedings of ESWC, pp. 104–118 (2015)

23. Selsam, D., Lamm, M., Bünz, B., Liang, P., de Moura, L., Dill, D.L.: Learning a sat solver from single-bit supervision. arXiv preprint arXiv:1802.03685 (2018)

24. Shaojie, L., Shudong, C., Xiaoye, O., Lichen, G.: Joint learning based on multi-shaped filters for knowledge graph completion. High Technol. Lett. **27**(1), 43–52 (2021)

25. Suchanek, F.M., Kasneci, G., Weikum, G.: YAGO: a large ontology from Wikipedia and wordnet. J. Web Sem. **6**(3), 203–217 (2008)

26. Trouillon, T., Welbl, J., Riedel, S., Gaussier, É., Bouchard, G.: Complex embeddings for simple link prediction. In: International Conference on Machine Learning, pp. 2071–2080. PMLR (2016)
27. Wang, X., He, X., Cao, Y., Liu, M., Chua, T.-S.: KGAT: knowledge graph attention network for recommendation. In: Proceedings of the 25th ACM SIGKDD International Conference on Knowledge Discovery & Data Mining, pp. 950–958 (2019)
28. Yang, B., Yih, W.-T., He, X., Gao, J., Deng, L.: Embedding entities and relations for learning and inference in knowledge bases. arXiv preprint arXiv:1412.6575 (2014)
29. Zhou, X., Peng, Y., Liu, B.: Text mining for traditional Chinese medical knowledge discovery: a survey. J. Biomed. Inform. 43(4), 650–660 (2010)
30. Zhou, Z., Qi, G., Glimm, B.: Parallel tractability of ontology materialization: technique and practice. J. Web Seman. 52, 45–65 (2018)

Incorporating Uncertainty of Entities and Relations into Few-Shot Uncertain Knowledge Graph Embedding

Jingting Wang, Tianxing Wu[✉], and Jiatao Zhang

Southeast University, Nanjing, China
{jtwang,tianxingwu,zjt}@seu.edu.cn

Abstract. In this paper, we study the problem of embedding few-shot uncertain knowledge graphs. Observing the existing embedding methods may discard the uncertainty information, or require sufficient training data for each relation, we propose a novel method by incorporating the inherent uncertainty of entities and relations (i.e. element-level uncertainty) into uncertain knowledge graph embedding. We introduce different metrics to quantify the uncertainty of different entities and relations. By employing a metric-based framework, our method can effectively capture both semantic and uncertainty information of entities and relations in the few-shot scenario. Experimental results show that our proposed method can learn better embeddings in terms of the higher accuracy in both confidence score prediction and tail entity prediction.

Keywords: Uncertain knowledge graph · Knowledge graph embedding · Few-shot learning

1 Introduction

Knowledge graphs (KGs) [1] describe the real-world facts in the form of triples *(head entity, relation, tail entity)*, indicating that two entities are connected by a sepecific relation. In addition to deterministic KGs (DKGs), much recent attention has been paid to uncertain KGs (UKGs). UKGs, such as Probase [2], NELL [3] and ConceptNet [4], associate each fact (or triple) with a confidence score representing the likelihood of that fact to be true, e.g. *(Twitter, competeswith, Facebook, 0.85)*. Such uncertain knowledge representations can capture the uncertain nature of reality, and provide more precise reasoning.

KG embedding models are essential tools for incorporating the structured knowledge representations in KGs into machine learning. These models encode entities and relations into continuous vector spaces, so as to accurately capture the similarity of entities and preserve the structure of KGs in the embedding space. Inspired by the works about DKG embeddings [5–8], some efforts have been devoted to UKGs [9–12] embedding. Existing methods usually assume the availability of sufficient training examples for all relations. However, the frequency distributions of relations in real datasets often have long tails, which

M. Sun et al. (Eds.): CCKS 2022, CCIS 1669, pp. 16–28, 2022.
https://doi.org/10.1007/978-981-19-7596-7_2

means that a large potion of relations appear in only a few triples in KGs. It is important and challenging to deal with the relations with limited number of triples, leading to the few-shot UKG embedding problem.

To our knowledge, GMUC [13] is the first and the only embedding method designed for few-shot UKGs. GMUC represents each entity and relation as a multi-dimensional Gaussian distribution, and utilizes a metric-based framework to learn a matching function for completing missing facts and their confidence scores. In light of the success of GMUC, we further find an important issue to be solved. Although the variance vectors in Gaussian distribution are claimed to represent entities' or relations' uncertainty, it lacks rational explanations and how such a setting influences the process of UKG embedding is unpredictable, which may lead to the imprecise modeling of entities and relations.

To alleviate this problem, we consider the uncertainty of an entity/relation on its semantic level. Table 1 shows an example in NELL. For relation *museumincity*, the head entity must be a museum, and the corresponding tail entity must be a city. In contrast, relation *atlocation* provides more rich semantics because it can represent the connection between company and city, country and continent, or person and country, etc. Obviously, *atlocation* has higher uncertainty than *museumincity*. Similarly, different entities has different uncertainty extents. For example, *Alice* is more certain than *artist*, since there are much more persons belong to *artist* category. To summarize, the uncertainty of an entity/relation can be measured by its semantic imprecision. In contrast to triple-level uncertainty (i.e., the confidence score of a triple), we call this kind of uncertainty as *element-level* uncertainty of UKGs.

Table 1. Example facts of relations *museumincity* and *atlocation* in NELL.

Relation: museumincity	Relation: atlocation
(Gotoh Museum, Tokyo, 1.0)	(Air Canada, Vancouver, 0.92)
(Decordova, Lincoln, 0.96)	(Albania, Europe, 1.0)
(Whitney Museum, New York, 0.93)	(Queen Victoria, Great Britain, 0.93)

In this paper, we propose a new few-shot UKG embedding model by incorporating the inherent uncertainty of entities and relations. In order to capture the element-level uncertainty in UKGs, we design different metrics for quantification. We use intrinsic information content (IIC) to measure an entity's uncertainty. In the taxonomy of entities, the closer an entity is to the root (i.e. the more abstract this entity is), the higher uncertainty it contains. We use domain and range to measure a relation's uncertainty: the richer entity types a relation links to, the more uncertainty it contains. Following [13], we represent each entity and relation by a Gaussian distribution, while the mean vector denotes its position and the diagonal covariance matrix denotes its uncertainty. To combine the element-level uncertainty into UKG embedding, we design a constraint between measurement and variance in Gaussian distribution and add it into parameter optimization process. We also use a metric-based framework, with the purpose of learning a similarity function that can effectively infer the true facts and their corresponding confidence scores given the few-shot support sets for each relation.

We conducted extensive experiments using two open uncertain knowledge graph datasets on two tasks: (i) tail entity prediction, which focuses on complete tail entities for the query; and (ii) confidence prediction, which seeks to predict confidence scores of unseen relation facts. Our method consistently outperforms the baseline models, justifying the efficacy of incorporation of the uncertainty information of entities and relations.

The rest of the paper is organized as follows. We first review the related work in Sect. 2, then provide the problem definition and propose our method in the next two sections. In Sect. 5, we present our experiments. Finally, we conclude the paper in Sect. 6.

2   Related Work

Here we survey three topics relevant to this work: deterministic KG embedding, uncertain KG embedding, and few-shot KG embedding.

2.1   Deterministic Knowledge Graph Embedding

Deterministic KG embedding methods have been extensively explored by recent works. There are two representative families of models, i.e. translation distance models and semantic matching models. For the former, a relation embedding is usually a transition or mapping for entity embeddings. Representative works include TransE [5], TransH [6], KG2E [14], and RotatE [15]. KG2E [14] represents entities and relations as multi-dimensional Gaussian distributions, but it cannot be used for embedding UKGs. For semantic matching methods, the scoring function evaluates the plausibility based on the latent semantics of entities given a triple. Representative works include RESCAL [16], DistMult [7], and ComplEx [8]. Recently, deep neural network based models like R-GCN [17] and KG-BERT [18] have been presented for further improvement.

2.2   Uncertain Knowledge Graph Embedding

UKGE [9] is the first work on embedding uncertain KGs, which utilizes a mapping function to transform plausibility scores to confidence scores and boosts its performance by applying probabilistic soft logic. GTransE [12] uses confidence-aware margin loss to deal with the uncertainty of triples in UKGs. PASSLEAF [10] extends UKGE for other types of scoring functions and includes pool-based semi-supervised learning to alleviate the false-negative problem for training.

2.3   Few-Shot Knowledge Graph Embedding

Recently, few-shot learning has been applied to KG completion. Xiong et al. [19] presented GMatching model for one-shot DKG embedding, which introduces a metric-based framework for relational learning. FSRL [20] proposed a more effective heterogeneous neighbor encoder under the few-shot learning setting. GMUC is the first work to study the few-shot UKG embedding problem, which utilizes metric-based learning to model entities and relations as multi-dimensional Gaussian distributions.

None of these models pays close attention to the uncertainty of entities and relations, which is the key problem we aim to solve in this paper.

3   Problem Definition

In this section, we formally define the uncertain knowledge graph embedding task and detail the corresponding few-shot learning settings.

3.1   Uncertain Knowledge Graph Embedding

An *uncertain knowledge graph* can be denoted by $\mathcal{G} = \{(h, r, t, s) | h, t \in \mathcal{E}, r \in \mathcal{R}, s \in [0, 1]\}$, where $\mathcal{E}$ is the entity set, $\mathcal{R}$ is the relation set, and s is the corresponding confidence score. Given an uncertain KG $\mathcal{G}$, the embedding model aims to encode each entity and relation in a low-dimensional space in which the structure information and confidence scores of facts are both preserved.

3.2   Few-Shot Learning Settings

In contrast to the most previous work [9,10,12] that usually assumes enough triples for each relation are available for training, this work studies the case where only few-shot triples (support set) are available. The goal of our work is to learn a metric that could be used to predict new facts with few examples.

Following the standard few-shot learning settings [21], we assume access to a set of training tasks. In our problem, each training task corresponds to a KG relation $r \in \mathcal{R}$, and has its own training/testing data: $T_r = \{S_r, Q_r\}$, where S_r is the support set for training, Q_r is the query set for testing. We denote this kind of task set as meta-training set, $\mathcal{T}_{meta-train}$. To imitate the few-shot relation prediction at evaluation period, there are only few-shot triples in each S_r. Besides, Q_r consists of the testing triples of r with ground-truth tail entities t_i and confidence scores s_i for each query (h_i, r), as well as the corresponding tail entity candidates $\mathcal{C}_{h_i,t} = \{t_{ij}\}$ where each t_{ij} is an entity in $\mathcal{G}$. The metric model can thus be tested on this set by ranking the candidates or predicting their confidence scores given the test query (h_i, r) and the support triples in S_r.

Once trained, we can use the model to predict on new relations, which is called the meta-testing step in literature. These meta-testing relations are unseen from meta-training. Each meta-testing relation also has its own few-shot training/testing data. These meta-testing relations form a meat-test set $\mathcal{T}_{meta-test}$.

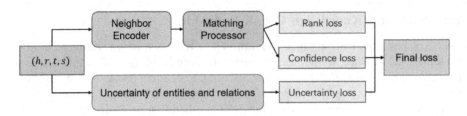

Fig. 1. The framework of our model.

Moreover, we leave out a subset of relations in $\mathcal{T}_{meta-train}$ as the meta-validation set $\mathcal{T}_{meta-val}$. Finally, we assume that the method has access to a background knowledge graph $\mathcal{G}'$, which is a subset of $\mathcal{G}$ with all the relations from $\mathcal{T}_{meta-train}$, $\mathcal{T}_{meta-test}$ and $\mathcal{T}_{meta-val}$ removed.

4   Methodology

In this section, we firstly introduce how we measure the uncertainty of entities and relations. We then present the framework for learning KG embedding and the learning strategy, as illustrated in Fig 1.

4.1   Uncertainty of Entities and Relations

We consider that the uncertainty of one entity/relation represents its semantic imprecision. The more imprecise semantic an entity/relation has, the higher uncertainty it contains. We utilize Intrinsic Information Content (IIC) to measure an entity's uncertainty, and utilize domain and range to measure a relation's uncertainty.

Uncertainty of Entities. IIC is used to measure an entity's uncertainty, and the lower IIC value one entity has, the more uncertainties it contains.

Information Content (IC) is an important dimension of word knowledge when assessing the similarity of two terms or word senses. The conventional way of measuring the IC of word senses is to combine knowledge of their hierarchical structure from an ontology like WordNet [22] with statistics on their actual usage in text as derived from a large corpus. However, IIC relies on hierarchical structure alone without the need for external resources. The calculation formula of IIC is defined as:

$$IIC(c) = 1 - \frac{\log(hypo(c) + 1)}{\log(N)} \tag{1}$$

where c is an arbitrary concept (essentially a node) in a taxonomy, N is a constant that is set to the maximum number of concepts that exist in the taxonomy, the function *hypo* returns the number of hyponyms of a given concept. The core idea behind IIC is that the more hyponyms a concept has the less information it expresses, otherwise there would be no need to further differentiate it.

Our method of obtaining an entity's uncertainty rests on the assumption that the taxonomic structure of entities in KG is organized in a meaningful and principled way, where entities near the root are more abstract than entities that are leaves. We argue that the more hyponyms an entity has, i.e. the lower IIC value, the higher uncertainty is contains. Considering the IIC value belongs to $[0, 1]$, we define the uncertainty value of an entity as:

$$UC_e(h) = 1 - IIC(h) \tag{2}$$

where h denotes an arbitrary entity in KG, $IIC(h)$ is its information content calculated by Eq. 1.

Uncertainty of Relations. We use domain and range to measure a relation's uncertainty. The richer the domain and range of a relation, the more uncertainties it contains.

RDF-Schema (RDFs) provides *rdfs:domain* and *rdfs:range* properties to declare the class of entities for relations. Domain restricts the class of head entities and range restricts the class of tail entities. We argue that if a relation links more entity classes, i.e. the domain and range are more diverse, it contains higher uncertainty. We introduce two different functions to calculate relation's uncertainties. One way utilizes the size of domain and range:

$$UC_r(r) = |D_r| \times |R_r| \tag{3}$$

where $|D_r|$ and $|R_r|$ are the size of domain and range set of relation r. The second one leverages the uncertainty of linked entity pairs:

$$UC_r(r) = \sum_{h \in D_r, t \in R_r} (UC_e(h) + UC_e(t)) \tag{4}$$

where h and t denote the entity class belongs to domain and range of relation r, respectively.

To incorporate the uncertainty of entities and relations into UKG embedding, we represent each of them as a multi-dimensional Gaussian distribution $\mathcal{N}(\mu, \Sigma)$, where $\mu \in \mathbb{R}^d$ is the mean vector indicating its position, $\Sigma = \sigma I$ ($\sigma \in \mathbb{R}^d$) is the diagonal covariance matrix indicating its uncertainty. We denote it by $\mathcal{N}(\mu, \sigma)$ for convenience. We argue that the norm of variance vector is proportional to the uncertainty value for each entity/relation, and design a loss function $\mathcal{L}_{uc}$ as a constraint on variance vectors:

$$\mathcal{L}_{uc} = \sum_{i \in \mathcal{R}} \sum_{i \in \mathcal{E}} (w \cdot \|\sigma_i\|_2 + b - UC_{r/e}(i)) \tag{5}$$

where $\|\sigma_i\|_2$ is the l_2 norm of variance vector σ in Gaussian distribution, w and b are learnable parameters.

4.2   Model

Inspired by [20], we use a metric-based KG embedding framework composed of two major parts: (i) *Neighbor Encoder* utilizes local graph structure (i.e. one-hop neighbors) to enhance representation for each entity; (ii) *Matching Processor* calculates the similarity between a query and support set for relation prediction.

Neighbor Encoder. Considering different impacts of heterogeneous neighbors which may help improve entity embedding, we use heterogeneous neighbor encoder [20] to enhance the representation of given entity. Specifically, we denote the set of relational neighbors of given head entity h as $N_h = \{(r_i, t_i, s_i)|(h, r_i, t_i, s_i) \in \mathcal{G}'\}$, where $\mathcal{G}'$ is the background KG, r_i, t_i and s_i represent the i-th relation, corresponding tail entity and confidence score, respectively. The Neighbor Encoder should be able to encoder N_h and output a feature representation of h. We denote the output representation of h by $\mathcal{N}(\mathcal{F}_{NE}^{\mu}(h), \mathcal{F}_{NE}^{\sigma}(h))$, where $\mathcal{F}_{NE}^{\mu}(\cdot)$ and $\mathcal{F}_{NE}^{\sigma}(\cdot)$ are two heterogeneous neighbor encoders respectively for mean embedding and variance embedding.

By applying the neighbor encoder $\mathcal{F}_{NE}$ to each entity, we then concatenate head and tail entity embeddings to obtain the representation of each triple in the form of $\mathcal{N}(\mu_i, \sigma_i)$, where $\mu_i = [\mathcal{F}_{NE}^{\mu}(h) \oplus \mathcal{F}_{NE}^{\mu}(t)]$, $\sigma_i = [\mathcal{F}_{NE}^{\sigma}(h) \oplus \mathcal{F}_{NE}^{\sigma}(t)]$ and $\oplus$ is the concatenation operation. In this way, we can get the Gaussian representation of each query, $\mathcal{N}(\mu_q, \sigma_q)$. Since there are few-shot triples in support set, we utilize mean-pooling to aggregate them into one multi-Gaussian distribution $\mathcal{N}(\mu_s, \sigma_s)$.

Matching Processor. After the above operations, we can get two Gaussian distributions for each query and each support set. In order to measure the similarity between them, we employ the LSTM-based [23] recurrent processing block [24] to perform multi-step matching. We use two matching processors $\mathcal{F}_{MP}^{\mu}$ and $\mathcal{F}_{MP}^{\sigma}$ to calculate mean similarity sim_{μ} and variance similarity sim_{σ} respectively. To predict missing triples and their confidence scores, we define $s_{rank} = sim_{\mu} + \lambda sim_{\sigma}$ as ranking scores and $s_{conf} = sigmoid(w \cdot sim_{\sigma} + b)$ as confidence scores, where w and b are learnable parameters, and λ is a hyper-parameter.

4.3   Learning

For the query relation r, we randomly sample a set of few positive triples and regard them as the support set $\mathcal{S}_r = \{(h_i, t_i, s_i)|(h_i, r, t_i, s_i) \in \mathcal{G}\}$. The remaining positive triples are utilized as positive queries $\mathcal{Q}_r = \{(h_i, t_i, s_i)|(h_i, r, t_i, s_i) \in \mathcal{G} \cap (h_i, t_i, s_i) \notin \mathcal{S}_r\}$. Besides, we construct a group of negative triples $\mathcal{Q}_r' = \{(h_i, t_i')|(h_i, r, t_i', *) \notin \mathcal{G}\}$ by polluting the tail entities. Therefore, the ranking loss is formulated as:

$$\mathcal{L}_{rank} = \sum_r \sum_{(h,t,s) \in \mathcal{Q}_r} \sum_{(h,t',s') \in \mathcal{Q}_r'} s \cdot [\gamma + s_{rank} - s_{rank}']_+ \tag{6}$$

where $[x]_+ = \max[0, x]$ is standard hinge loss and γ is margin distance, s_{rank} and s'_{rank} are rank scores between query $(h_i, t_i/t'_i)$ and support set $\mathcal{S}_r$.

To reduce the difference between the ground truth confidence score s_i and our predicting confidence score s_{conf}, we utilize mean squared error (MSE) between them as the MSE loss $\mathcal{L}_{mse}$. Specifically, $\mathcal{L}_{mse}$ is defined as:

$$\mathcal{L}_{mse} = \sum_r \sum_{(h_i, t_i, s_i) \in \mathcal{Q}_r} (s_{conf} - s_i)^2 \tag{7}$$

By leveraging the uncertainty loss $\mathcal{L}_{uc}$ of entities and relations, we define the final objective function as:

$$\mathcal{L}_{joint} = w_1 \mathcal{L}_{rank} + w_2 \mathcal{L}_{mse} + w_3 \mathcal{L}_{uc} \tag{8}$$

where w_1, w_2 and w_3 are trade-off factors. To minimize $\mathcal{L}_{joint}$ and optimize model parameters, we take each relations as a task and design a batch sampling based meta-training procedure.

5   Experiments

In this section, we evaluate our models on two tasks: tail entity prediction and confidence score prediction. Ablation studies are followed to verify the impact of each module.

5.1   Datasets

The evaluation is conducted on two datasets named as NL27 k and CN15 k [9]. Table 2 gives the statistics of the datasets. NL27 k is extracted from NELL [3], an uncertain knowledge graph obtained from web pages. CN15 k is a subgraph of the common sense KG ConceptNet [4]. CN15 k matches the number of nodes with FB15 k - the widely used benchmark dataset for DKG embeddings, while NL27 k is a larger and more general dataset.

Entity's type and taxonomy structure are needed for calculating the uncertainty value of each entity/relation. For NL27 k, we utilize NELL's ontology to get the entity taxonomy. For CN15 k, since there is no ontology for ConceptNet, we align all entities in CN15k to DBpedia through the *ExternalURL* relation (one relation defined in ConceptNet) and string matching. Then, we leverage DBpedia's ontology to get the entity taxonomy. Meanwhile, both ontologies provide the type information for each entity. Then, we extract the domain and range of each relation from raw triple data.

We select the relations with less than 500 but more than 50 triples as few-shot tasks. There are 134 tasks in NL27 k and 11 tasks in CN15 k. In addition, we use 101/13/20 task relations for training/validation/testing in NL27k and the division is set to 8/1/2 in CN15 k. We refer the rest of the relations as background relations. According to Eq. 2, 3 and 4, we calculate the corresponding uncertainty values of entities and relations in both datasets and apply z-score normalization to maintain the scale consistency.

Table 2. Statistics of datasets. #Ent., #Rel., #Tri., #Task denote the number of entities, relations, triples, and tasks, respectively. Avg(s) and Std(s) are the average and standard deviation of the confidence scores, respectively.

Dataset	#Ent	#Rel	#Tri	#Task	Avg(s)	Std(s)
NL27k	27,221	404	175,412	134	0.797	0.242
CN15k	15,000	36	241,158	11	0.629	0.232

5.2   Baselines

In our comparison, we consider the following embedding-based methods: (i) UKGE, the first UKG embedding models, (ii) FSRL, a few-shot DKG embedding models, and (iii) GMUC, the first few-shot UKG embedding models. When evaluating UKGE, we use not only the triples of background relations but also all the triples of the training relations and the few-shot training triples of those in validate/test relations. When evaluating FSRL, we set a threshold $\tau = 0.75$ to distinguish high-confidence triples for training.

5.3   Experimental Setup

We tune hyper-parameters based weighted mean reciprocal rank (WMRR) on the validation datasets. The embedding dimension is set to 100 and 50 for NL27 k and CN15 k dataset, respectively. The maximum number of local neighbors in Neighbor Encoder is set to 30. In addition, the dimension of LSTM's hidden state is set to twice the embedding dimension. The number of matching steps equals 2. The margin distance γ is set to 5.0 for NL27 k and 6.0 for CN15 k. The initial learning rate equals 0.001 and the weight decay is 0.25 for each 10 k training steps. The batch size equals 256 and 64 for NL27 k and CN15 k. In entity candidate set construction, we set the maximum size to 1000 for both datasets. The few-shot size is set to 3 for the following experiments. The trade-off factors in the objective function are set to $w_1 = 1, w_2 = 1.1, w_3 = 0.01$.

5.4   Tail Entity Prediction

Tail entity prediction is a conventional evaluation task for knowledge graph embedding. The goal is to predict the tail entities given a head entity and a relation, which can be formulated as $(h, r, ?t)$.

Evaluation Protocol. Relations and their triples in training data are utilized to train the model while those of validation and test data are respectively used to tune and evaluate model. We use the top-k hit ratio (Hits@k), weighted mean rank (WMR), and mean reciprocal rank (WMRR) to evaluate performances of different methods. The k is set to 1, 5 and 10. The mean rank and mean reciprocal rank are linearly weighted by the confidence score.

Results. The performance of all models are reported in Table 3. We refer to the variant that adopt Eq. 3 to calculate relation's uncertainties as $Ours_1$ and name the one using Eq. 4 as $Ours_2$. We can see that our method produces consistent improvements over various embedding models on NL27 k and the superiority is lighter on CN15 k but still gets higher WMRR. UKGE performs much worse than the remaining models, proving that the metric-based framework is very effective in few-shot scenario. The Gaussian distribution representation is better than the point-based one, indicating that it is necessary to consider the uncertainty of entities and relations in UKGs. Our method outperforms GMUC, which demonstrates the rationality of the proposed uncertainty metrics for entities and relations. The results of $Ours_1$ are close to $Ours_2$, indicating that the two ways for calculating relation's uncertainties are both reasonable and effective. Comparing the model's performance on different datasets, all testing results on NL27 k are much better than those on CN15 k, which is caused by the metric-based learning process. Metric-based models aim to learn a matching function between support sets and queries to calculate their similarities, so they need (support set, query) pairs as many as possible, i.e., more training tasks. Nevertheless, CN15 k contains only 11 tasks, lesser than 134 tasks in NL27 k. Therefore, it not surprising that the evaluation results on CN15 k dataset are poor.

Table 3. Results of tail entity prediction

Dataset	Model	Hits@1	Hits@5	HIts@10	WMR	WMRR
NL27k	UKGE	0.031	0.038	0.046	489.537	0.037
	FSRL	0.216	0.373	0.490	81.728	0.294
	GMUC	0.363	0.549	0.626	65.146	0.455
	$Ours_1$	0.379	**0.598**	**0.670**	**50.940**	**0.481**
	$Ours_2$	**0.386**	0.573	0.663	51.539	0.474
CN15k	UKGE	**0.014**	0.019	0.028	496.185	0.022
	FSRL	0.006	0.025	0.041	374.439	0.023
	GMUC	0.002	0.027	0.089	382.188	0.027
	$Ours_1$	0.010	**0.042**	0.090	378.854	0.029
	$Ours_2$	0.013	0.037	**0.094**	**367.456**	**0.034**

5.5   Confidence Score Prediction

Confidence score prediction is to predict the confidence score given a triple, requiring the model to be uncertainty-aware. This task can be formulated as $(h, r, t, ?s)$.

Evaluation Protocol. For each uncertain relation fact (h, r, t, s) in the test query set, we predict the confidence score of (h, r, t) and report the mean squared error (MSE) and mean absolute error (MAE).

Results. Results are reported in Table 4. Since FSRL cannot predict the confidence scores of triples, we only compares with UKGE and GMUC. Our model also achieves the best performance in the this task. The results of UKGE are still worse, indicating that the metric-based few-shot KG embedding framework can also improve the accuracy of confidence prediction. Our method outperforms GMUC, illustrating that incorporating the uncertainty of entities and relations helps the model to predict the uncertainty of facts. The performances of $Ours_1$ and $Ours_2$ are very close, demonstrating the effectiveness of both methods for measuring the relation uncertainty. In the confidence prediction task, the results on two datasets are not much different, showing that confidence score information is easier to learn than the ranking information.

Table 4. Results of confidence score prediction

Dataset	NL27k		CN15k	
Metric	MSE	MAE	MSE	MAE
UKGE	0.468	0.636	0.350	0.541
GMUC	0.017	0.100	0.021	0.112
$Ours_1$	0.015	0.094	0.017	0.082
$Ours_2$	**0.015**	**0.092**	**0.017**	**0.079**

5.6   Ablation Studies

To investigate the contributions of different modules, we conduct the following ablation studies from three perspectives: (i) remove the Neighbor Encoder, denoted by No $\mathcal{F}_{NE}$, (ii) replace the LSTM-based Matching Network with the cosine similarity, denoted by No $\mathcal{F}_{MP}$, and (iii) exclude the uncertainty loss of entities and relations, denoted by No $\mathcal{L}_{uc}$.

Table 5. Results of ablation studies on different components.

Configuration	Hits@1	Hits@5	Hits@10	WMR	WMRR
No $\mathcal{F}_{NE}$	0.091	0.154	0.204	175.535	0.148
No $\mathcal{F}_{MP}$	0.129	0.239	0.317	118.207	0.203
No $\mathcal{L}_{uc}$	0.198	0.406	0.488	58.937	0.313
$Ours_1$	**0.234**	**0.450**	**0.540**	**49.093**	**0.346**

Table 5 shows the results of tail entity prediction in NL27k validate set and best results are highlighted in bold. We can see that removing any module will weaken the overall effect of our method, and the Neighbor Encoder has the greatest contribution. In addition, the results of No $\mathcal{L}_{uc}$ is worse than Ours$_1$, indicating that constraining the variance vector in Gaussian distribution by quantified element-level uncertainty can also boost the performance.

6 Conclusion

This paper introduces a few-shot uncertain knowledge graph embedding method by incorporating the uncertainty of entities and relations. We propose the corresponding metrics to measure the inherent element-level uncertainty of each entity and relation in UKGs and incorporate it into a few-shot metric-based framework to capture both semantic and uncertainty information. The extensive experiments on two public datasets demonstrate that our proposed method can outperform the state-of-the-art baseline models. Our future work might consider extending the metrics for element-level uncertainty into deterministic knowledge graphs to improve the learned embeddings.

Acknowledgements. This work is supported by the NSFC (Grant No. 62006040), the Project for the Doctor of Entrepreneurship and Innovation in Jiangsu Province (Grant No. JSSCBS20210126), the Fundamental Research Funds for the Central Universities, and ZhiShan Young Scholar Program of Southeast University.

References

1. Mao, Z., Wang, B., Guo, L., Wang, Q.: Knowledge graph embedding: a survey of approaches and applications. IEEE Trans. Knowl. Data Eng. **29**(12), 2724–2743 (2017)
2. Wu, W., Li, H., Wang, H., Zhu, K.: Probase: for text understanding. In: Proceedings of SIGMOD, pp. 481–492 (2012)
3. Carlson, A., Betteridge, J., Kisiel, B., Settles, B., Hruschka, E.R., Mitchell, T.M.: Toward an architecture for never-ending language learning. In: Proceedings of AAAI (2010)
4. Speer, R., Chin, J., Havasi, C.: ConceptNet 5.5: an open multilingual graph of general knowledge. In: Proceedings of AAAI, pp. 4444–4451 (2017)
5. Bordes, A., Usunier, N., García-Durán, A., Weston, J., Yakhnenko, O.: Translating embeddings for modeling multi-relational data. In: Proceedings of NeurIPS, pp. 2787–2795 (2013)
6. Wang, Z., Zhang, J., Feng, J., Chen, Z.: Knowledge graph embedding by translating on hyperplanes. In: Proceedings of AAAI, pp. 1112–1119 (2014)
7. Yang, B., Yih, W., He, X., Gao, J., Deng, L.: Embedding entities and relations for learning and inference in knowledge bases. In: Proceedings of ICLR (Poster) (2015)
8. Trouillon, T., Welbl, J., Riedel, S., Gaussier, E., Bouchard, G.: Complex embeddings for simple link prediction. In: Proceedings of ICML, pp. 2071–2080 (2016)
9. Chen, X., Chen, M., Shi, W., Sun, Y., Zaniolo, C.: Embedding uncertain knowledge graphs. In: Proceedings of AAAI, pp. 3363–3370 (2019)

10. Chen, Z., Yeh, M., Kuo, T.: PASSLEAF: a pool-based semi-supervised learning framework for uncertain knowledge graph embedding. In: Proceedings of AAAI, pp. 4019–4026 (2021)
11. Chen, X., Boratko, M., Chen, M., Dasgupta, S., Li, X., McCallum, A.: Probabilistic box embeddings for uncertain knowledge graph reasoning. In: Proceedings of NAACL-HLT, pp. 882–893 (2021)
12. Kertkeidkachorn, N., Liu, X., Ichise, R.: GTransE: generalizing translation-based model on uncertain knowledge graph embedding. In: Proceedings of JSAI, pp. 170–178 (2019)
13. Zhang, J., Wu, T., Qi, G.: Gaussian metric learning for few-shot uncertain knowledge graph completion. In: Jensen, C.S., et al. (eds.) DASFAA 2021. LNCS, vol. 12681, pp. 256–271. Springer, Cham (2021). https://doi.org/10.1007/978-3-030-73194-6_18
14. He, S., Liu, K., Ji, G., Zhao, J.: Learning to represent knowledge graphs with Gaussian embedding. In: Proceedings of CIKM, pp. 623–632 (2015)
15. Sun, Z., Deng, Z., Nie, J., Tang, J.: Rotate: knowledge graph embedding by relational rotation in complex space. In: Proceedings of ICLR (Poster) (2019)
16. Nickel, M., Tresp, V., Kriegel, H.: A three-way model for collective learning on multi-relational data. In: Proceedings of ICML, pp. 809–816 (2011)
17. Schlichtkrull, M., Kipf, T.N., Bloem, P., van den Berg, R., Titov, I., Welling, M.: Modeling relational data with graph convolutional networks. In: Gangemi, A., et al. (eds.) ESWC 2018. LNCS, vol. 10843, pp. 593–607. Springer, Cham (2018). https://doi.org/10.1007/978-3-319-93417-4_38
18. Yao, L., Mao, C., Luo, Y.: KG-BERT: BERT for knowledge graph completion. CoRR abs/1909.03193 (2019)
19. Xiong, W., Yu, M., Chang, S., William Yang Wang, X.G.: One-shot relational learning for knowledge graphs. In: Proceedings of EMNLP, pp. 1980–1990 (2018)
20. Zang, C., Yao, H., Huang, C., Jiang, M., Li, Z., Chawla, N.V.: Few-shot knowledge graph completion. In: Proceedings of AAAI, pp. 3041–3048 (2020)
21. Ravi, S., Larochelle, H.: Optimization as a model for few-shot learning. In: Proceedings of ICLR (2017)
22. Miller, G.A.: WordNet: a lexical database for English. Commun. ACM **38**(11), 39–41 (1995)
23. Hochreiter, S., Schmidhuber, J.: Long short-term memory. Neural Comput. **9**(8), 1735–1780 (1997)
24. Vinyals, O., Blundell, C., Lillicrap, T., Kavukcuoglu, K., Wierstra, D.: Matching networks for one shot learning. In: Proceedings of NeurIPS, pp. 3630–3638 (2016)

Knowledge Acquisition and Knowledge Base Construction

TraConcept: Constructing a Concept Framework from Chinese Traffic Legal Texts

Xinyu Cai[1], Peng Gao[2], and Xiang Zhang[2,3]([✉])

[1] School of Cyber Science and Engineering, Southeast University, Nanjing, China
xycai@seu.edu.cn
[2] School of Computer Science and Engineering, Southeast University, Nanjing, China
{gao_peng,x.zhang}@seu.edu.cn
[3] Research Center for Judicial Big Data, Supreme Court of China, Nanjing, China

Abstract. To construct a legal knowledge graph to support the intelligent computing in the domain of law, a conceptual framework of this domain needs to be set up first. This framework usually comprises domain-specific inter-related concepts, their relations, and their attributes, to achieve a comprehensive understanding of the subject domain. While some of the topics in the task of concept framework construction had been studied, such as the identification of hypernymy/hyponymy relations, other key parts in this task have not been fully investigated. In this work, we propose a system TraConcept, in which we use PLM to encode traffic concept pairs with context to alleviate the "lexical memorization" problem. In addition, we model this task as a multi-relation identification problem and use a Siamese Network with a tensor layer to solve this problem. Compared with state-of-the-art methods, our method is more effective in detecting multi-relations between Chinese traffic concepts and finding attributes of these concepts in a large corpus of traffic legal texts.

Keywords: Concept framework · Hypernymy/hyponymy relation · Traffic legal text

1 Introduction

To construct a legal knowledge graph to support intelligent computing in the domain of law, a conceptual framework for this domain needs to be set up first. The construction of such a framework will greatly facilitate the organization and representation of shareable knowledge in the law domain, and thus promote the upper-level knowledge-enhanced applications, such as the "Smart Court". This framework usually comprises domain-specific inter-related concepts, their relations, and their attributes, to achieve a comprehensive understanding of the subject domain. As shown in Fig. 1, a conceptual framework constructed from traffic legal texts comprises several traffic concepts, such as "机动车(MotorVehicle)"

M. Sun et al. (Eds.): CCKS 2022, CCIS 1669, pp. 31–42, 2022.
https://doi.org/10.1007/978-981-19-7596-7_3

and "小轿车(Car)" , the hypernymy or hyponymy relations between these concepts, and their attributes, such as "颜色(color)" and "品牌(brand)" . Concepts, relations, and attributes play fundamental roles in building a hierarchical concept framework [2]. In the research of taxonomy learning [13], pattern-based methods [5,9] and distributional approaches [10] were two major paradigms to predict hypernymy/hyponymy relations between terms. The problem of pattern-based methods is that relation between two terms can only be identified when they co-occur in the same sentence. Distributional approaches alleviate this problem and directly use the distributed representation of the two terms as the input features of the learning model to infer whether the two terms have a certain relation. However, distributional approaches suffer from the problem of "lexical memorization" [6], in which relation classifiers are prone to identify the relationship by learning the lexical features, not the semantic features. In addition, existing methods generally aim at binary relation classification, while concept attributes are usually ignored in constructing the conceptual framework.

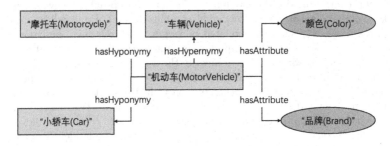

Fig. 1. Example of a simple Concept Framework

In this paper, we model the task of concept framework construction as a multi-relation identification problem. A system of TraConcept is proposed to resolve this problem by identifying multiple concept-concept relations and concept-attribute relations from massive Chinese traffic legal texts. Our contributions can be summarized as follows:

1) We use a Pre-training Language Model to encode domain term pairs with context. This encoding can effectively alleviate the problem of "lexical memorization";
2) We use a Siamese Network with a tensor layer and a double affine operation to accurately capture multiple relations among traffic legal concepts and their attributes.

2   Related Work

Hearst et al. [5] pioneered the line of pattern-based hypernymy discovery methods which leverage hand-crafted lexico-syntactic patterns to extract explicitly mentioned hypernymy pairs from a text corpus. Snow et al. [11] trained a logistic regression classifier to find the dependency path related to the hypernymy and then used this classifier to identify the new hypernymy on the new corpus. Liu et al. [7] used two syntactic templates with high quality and high coverage to identify Chinese hypernymy. To overcome occurrence sparsity [9], distributional approaches model the degree of hypernymy within a term pair. The earliest use of this approaches for hypernymy discovery only focused on the relevance between a term pair. More recently, Distributional Inclusion Hypothesis (DIH) is the premise of these approaches. It means that the semantics of the hypernym is often broader than the semantics of the corresponding hyponyms. An example of a successful DIH is WeedsPrec [15].

3   Problem Statement

Constructing a conceptual framework in the traffic legal area can be depicted in two major steps: 1) identifying domain concepts in a relevant corpus; 2) extracting concept-concept and concept-attribute relations from the corpus.

We use a distant supervision paradigm to identify domain concepts in a traffic legal corpus we collected. If domain concept can be matched to the knowledge base as a positive example, if not as a negative example. By random forest, frequent and subject-relevant n-gram are extracted from the corpus. Then phrases are automatically labeled with syntactic information to characterize their popularity, consistency, informativeness, and completeness. These syntactic features are exploited in a domain concept classifier, to assign a pseudo label to each phrase. Since concept identification is not the focus of this paper, and there is a length limitation of this paper, we omit the details here.

Constructing Concept Framework as a Multi-Relation Identification Task. Corpus is a large-scale electronic text library. Concepts are abstractions of the essence of things and concept pairs are two related concepts. A knowledge base is a collection of domain knowledge defined by experts.

Given a set of corpus D, we extract a set of concepts C using the above method. Then We combine knowledge base K and C to extract concept pairs $C_p = <c_i, c_j>$ of hypernymy and concept-attribute. We mix five relations in a 1:1 ratio to get a set of relations R and randomly select concepts in the C for pairing to get negative samples. These five relations include: <hypernym, hyponym>, <hyponym, hypernym>, <concept, attribute>, <attribute, concept> and other relations. In multi-relation identification, our task is to learn a classifier f to map any given concept pair C_x to relations set R.

4   TraConcept

Previous models usually encode the domain terms with word embeddings, which may trigger the "lexical memorization" problem [6]. To address this problem,

Verga et al. [12] tried to learn a contextual embedding for a given domain term occurring in a contextual description. In TraConcept, we use a Siamese Network [8], which has an architecture containing a couple of networks with shared parameters. We use the Siamese Network to capture the features of given domain terms with contexts and to produce a comparable output to reflect a potential relationship between this pair of domain terms. For each domain term in the pair, a set of context sentences describing this term is extracted and fed into the encoding layer. Term mentions at different positions in a contextual description have different degrees of importance, so we use the attention mechanism to learn how each mention contributes to the contextual embedding.

For the identification of relations and attributes, a multi-relation classifier is needed. Glava et al. [4] used a tensor model to learn representations in the task of hyponymy detection. It showed the effectiveness of the tensor model in characterizing multi-relational data. Inspired by this work, we put a bi-affine operation in a tensor layer to decide which relation a given domain term holds. The network architecture of TraConcept is shown in Fig. 2.

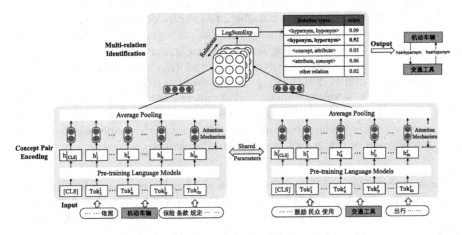

Fig. 2. The Network Architecture of TraConcept.

4.1 Domain Terms Encoding

Given a domain term pair $<c_1, c_2>$, the first step is to separately get a contextual description of c_1 and c_2. We use the keyword search to retrieve a set of term-related sentences from the corpus, and randomly select 3 sentences to form a contextual description to represent the context for each domain term. The contextual description of each domain term will be further divided into tokens $\{Tok_1^l, Tok_2^l, ..., Tok_m^l\}$ and $\{Tok_1^r, Tok_2^r, ..., Tok_m^r\}$, where l and r stand for the left domain term c_1 and the right domain term c_2 in a pair. For example, given the pair <机动车辆, 交通工具 > having a hypernymy relation and the pair

<电动自行车, 车速 > having a concept-attribute relation, part of their contextual description are shown in Table 1.

Table 1. Example table of conceptual description corresponding to domain term

Domain term	Conceptual description
机动车辆	依照《机动车辆保险条款》规定, ...
交通工具	... 鼓励公众使用清洁能源交通工具出行, ...
电动自行车	（一）驾驶自行车、电动自行车、三轮车在路段上横过机动车道时...
车速	... 最大设计车速小于或等于50公里/小时的四个车轮的机动车。...

We adopt PLM(Pre-training Language Model) to encode the contextual description of a given concept or attribute separately. We can get two encoded contextual description: $(O^l_{[CLS]}, O^l_1, O^l_2, ..., O^l_m)$ and $(O^r_{[CLS]}, O^r_1, O^r_2, ..., O^r_m)$, where $O^l_{[CLS]}$ and $O^r_{[CLS]}$ are the head label information of the contextual description; $O_i \in \mathcal{R}^d$; d denotes the dimension of the encoded words.

Domain term mention at different positions in the contextual description have different degrees of importance, so it is helpful to learn how domain term mention in different locations contributes to the final contextual embedding. For example, in the sentence "依照《机动车辆保险条款》规定, ...", "机动车辆" are subordinate to another domain term "机动车辆保险条款". However, in this sentence "（五）非法拦截、扣留机动车辆, ...", "机动车辆" is a separate domain term, so its importance is higher than "机动车辆" in the previous sentence. In our model, we introduce an attention mechanism to improve detection performance.

As illustrated in Fig. 2, we use this method to construct the contextual embedding of the domain term mention. Firstly, we construct a mask sequence according to the position of the domain term mention in the contextual description, which is used to filter the coding information passed from the pre-training encoding module. Then we can get two sequences: $h^l = (h^l_{[CLS]}, h^l_1, h^l_2, ..., h^l_m)$ and $h^r = (h^r_{[CLS]}, h^r_1, h^r_2, ..., h^r_m)$. Then, we use the attention mechanism to calculate the contribution of domain term mention in different positions to the final contextual embedding, which is computed as follows:

$$W_S = Softmax(\frac{(HW_K)(HW_Q)^T}{\sqrt{d'}}) \tag{1}$$

$$\theta_i = W_S H W_V \tag{2}$$

$$A = [\theta_1; \theta_2; ...; \theta_t]W_O \tag{3}$$

Here, H is the output sequence of the mask layer, d' denotes the dimension of the output of a single attention head, and W_K, W_V, W_Q and W_O are the parameters of the network. Finally, we use pooling operations to compress data and parameters to reduce the risk of overfitting.

4.2   Multi-relation Identification

To detect multi-relations between domain terms, we use a tensor layer to capture semantic features through double affine operations. Through the last module, we get the contextual embedding A^l , A^r of h^l , h^r:

$$A^l = (a_1^l, a_2^l, ..., a_{m+1}^l)$$

$$A^r = (a_1^r, a_2^r, ..., a_{m+1}^r)$$

We use a bi-affine operator to calculate an $(m+1) \times L \times (m+1)$ tensor W_T, which is the raw score of domain term pairs:

$$W_T = A^l W_L (A^r)^T \tag{4}$$

where W_L is a $d \times L \times d$ tensor, a learned embedding matrix for each of the L relations. Then we use the Softmax function to normalize the dimension representing the initial score of the relation. For each domain term pair$<c_1, c_2>$, we use the LogSumExp function [1] to get the score in each relation category:

$$score(c_1, c_2) = log \sum_{k=1}^{m+1} \sum_{i=1}^{m+1} exp(Softmax(W_{T_{ijk}})) \tag{5}$$

The LogSumExp scoring function is a smooth approximation to the max function and has the benefits of aggregating information from multiple predictions and propagating dense gradients as opposed to the sparse gradient updates of the max. Finally, we can directly use Argmax to get the final relation category.

4.3   Model Training

We use the maximum likelihood function as the objective function based on the score calculated by the LogSumExp function. In addition, for the detection of binary classification relations, we will calculate the contrast loss function between contextual embeddings based on the current objective function $\mathcal{L}_1$:

$$\mathcal{L}_1 = \beta_1 \frac{1}{L} \sum_{i=1}^{L} log P(r_i | score(c_1, c_2)) + \beta_2 \mathcal{L}_2 \tag{6}$$

$$\mathcal{L}_2 = \sum_{A'} \eta * label * d^2 + (1 - label) * Relu(margin - d)^2 \tag{7}$$

where L refers to the number of relations. r_i is the type of relation. $\mathcal{L}_2$ is the contrastive Loss, and $d = cos(A^r, A^l)$ is the cosine similarity of contextual embedding. β_1, β_2, η and $margin$ are hyperparameter.

5   Experiments

In this section, we conduct extensive experiments to evaluate our model over various benchmarks. We also compare it with state-of-the-art to show its effectiveness.

5.1 Experimental Setup

Dataset. Our model is evaluated on a Chinese traffic legal text corpus HITT, which was constructed in our previous work [3]. Since the previous model was only used to detect single relations, this corpus was divided into two parts: HITT-h and HITT-a, in which the HITT-h dataset is used for hypernymy/hyponymy identification, and the HITT-a dataset is used for concept attribute relation detection. The ratio of positive and negative samples is 1:4. To perform experiments on multi-relation detection, we mixed HITT-h and HITT-a to obtain HITT-m dataset. This dataset has five categories, including <hypernym, hyponym>, <hyponym, hypernym>, <concept, attribute>, <attribute, concept> and other relation. The ratio of each category is 1: 1. The number of sentences included in each dataset is shown in Table 2. The dataset and code are available in https://github.com/wds-seu/TraConcept for reproducibility.

Table 2. The statistical characteristics of datasets

Dataset	Train	Validation	Test
HITT-h	18,847	6,302	6,292
HITT-a	40,412	13,449	13,451
HITT-m	19,100	6,120	6,515

Metrics. In the following experiments, widely-used performance measures such as precision (P), recall (R), F1-score (F1), and accuracy (A) are used to evaluate the methods. For multi-relation detection experiments, we use Micro-P, Micro-R, and Micro-F1 to measure performance.

5.2 Comparison with State-of-the-Art Models

In the experiments, we compare our model with state-of-the-art methods. These reference algorithms can be roughly divided into two categories: three methods of single relation detection and two methods for multi-relation detection.

The Methods dedicated to detecting single relations used in this paper are listed as follows:

1) U_Teal [14] is an unsupervised method that uses the projection network model trained by the taxonomy to classify the set of concept pairs of binary relations;
2) S_Teal [14] is a supervised method, which classifies concept pairs by using a word embedding learned from the corpus and artificially labeled training sets;
3) AS_Teal [14] uses two adversarial classifiers to train the prediction model through the competition between the S_Teal model and the projection network constructed by the Taxonomy, thereby further improving the classification performance of the model

For multi-relation detection, we selected two methods, which can detect multi-relation and single relation detection. These methods are:

1) D-Tensor [4] uses two tensors to convert concept embeddings at different positions into vectors in a specific semantic space for comparison;
2) Bran [12] uses Transformer to encode the spliced contextual description, and then directly uses the double affine operation to calculate the score between context embeddings, which is used to classify the semantic relation between concepts;

Table 3 summarizes the comparative results of our model and five reference algorithms on the HITT-h and HITT-a. From the table, we observe that our model outperforms these reference algorithms. More specifically, our model achieves the best F1 scores on HITT-h compared with all reference algorithms. While for the performance in terms of recall and precision, our model is also highly competitive. For the adapted reference algorithms, we observe that the accuracy (93.36%) and precision (88.67%) of AS_Teal are higher than the model proposed in this article on the HITT-h, and its F1-score on the HITT-a is higher than our model. However, AS_Teal uses additional knowledge base information to train the adversarial network, which can capture the structural information in the knowledge base. We extract the corresponding knowledge base information from CN-DBpedia and CN-Probase respectively to train its projection network. However, we have achieved considerable results without the help of knowledge base information.

Table 3. Comparative results of our model and reference methods. The Method with * uses additional knowledge base information

	HITT-h				HITT-a			
	A	P	R	F1	A	P	R	F1
D-Tensor (Glavaš et al. 2017)	87.78	74.88	61.56	67.45	83.27	70.15	60.18	65.38
Bran (Verga et al. 2018)	91.52	82.31	79.68	81.32	85.34	71.25	65.48	68.56
U_Teal (Wang et al. 2019)	91.52	82.31	79.68	81.32	85.34	71.25	65.48	68.56
S_Teal (Wang et al. 2019)	90.85	87.03	84.31	85.56	89.90	74.22	73.44	73.83
AS_Teal (Wang et al. 2019)*	**93.36**	**88.67**	86.22	87.89	**92.92**	**80.89**	79.60	**79.70**
Ours	93.00	87.88	**89.79**	**88.18**	91.09	77.66	**81.02**	79.31

We also conduct experiments on multi-relation detection tasks on the HITT-m dataset, and the overall experimental results are shown in Table 4. In the baseline model, D-Tensor, and Bran can perform multi-relation phrase pair detection like our model. It can be seen that our model achieves highly competitive performance on multi-relation domain terms detection compared with these two reference baselines. The reason is that we adopted an advanced PLM, which significantly improved the effect. Besides, we use the attention mechanism to encode the contextual embedding of domain terms, which can effectively capture the semantic relation between domain terms.

Table 4. Comparative results of our model and reference methods on multi-relation detection

	HITT-m			
	A	Macro_P	Macro_R	Macro_F1
D-Tensor (Glavaš et al. 2017)	75.30	76.52	73.34	74.78
Bran (Verga et al. 2018)	78.89	79.32	75.18	77.56
Ours	**81.57**	**82.23**	**81.56**	**81.80**

5.3   Effectiveness of the Domain Term Pair Encoding

To eliminate lexical memorization, we do not directly encode the domain term but use the contextual description corresponding to the domain term to obtain the contextual embedding corresponding to the domain term. Therefore, the problem of lexical memorization can be effectively eliminated. To investigate the effectiveness of our method, we use a traditional neural network to directly encode the domain term to capture the semantic relation between domain terms for analysis. Based on three datasets, we compare some encode methods.

Table 5 shows the comparative results of some different encoding methods on three datasets. The performance of our sequence encoding with the Pre-training Language Model is better than other encoding methods. Our model improved by about 11.3%, 8.86%, and 9.4% accuracy rate to the best baseline model on the three datasets. The experimental results show that encoding contextual descriptions of domain terms can effectively improve the overall performance of our model.

Table 5. Comparative results of several encoding methods

	HITT-h	HITT-a	HITT-m
CNN	74.38	78.67	68.32
RNN	76.81	80.22	69.84
fastText	79.61	80.36	70.60
Transformer	79.59	80.33	70.53
Seq2Seq+Attention	79.45	80.36	70.84
Ours	**93.00**	**91.09**	**81.57**

In addition, we also verified the effectiveness of the PLM used in our model. Based on three datasets, we empirically compare BiLSTM and five Pre-training Language Models.

The experimental results are shown in Fig. 3. It can be seen that the relation detection results using Pre-training Language Models are better than those using traditional BiLSTM for contextual description encoding. We also observe that

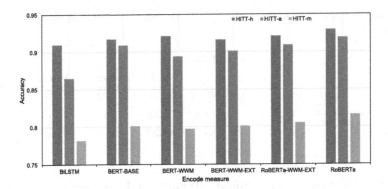

Fig. 3. The accuracy of relation detection in the different Pre-training Language Models

RoBERTa achieves better performance than BERT overall. The experimental results also show that the use of Whole Word Masking (WWM) does not necessarily improve the overall performance of the model. We think that the main reason is that the word segmentation method of WordPiece is used when the model is tuned, and the character-level word segmentation method is still used for Chinese sequences, so the performance of WWM is not effectively used.

5.4 Effectiveness of the Tensor Layer

This section is devoted to investigating the effectiveness of our tensor layer. To test the performance of our model, we designed the four variants to replace the tensor layer.

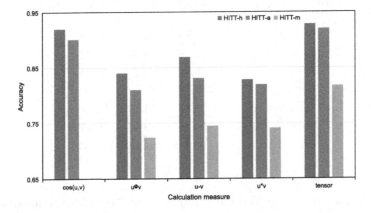

Fig. 4. The accuracy of relation detection of different relation capture modules

The experimental results are shown in Fig. 4. We can observe that calculating the cosine similarity between context embeddings to single relation detection can experimental results comparable to the model in this paper on the HITT-h and HITT-a datasets. In terms of multi-relation detection, in addition to the method proposed in this paper, vector subtraction operations between context embeddings have achieved the best experimental results on the HITT-m dataset.

5.5 Error Inspection

Although our model achieves good results in relation detection, we observed several common errors which are useful for further research. Error statistics are shown in Table 6. In the three datasets, the majority of the sources of the errors are contextual description problems. Such cases include <新能源汽车，汽车型号 >, <政治权利，法规 >, etc. For these concepts and attributes, the corresponding contextual description lacks sufficient scale or cannot provide effective information. Another major error is the domain terms of error contained in three datasets. Such cases include <会计师事务所，奔驰公司 >, <庐阳区人民法院，前身 >, etc. This is an error in our domain terms identification task, which leads to the inclusion of wrong domain terms in the datasets.

Table 6. Error statistics

	HITT-h	HITT-a	HITT-m
Problems with contextual description	0.22	0.42	0.46
Wrong domain terms	0.26	0.24	0.16
Similar domain terms	0.24	0.12	0.04
Related domain terms	0.18	–	0.10
Wrong label	0.08	0.12	0.16
Other	-	0.10	0.08

6   Conclusion and the Future Work

In this paper, we propose a system TraConcept for constructing a Concept Framework. Instead of directly operating on the word embedding representation of the domain term, we use a PLM to encode the input sequence, which effectively prevents the problem of lexical memorization. In addition, our model can detect multi-relations of domain terms by combining the tensor model. We conduct extensive experiments on three datasets we built to validate the effectiveness of the proposed model. Experimental results show that our model overwhelmingly outperforms state-of-the-art baselines over different scenarios, especially on multi-relation detection. In the future, we plan to explore more domain term relations to construct a more complete Concept Framework in the field of Chinese traffic legal.

Acknowledgments. This work was supported by the National Key R&D Program of China (2019YFB2101802).

References

1. Das, R., Neelakantan, A., Belanger, D., McCallum, A.: Chains of reasoning over entities, relations, and text using recurrent neural networks. arXiv preprint arXiv:1607.01426 (2016)
2. Fu, R., Guo, J., Qin, B., Che, W., Wang, H., Liu, T.: Learning semantic hierarchies via word embeddings. In: Proceedings of the 52nd Annual Meeting of the Association for Computational Linguistics (Volume 1: Long Papers), pp. 1199–1209 (2014)
3. Gao, P., Zhang, X., Qi, G.: Discovering hypernymy relationships in Chinese traffic legal texts. In: Wang, X., Lisi, F.A., Xiao, G., Botoeva, E. (eds.) Semant. Technol., pp. 109–116. Springer, Singapore (2020)
4. Glavaš, G., Ponzetto, S.P.: Dual tensor model for detecting asymmetric lexico-semantic relations. Association for Computational Linguistics (2017)
5. Hearst, M.A.: Automatic acquisition of hyponyms from large text corpora. In: The 14th International Conference on Computational Linguistics COLING 1992, vol. 2 (1992)
6. Levy, O., Remus, S., Biemann, C., Dagan, I.: Do supervised distributional methods really learn lexical inference relations? In: Proceedings of the 2015 Conference of the North American Chapter of the Association for Computational Linguistics: Human Language Technologies, pp. 970–976 (2015)
7. Liu, L., Zhang, S., Diao, L.H., Cao, C.: An iterative method of extracting Chinese is a relations for ontology learning. J. Comput. **5**(6), 870–877 (2010)
8. Reimers, N., Gurevych, I.: Sentence-Bert: sentence embeddings using siamese Bert-networks. arXiv preprint arXiv:1908.10084 (2019)
9. Roller, S., Kiela, D., Nickel, M.: Hearst patterns revisited: automatic hypernym detection from large text corpora. arXiv preprint arXiv:1806.03191 (2018)
10. Shwartz, V., Goldberg, Y., Dagan, I.: Improving hypernymy detection with an integrated path-based and distributional method. arXiv preprint arXiv:1603.06076 (2016)
11. Snow, R., Jurafsky, D., Ng, A.: Learning syntactic patterns for automatic hypernym discovery. In: Advances in Neural Information Processing Systems, vol. 17 (2004)
12. Verga, P., Strubell, E., McCallum, A.: Simultaneously self-attending to all mentions for full-abstract biological relation extraction. arXiv preprint arXiv:1802.10569 (2018)
13. Wang, C., He, X., Zhou, A.: A short survey on taxonomy learning from text corpora: issues, resources and recent advances. In: Proceedings of the 2017 Conference on Empirical Methods in Natural Language Processing, pp. 1190–1203 (2017)
14. Wang, C., He, X., Zhou, A.: Improving hypernymy prediction via taxonomy enhanced adversarial learning. In: Proceedings of the AAAI Conference on Artificial Intelligence, vol. 33, pp. 7128–7135 (2019)
15. Weeds, J., Weir, D.: A general framework for distributional similarity. In: Proceedings of the 2003 Conference on Empirical Methods in Natural Language Processing, pp. 81–88 (2003)

Document-Level Relation Extraction with a Dependency Syntax Transformer and Supervised Contrastive Learning

Ming Yang[1], Yijia Zhang[1(✉)], Santosh Kumar Banbhrani[2], Hongfei Lin[2], and Mingyu Lu[1]

[1] School of Information Science and Technology, Dalian Maritime University, Dalian 116024, Liaoning, China
zhangyijia@dlmu.edu.cn
[2] School of Computer Science and Technology, Dalian University of Technology, Dalian 116023, Lioaoning, China

Abstract. Document-level Relation Extraction is more challenging than its sentence-level counterpart, extracting unknown relational facts from a plain text at the document level. Studies have shown that the Transformer architecture models long-distance dependencies without regard to the syntax-level dependencies between tokens in the sequence, which hinders its ability to model long-range dependencies. Furthermore, the global information among relational triples and local information around entities is critical. In this paper, we propose a **D**ependency **S**yntax **T**ransformer and **S**upervised **C**ontrastive Learning model (DSTSC) for document-level relation extraction. Specifically, dependency syntax information guides Transformer to enhance attention between tokens with dependency syntax relation in the sequence. The ability of Transformer to model document-level dependencies is improved. Supervised contrastive learning with fusion knowledge captures global information among relational triples. Gaussian probability distributions are also designed to capture local information around entities. Our experiments on two document-level relation extraction datasets, CDR and GDA, have remarkable results.

Keywords: Document-level relation extraction · Transformer model · Dependency syntax · Supervised contrastive learning · Gaussian probability

1 Introduction

Relation extraction (RE) extracts unknown relational facts from plain text, which is a significant step in text mining. Earlier research focused on predicting relations between entities in a single sentence [3,8]. However, large amounts of relational information between entities, such as biomedical literature, are inferred from multiple long sentences in real-world applications. Therefore, relation extraction gradually extends to the document level [6,9,13].

© The Author(s), under exclusive license to Springer Nature Singapore Pte Ltd. 2022
M. Sun et al. (Eds.): CCKS 2022, CCIS 1669, pp. 43–54, 2022.
https://doi.org/10.1007/978-981-19-7596-7_4

Document-level RE is more challenging than sentence-level RE. Only one entity pare of a sentence is to be classified in the sentence-level RE. A document contains multiple entity pairs in document-level RE, each of which may have multiple relations. But in sentence-level RE, there is only one relation per entity pair. This multi-entity, multi-label (multiple relation types for a particular entity pair) and long sentence of document-level RE make it more difficult than sentence-level RE. Figure 1 shows an instance of the CDR dataset, where P1 describes the combination of four drugs, cis-platinum, Adriamycin, cyclophosphamide, and hexamethyl elamine, to treat ovarian cancer. P2 is the medication record of the patient. P3 said that the patient showed anemia after taking the drug. It can be inferred that CPDD induces anemia and other CID relation. However, P2 and P3 are separated by multiple sentences, which requires the model to have excellent modeling ability for long sentence dependencies. Moreover, it requires the model to infer the relation between target entity pair by integrating important information, such as entity-local and entity-global information, in the document.

[P1] Treatment of ovarian cancer with a combination of cis - platinum , adriamycin , cyclophosphamide and hexamethylmelamine.
[P2] During the last 2 1 / 2 years , 38 patients with ovarian cancer were treated with a combination of cisplatinum (CPDD) , 50 mg / m2 , adriamycin , 30 mg / m2 , cyclophosphamide , 300 mg / m2 , on day 1 ; and hexamethylmelamine (HMM) , 6 mg / kg daily , for 14 days .Each course was repeated monthly .
...

[P3] Hematologic toxicity was moderate and with reversible anemia developing in 71 % of patients .
[P4] Gastrointestinal side effects from CPDD were universal . HMM gastrointestinal toxicity necessitated discontinuation of the drug in 5 patients .
...

Fig. 1. An illustrative instance in the CDR dataset.

The Transformer model has been used in natural language processing (NLP) to tackle the above problems and achieved excellent results [12]. The Transformer models rely on attention mechanisms to draw global dependencies between input and output. Attention mechanisms allow the modeling of dependencies without regard to the syntax-level dependencies between tokens dependencies at the syntax level in the sequence. This prevents the Transformer from modeling dependencies of sentences in long-range and reasoning relation between entities.

Dependency trees have been used particularly effectively in tasks to capture long-distance relations among entities in RE. The existing method is that graph convolutional networks(GCN) use dependency trees to update entity information through propagation [9]. However, most of these methods are difficult to apply to different models, significantly when the model's overall structure has changed or when new suggestions are made to insert the dependency tree information. Nor can it change the Transformer model to model the dependency relation between tokens in articles. In addition, some relational triples can provide information to each other due to the relevance of the information within the exact text, especially biomedical information. Local information around entities is particularly beneficial for inferential relationships.

Inspired by the above, we propose a **D**ependency **S**yntax **T**ransformer and **S**upervised **C**ontrastive Learning with Fused Knowledge model (DSTSC) for document-level relation extraction. Specifically, a decomposed linear transformation is used to introduce dependency syntax information into the Transformer to enhance the attention between tokens with dependency syntax in a sentence. The dependency syntax guides the self-attention part of the Transformer model to improve the Transformer model's ability to model dependencies in long sentences. Supervised contrastive learning with domain knowledge captures global information among relational triples. Based on knowledge guidance, automatically pull into the same category relational triplet and learn similar data characteristics. In addition, Gaussian probability distributions are also designed to capture local information around entities. Our research contributions can be summarized as follows:

- We propose a Transformer model guided by dependency syntax information to enhance the Transformer model's ability to model dependencies on long-distance text.
- We propose a Supervised contrastive loss with fused knowledge to capture global information among relational triples and Gaussian probability distributions to capture local information around entities.
- Experimental results on two public document-level relation extraction datasets, CDR and GDA, demonstrate the effectiveness of our DSTSC model and achieve SOTA performance on both datasets. DSTSC model facilitates document-level relation extraction.

2   Method

2.1   Overview

In this section, we will detail the various modules of DSTSC. The overall structure of the model is shown in Fig. 2. The DSTSC model consists of three main components: (1) **Dependency syntax Transformer model layer**, a Transformer model guided by dependency syntax information to enhance its ability to model long-distance dependencies. First, the dependency syntax tree of a sentence is obtained by using the dependency syntax parsing tool, such as Stanford CoreNLP[1]. Then the dependency syntax tree of the whole article is designed. Finally, the dependency syntax tree is used to guide the attention direction of the Transformer model. (2) **Guass enhancement layer**, a way to capture local information around an entity. (3) **Supervision contrastive losses with knowledge layer**, a supervised contrastive loss with fused knowledge for capturing global information among relational triples.

---

[1] https://stanfordnlp.github.io/CoreNLP/.

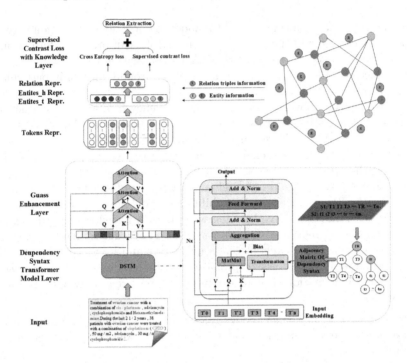

Fig. 2. The overall structure of the DSTSC model.

2.2 Dependency Syntax Pretraining Model Layer

2.2.1 Document-Level Dependency Syntax Tree

The dependency syntax relation between tokens in a sentence can be expressed as a dependency syntax tree with only one root node. This paper uses Stanford CoreNLP to parse the dependency syntax information for each sentence. To obtain the dependency syntax tree of the whole article, we link the root node of the dependency syntax tree of the latter sentence to the root node of the dependency syntax tree of the former sentence. Finally, the dependency syntax tree of the whole article is transformed into the corresponding adjacency matrix A.

2.2.2 Dependency Syntax Transformer

Let $x = (x_1, x_2, x_3, ..., x_n)$ be the token sequence of a document as input to Transformer, where $x_i (1 \leq i \leq n)$ is the i_{th} word in it. The overall framework of the Transformer comprises several layers of the encoder, which relies entirely on attention mechanisms to draw global dependencies between inputs and outputs. In the l_{th} layer, the token embedding $x_i^l \in R^{d_{in}}$ is mapped to query, key and value vectors, respectively:

$$q_i^l = x_i^l W_i^Q, k_i^l = x_i^l W_i^K, v_i^l = x_i^l W_i^V \tag{1}$$

where $W_i^Q, W_i^K, W_i^V \in R^{d_{in} \times d_{out}}$. The attention score between x_i^l and x_j^l is calculated as follows:

$$e_{ij}^l = \frac{q_i^l k_j^{l^T}}{\sqrt{d}} \qquad (2)$$

The attention mechanism allows dependencies to be modeled without regard to their dependencies information at the syntax level in the sequence. Instead, attention between tokens with dependencies in a sequence should be significant. Dependency syntax information guides the flow of attention in the Transformer model by enhancing attention between tokens with dependency syntax in the sentence. Dependency syntax information runs through the whole Transformer. Moreover, Decomposed Linear Transformation is used to introduce dependency syntax information into the Transformer model, with details as follows.

Decomposed Linear Transformation. Inspired by how to decompose the word embedding and position embedding in Transformer, decomposed linear transformation parameterizes the dependency syntax matrix on q and k, respectively. It's the principle of automatically preserving a moderate amount of inter-token attention with dependency syntax.

$$Bias\_e_{ij}^l = (q_i^l K_l^T + Q_l k_j^{l^T}) * A_{ij} + b_{l,A_{ij}} \qquad (3)$$

where $K_l, Q_l \in R^{d_{in} \times d_{out}}$ are trainable parameterization matrices assigned to the query and key vector. A_{ij} indicates whether x_i is dependent on x_j, A_{ij} is 1 if there is a dependency. Otherwise, it is 0. $b_{l,A_{ij}}$ is a bias.

The final attention score can be calculated as Eq. 4. We softmax a_{ij}^l and aggregate it with the value vector in Eq. 5.

$$a_{ij}^l = e_{ij}^l + Bias\_e_{ij}^l \qquad (4)$$

$$x_i^{l+1} = \sum_{j=1}^{n} \frac{\exp a_{ij}^l}{\sum_{k=1}^{n} \exp a_{ij}^l} v_j^l \qquad (5)$$

where $x_i^{l+1} \in R^{d_{out}}$ is the result of the update of x_i^l.

2.3   Guass Enhancement Layer

We use the Gaussian probability distribution method used in [11] to enhance the ability of the model to capture local information by increasing the weight of the target entity and its adjacent words. First, the relative distance list between non-entity tokens and nearby entity tokens in the sequence is obtained. The probability of each token is calculated using the Gaussian probability distribution function. Then the probability of the token is multiplied by the corresponding token in the sequence. The token guided by Gaussian probability information is represented y_i^{l+1}. In addition, the multi-top attention mechanism is used to compute the correlation of textual semantic vectors between the x_i^{l+1} and y_i^{l+1}.

x_i^{l+1} is used as the query vector and y_i^{l+1} as the key vector and the value vector. The final representation g_i^{l+1} with Gaussian enhancement is obtained.

$$y_i^{l+1} = GP(x_i^{l+1}) * x_i^{l+1} \tag{6}$$

$$g_{i_k}^{l+1} = Attention(x_i^{l+1}, y_{i_{k-1}}^{l+1}, y_{i_{k-1}}^{l+1}) \tag{7}$$

where GP is the Gaussian probability distribution function, and k is the number of hops in attention. In this paper, k = 2 is the best effect.

2.4   Supervision Contrastive Losses with Fused Knowledge Layer

As shown in Fig. 2, the domain knowledge trained by the RotatE model is used to enhance the learning ability of the model. After enrichment with domain knowledge, the entity information is enriched and more information can be shared among relational triples. In this case, supervised contrastive loss to capture the global information among relational triples is an excellent choice.

Contrastive learning focuses on learning the common features between similar instances and differentiating the differences between non-similar instances. Supervised contrastive learning makes the distance between features belonging to the same labels of entity pair as close as possible and the distance between different labels of entity pair as far as possible. Supervised contrastive learning works as follows:

$$SConL = -\sum_{i=1}^{M} \frac{1}{M_{y_i} - 1} \sum_{j=1}^{M} l_{i \neq j} l_{y_i = y_j} \ln(\frac{exp(\frac{S_{i,j}}{t})}{exp(\frac{S_{i,j}}{t}) + \sum_{k=1}^{M} l_{y_i \neq y_j} exp(\frac{S_{i,k}}{t})}) \tag{8}$$

where M represents a batch size, y_i and y_j represent the label of the anchor sample i and the sample j, respectively. M_{y_i} represents the number of samples whose label is y_i in a batch. $l_{i \neq j} \in \{0, 1\}$, $l_{y_i = y_j}$ and $l_{y_i \neq y_j}$ are similar indicator functions. $S_{i,j}$ is the cosine similarity between the sample i and the sample j.

We use the cross-entropy loss function to calculate the gap between the predicted and real data.

$$CroEL = \sum_{<h,t>} \sum_{r} CrossEntropy(P_r(e_h, e_t), \overline{y}_r(e_h, e_t)) \tag{9}$$

where e_h and e_t are head and tail entities, respectively. P_r is the predicted label, $\overline{y}_r$ is the target label. Summing the two-loss functions as the final function.

$$L = SConL + CroEL \tag{10}$$

3   Experiments

3.1   Dataset

We evaluate the DSTSC model on two biomedical datasets, CDR and GDA. The dataset details are in Table 1.

Table 1. Details of CDR and GDA dataset.

Dataset	Train	Dev	Test	Entities/Article	Mentions/Article	Relation
CDR	500	500	500	6.8	19.2	1
GDA	23353	5839	1000	4.8	18.5	1

Table 2. Hyperparamters setting.

Pretraining model	BERT	SciBERT/BioBERT
Hyperparamters	Value	Value
Batch size	4	4
Learning rate	2e−5	2e−5
Epoch	40	40
Seed	42	42
k	2	2
Knowledge dim	64	64

CDR. The Chemical-Disease Relations dataset is a biomedical dataset constructed by PubMed abstract, which contains 1500 human-annotated documents with 4409 annotated chemicals, 5818 diseases and 3116 chemical-disease interactions. It is evenly divided into the training set, development set and test set. The task is to predict binary interactions between Chemical and Disease concepts.

GDA. The Gene-Disease relation dataset is a large-scale dataset in the biomedical domain composed of 30192 MEDLINE abstracts, divided into 29192 training articles and 1000 test articles. It contains 10697 genes, 12774 diseases and 74928 gene-diseases associations. We follow [16] to split the training set into 80/20 sections as training and development sets. The task is to predict the binary interactions between Gene and Disease concepts.

3.2 Experimental Setting

The pretraining models based-Transformer used in this paper are BERT, SciBERT and BioBERT. SciBERT is a pretrained language model based on BERT to address the lack of a high-multi-domain corpus of scientific publications to improve performance on downstream scientific NLP tasks. BioBERT, Bidirectional Encoder Representations from Transformers for Biomedical Text Mining, is a domain-specific language representation model pre-trained on large-scale biomedical corpora. BioBERT and SciBERT largely outperform BERT and previous state-of-the-art models in various biomedical text mining tasks. Some essential hyperparameters are listed in Table 2.

Table 3. Main results (%) on the development and test set of CDR.

Model	Dev	Test	
	F1	Precision/Recall	F1
Without KBs			
CNN+SDP [6]	–	58.02/76.20	65.88
BRAN [13]	–	55.60/70.80	62.10
Bio-Seq [7]	–	60.00/58.60	63.50
LSR [9]	–	–/–	64.80
SciBERT	66.01	61.00/68.42	64.50
DSTSC_SciBERT (ours)	68.33	65.80/68.30	67.03
Without KBs			
CAN(+CTD) [15]	–	60.52/80.48	69.08
LSTM+CNN(+CTD) [14]	–	65.80/68.30	69.60
DSTSC_BERT (ours)	70.89	57.60/73.81	68.65
DSTSC_SciBERT (ours)	**72.16**	66.24/76.14	**70.85**
DSTSC_BioBERT (ours)	71.34	65.54/73.33	69.22

Table 4. Main results (%) on the development and test set of GDA.

Model	Dev	Test	
	F1	F1_cross/F1_noncross	F1
Without KBs			
EOG [2]	–	49.30/85.20	81.50
LSR [9]	–	51.10/85.40	82.20
SciBERT	81.30	50.80/85.60	81.25
DSTSC_SciBERT (ours)	82.90	51.90/86.80	83.60

Note: F1_cross represents F1 across sentences, while F1_noncross is F1 within sentences.

3.3   CDR and GDA Results

To evaluate our approach, we compared the DSTSC model with sequence-based models, graph-based models, and Transformer-based models. As shown in Table 3, the models compared are divided into two categories on the CDR dataset. One is the method without the knowledge base. The other is the method with the knowledge base.

Sequence-Based Models. CNN+SDP proposes to use CNN to learn the features of diseases and chemicals on the shortest dependency path to extract the CID relation between them. Our model uses a dependency syntax tree to enhance the attention between entities with dependencies in the whole article to alleviate the difficulty of the Transformer model in handling document-level tasks. Compared with CNN+SDP, the DSTSC_SciBERT model increased by 1.15%. The

Table 5. Ablation Study of The DSTSC Model on CDR.

Model	Dev F1	Test F1	F1_cross/F1_noncross
DSTSC_SciBERT	72.16	70.85	57.34/75.82
- Dependency information	70.36	68.71	54.60/75.15
- Guess enhancement layer	71.22	69.07	55.67/75.20
- Contrast loss layer	71.43	69.52	56.93/75.32
- Knowledge	68.33	67.03	55.90/72.29
- all	66.01	64.50	51.25/70.73

DSTSC model was 2.53% higher than SciBERT. This suggests that Transformer guided by dependency syntax information is superior in long-range modeling dependencies than other uses of dependency syntax information.

Graph-Based Models. EoG and LSR models learn the underlying graph structure of the document to construct the document-graph, and Graph Convolutional Networks (GCNs) are used for information updating and inference. LSR and SciBERT have similar results in document-level RE. DSTSC_SciBERT is 2.23% higher than LSR. It shows that the DSTSC model based on the Transformer guide by dependency syntax information is better than graph structure in document-level RE.

Transformer-Based Models. BRAN encodes the token using Transformer, and then a biaffine operation is used to score all mentioned pairs. Followed by aggregating the mentioned pairs to form entities and finally predicting the relations between entities. DSTSC_SciBERT is also based on the Transformer structure, which is 4.93% higher than BRAN. It shows the validity of dependency syntax information in the Transformer model.

BERT, SciBERT and BioBERT are essential parts of the DSTSC model, respectively. The DSTSC model composed of SciBERT [1] performs best. The DSTSC model combined with the knowledge base has the most outstanding performance. Experiment results on the CDR dataset demonstrate that the DSTSC promotes document-level RE. Table 4 is the result of the DSTSC model on the GDA dataset, which shows the strong applicability and generality of the DSTSC model.

3.4 Ablation Study

The ablation study of the DSTSC model on the CDR dataset is presented in Table 5. We can obviously conclude that all four dependency terms contribute to the final improvement. The dependency syntax Transformer approach has the most significant impact in all dependency terms except domain knowledge, which leads to a drop of 2.14%. It shows that the Transformer model guided by dependency syntax information can overcome the difficulties of long-distance text modeling. Supervised contrastive loss for capturing global information and Gaussian probability enhancement for capturing local information are both effective.

3.5 Case Study

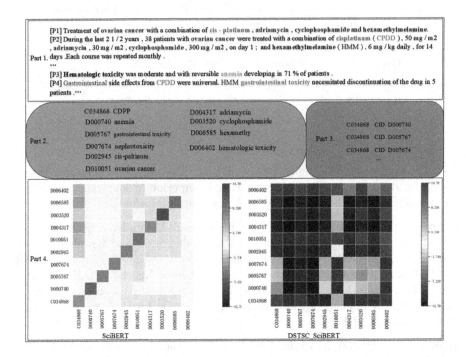

Fig. 3. Relational weights between entities in the baseline model and DSTSC model.

To analyze the model in detail, we visualized the weights of relation (relational triples in Part 3 of Fig. 3) between the entities (entities in Part 2) obtained in the baseline SciBERT and the DSTSC model. As detailed in Part 4. In Part4, the closer the color in each grid is to red, the greater the weight of the relation between the two entities judged by the model and vice versa. Obviously, the color difference obtained by the DSTSC model is quite distinct, while the color obtained by SciBERT model is not distinct. This demonstrates that SciBERT is prone to misjudgment. In this article, the DSTSC model determines that all red relational triples are correct. This effectively demonstrates the excellence of the DSTSC model in document-level relation extraction.

4 Related Work

4.1 Dependency Syntax Information

Dependency trees of input sentences are used in models and have proven to be very effective in RE. They capture long-term syntactic features that are difficult to obtain from surface forms alone. Traditional statistical models handle dependency information by combining different lexical, syntactic and semantic features [4]. However, sparse features and reliance on features created by external systems pose a significant challenge to the model processing task. Recent research has focused on document-level dependency graphs for encoding through dependent syntactic information combined with GCNs to capture useful long-range syntactic information [9]. Recently, Transformer models have shown excellent performance in NLP. However, the ability of Transformer [12] models to process long-distance text is hindered by not taking into account their dependency at the syntax level in the sequence.

4.2   Contrastive Learning

Contrastive learning aims to learn an encoder, which encodes similar data of the same kind and makes the encoding results of different kinds of data as different as possible. Self-supervised contrastive learning enhances the data and then compares the features of the data from the same source and the features of the data from different sources to make the data closer to the features of the data from the same source and farther away from the features of the data from different sources. Work [10] explored the method of employing contrastive learning to improve the text representation from the BERT model for relation extraction. However, self-supervised contrastive learning does not consider the correlation between data features belonging to the same class. Therefore, supervised comparative learning [5] makes the distance between features belonging to the same kind of data as close as possible and the distance between different kinds of data as far as possible.

5   Conclusion and Future Work

In this work, we propose the DSTSC model for document-level relation extraction, which features three novel methods. Dependency syntax Transformer model enhances the attention between tokens with dependency syntax relations, which enhances the Transformer's ability to model dependencies in long-range texts. The Gaussian enhancement module is designed to capture the local information around the entity. The supervised contrastive loss combined with domain knowledge to capture the global information among relational triples. Experiments on two biomedical datasets, CDR and GDA, demonstrate that the DSTSC model outperforms existing models in document-level relational extraction.

For future work, bridging the gap between the newly introduced dependency syntax parameters and the original Transformer model parameters is a potential research topic. It has hindered the improvement of DSTSC. Another is to explore more suitable methods to capture local and global information.

Acknowledgment. This work is supported by grant from the Natural Science Foundation of China (No. 62072070) and Social and Science Foundation of Liaoning Province (No. L20BTQ008).

References

1. Beltagy, I., Lo, K., Cohan, A.: SciBERT: a pretrained language model for scientific text. In: EMNLP-IJCNLP 2019, 3–7 November 2019, pp. 3613–3618 (2019). https://doi.org/10.18653/v1/D19-1371
2. Christopoulou, F., Miwa, M., Ananiadou, S.: Connecting the dots: document-level neural relation extraction with edge-oriented graphs. In: EMNLP-IJCNLP 2019, pp. 4924–4935 (2019). https://doi.org/10.18653/v1/D19-1498
3. Guo, Z., Zhang, Y., Lu, W.: Attention guided graph convolutional networks for relation extraction. In: ACL 2019, pp. 241–251 (2019). https://doi.org/10.18653/v1/P19-1024
4. Kambhatla, N.: Combining lexical, syntactic, and semantic features with maximum entropy models for information extraction. In: Proceedings of the ACL Interactive Poster and Demonstration Sessions, pp. 178–181 (2004). https://aclanthology.org/P04-3022/
5. Khosla, P., et al.: Supervised contrastive learning. In: NIPS 2020, vol. 33, pp. 18661–18673 (2020). https://proceedings.neurips.cc/paper/2020/hash/d89a66c7c80a29b1bdbab0f2a1a94af8-Abstract.html
6. Le, H., Can, D., Dang, T.H., Tran, M., Ha, Q., Collier, N.: Improving chemical-induced disease relation extraction with learned features based on convolutional neural network. In: KSE, pp. 292–297 (2017). https://doi.org/10.1109/KSE.2017.8119474
7. Li, Z., Yang, Z., Xiang, Y., Luo, L., Sun, Y., Lin, H.: Exploiting sequence labeling framework to extract document-level relations from biomedical texts. BMC Bioinform. **21**(1), 125 (2020). https://doi.org/10.1186/s12859-020-3457-2
8. Li, Z., Sun, Y., Zhu, J., Tang, S., Zhang, C., Ma, H.: Improve relation extraction with dual attention-guided graph convolutional networks. Neural Comput. Appl. **33**(6), 1773–1784 (2021). https://doi.org/10.1007/s00521-020-05087-z
9. Nan, G., Guo, Z., Sekulic, I., Lu, W.: Reasoning with latent structure refinement for document-level relation extraction. In: ACL 2020, 5–10 July 2020, pp. 1546–1557 (2020). https://doi.org/10.18653/v1/2020.acl-main.141
10. Su, P., Peng, Y., Vijay-Shanker, K.: Improving BERT model using contrastive learning for biomedical relation extraction. In: BioNLP@NAACL-HLT 2021, 11 June 2021, pp. 1–10 (2021). https://doi.org/10.18653/v1/2021.bionlp-1.1
11. Sun, C., et al.: Chemical-protein interaction extraction via Gaussian probability distribution and external biomedical knowledge. Bioinformatics **36**(15), 4323–4330 (2020). https://doi.org/10.1093/bioinformatics/btaa491
12. Vaswani, A., et al.: Attention is all you need. In: NIPS 2017, pp. 5998–6008 (2017). https://proceedings.neurips.cc/paper/2017/hash/3f5ee243547dee91fbd053c1c4a845aa-Abstract.html
13. Verga, P., Strubell, E., McCallum, A.: Simultaneously self-attending to all mentions for full-abstract biological relation extraction. In: NAACL-HLT, pp. 872–884 (2018). https://doi.org/10.18653/v1/n18-1080
14. Zheng, W., Lin, H., Liu, X., Xu, B.: A document level neural model integrated domain knowledge for chemical-induced disease relations. BMC Bioinform. **19**(1), 1–12 (2018). https://doi.org/10.1186/s12859-018-2316-x
15. Zhou, H., Ning, S., Yang, Y., Liu, Z., Lang, C., Lin, Y.: Chemical-induced disease relation extraction with dependency information and prior knowledge. CoRR (2020). http://arxiv.org/abs/2001.00295
16. Zhou, W., Huang, K., Ma, T., Huang, J.: Document-level relation extraction with adaptive thresholding and localized context pooling. In: AAAI 2021, vol. 35, pp. 14612–14620 (2021). https://ojs.aaai.org/index.php/AAAI/article/view/17717

KGSG: Knowledge Guided Syntactic Graph Model for Drug-Drug Interaction Extraction

Wei Du[1], Yijia Zhang[1(✉)], Ming Yang[1], Da Liu[1], and Xiaoxia Liu[2(✉)]

[1] Dalian Maritime University, Dalian 116024, Liaoning, China
zhangyijia@dlmu.edu.cn
[2] Stanford University, Stanford, CA 94305, USA
xxliu@stanford.edu

Abstract. The explosive growth of biomedical literature has produced a large amount of information on drug-drug interactions (DDI). How to effectively extract DDI from biomedical literature is of great significance for constructing biomedical knowledge and discovering new biomedical knowledge. Drug entity names are mostly nouns in specific fields. Most of the existing models can't make full use of the importance of drug entity information and syntax information for DDI extraction. In this paper, we propose a model that can reasonably use domain knowledge and syntactic information to extract DDI, which makes full use of domain knowledge to obtain an enhanced representation of entities and can learn sentence sequence information and long-distance grammatical relation. We conducted comparative experiments and ablation studies on the DDI extraction 2013 dataset. The experimental results show that our method can effectively integrate domain knowledge and syntactic information to improve the performance of DDI extraction compared with the existing methods.

Keywords: Drug-drug interaction · Biomedical literature · Domain knowledge syntactic features

1 Introduction

Drug-drug interaction relation extraction is a combination of many research achievements in bioinformatics, natural language processing and other fields. One drug can be affected by another drug, food, or environmental changes. Some DDI may threaten people's lives. The precise classification of DDI will have a positive effect on avoiding hazards [1]. DDI extraction is a multi-classification task. A sentence containing multiple drug entities in given biomedical literature is calculated to judge the relation between drug entities.

Biomedical relation extraction is of great significance for biomedical researchers to obtain domain knowledge and automatic processing of biomedical information. Nowadays, health professionals can retrieve a large amount of DDI information from Drug Interactions Facts, DrugBank, and Stockley, which contain rich DDI data. From this point of view, with the continuous growth of biomedical literature, if we can extract DDI

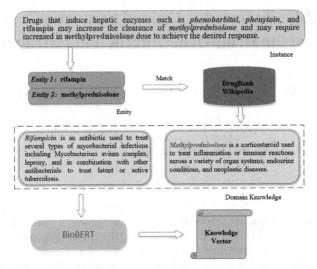

Drugs that induce hepatic enzymes such as *phenobarbital, phenytoin,* and rifampin may increase the clearance of *methylprednisolone* and may require increased in methylprednisolone dose to achieve the desired response.

Instance

Entity 1: rifampin

Entity 2: methylprednisolone

Match

DrugBank Wikipedia

Entity

Rifampicin is an antibiotic used to treat several types of mycobacterial infections including Mycobacterium avium complex, leprosy, and in combination with other antibacterials to treat latent or active tuberculosis.

Methylprednisolone is a corticosteroid used to treat inflammation or immune reactions across a variety of organ systems, endocrine conditions, and neoplastic diseases.

Domain Knowledge

BioBERT

Knowledge Vector

Fig. 1. The integration process of domain knowledge.

from a large amount of research literature, it can positively impact pharmacovigilance, and it will increase the speed of updating databases.

In recent years, many neural network methods have been applied to DDI interaction [2–5], and the classification of DDI interaction has made significant progress. However, most of the drug entities are professional nouns, and the existing models do not give full play to the importance of professional domain knowledge. The model may misjudge in predicting the relation of the DDI text containing multiple drug entities.

We incorporate domain knowledge of entities into the model to obtain an enhanced representation of the DDI texts. For example, the sentence in Fig. 1 contains multiple drug entities. The relation between rifampicin and methylprednisolone needs to be predicted. First, the drug information of two entities is extracted from the knowledge base, and then the model will learn the representation of the drug information, which will improve the performance of the model in predicting DDI texts containing multiple drug entities. Furthermore, as shown in Fig. 3, biomedical texts are mostly long and difficult sentences, so we integrate syntactic information into the model to improve the performance of the model in extracting long and difficult sentences.

In this paper, we propose a model that can reasonably use domain knowledge and syntactic information to extract DDI. First, the explanation information of DDI entities is crawled by DrugBank and Wikipedia. The interpretation information is converted into vectors by the pre-trained model to obtain the vector representation of domain knowledge. Then send the syntactic dependency matrix obtained by StanfordCoreNLP to graph neural networks to obtain the syntactic information representation. Finally, the final classification result is obtained through softmax. The experimental results show that domain knowledge and syntactic information can improve the performance of the model. In general, the contributions of this paper can be summarized as follows:

(1) We propose a model that integrates domain knowledge to obtain enhanced text representations, which can improve the performance in predicting the relation of the DDI text containing multiple drug entities
(2) We integrate the syntactic information into the model to improve the learning ability of the model to the sequence information of sentences and long-distance grammatical relations.
(3) We conduct extensive experiments on the DDI corpus. Experimental results suggest that our model achieves the state-of-the-art result for the DDI relation extraction task.

2 Related Work

In the early days, a rule-based method was used to extract DDI [6]. The rule-based method has many problems: low recall rate, high labor costs, and difficult design. Subsequently, researchers used many machine learning methods. Machine learning methods can be divided into traditional machine learning methods and deep learning methods. Support vector machines (SVM) with kernels are used on biomedical datasets and have achieved good performance [7]. Kim et al. [8] applied a feature-based method in the corpus.

As the neural network gradually moves into people's field of vision, people begin to pay attention to methods based on neural networks. The neural network can directly learn the feature representation from the training data, thus saving a lot of human resources and material resources. Liu et al. applied the convolutional neural networks (CNN) model [9] to DDI extraction and demonstrated the good performance of the model. The CNN [10–12] model can obtain local features so that the CNN-based method can obtain the semantic information and position information of the words very well. But in the long sentence, the CNN model ignores some syntactic information and the dependence between words. Then, the researchers found that the recurrent neural networks (RNN) model can better process sequence information, so the RNN model was applied to the DDI extraction task. Ramkanth et al. [13] applied the word-based RNN model and the character-based RNN model to DDI extraction tasks. The advantage of the RNN model is that it can alleviate the problem that the CNN model can only obtain local features.

However, the RNN model brings new problems of gradient disappearance and gradient explosion. Researchers have found that the long short-term memory (LSTM) model [14, 15] can effectively alleviate these problems. Huang et al. [16] applied a two-stage LSTM model to the DDI extraction task. The two-stage models are feature-based binary SVM classifier and LSTM-based multi-class classifier. Zheng et al. [17] used the attention mechanism to extract drug relations and proposed an attention-based BiLSTM (ATTBLSTM) model. Zhang et al. [18] applied the ASDP-LSTM model to the DDI extraction task. This model uses the shortest dependent path (SDP). The researchers found the graph convolutional neural network [19], has a good effect on the DDI extraction task. Peng et al. [20] applied the Bidirectional Encoder Representation from Transformers (BERT) model to the biomedical literature, and the experimental results showed that the BERT model has strong performance. BioBERT [21] is a pre-trained model trained using a large biomedical corpus. The pre-trained model has achieved the most advanced performance on some biomedical datasets. The R-BERT [22] model is a derivative model of BERT for relation extraction.

In the DDI extraction task, the BERT model only uses the semantic information of the text, ignoring the importance of expertise in the biomedical field. In order to improve the model's performance in predicting the relation of the DDI text containing multiple drug entities, we added entity explanation information to the model to learn enhanced text representations. The model can effectively distinguish different drug entities in the DDI text. Furthermore, the BERT model does not fully consider information such as part of speech and syntactic structure. Misjudgments may occur when predicting drug entity relation in complex sentence structures in biomedical texts. In this regard, we add syntactic information to improve this phenomenon.

3   Method

Figure 2 shows the structure of our model. The interpretation information of the drug entity crawled from Wikipedia and DrugBank is sent to the pre-trained model to obtain the vector representation document of knowledge. The interpretation information of the drug entity is taken as domain knowledge and integrated into the entity vector. Then the syntactic dependency of DDI sentences is obtained through StanfordCoreNLP. The syntactic features are extracted through the GCN model. The model fuses the semantic features obtained by BioBERT and the syntactic features obtained by the GCN model. The performance of our model has been further improved.

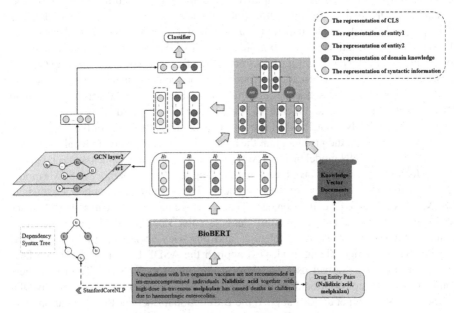

Fig. 2. The architecture of our model.

3.1 Input Layer

The input of our model consists of two parts. The first part is the sentences in the DDI dataset, and the second part is the interpretation information of the drug entity.

Encoding Sentences from the DDI Dataset. For a sentence in the DDI corpus, it is expressed as $S = \{W_1, W_2, W_3, ..., W_N\}$, where W_i is the i-th word, and N represents the length of the sentence. Each word in the sentence is segmented, and each token is represented by a d-dimensional vector. Moreover, an embedding ('[CLS]') is appended at the beginning of each sequence. In addition, special symbols are inserted on both sides of each drug entity. The special symbols on both sides of the first entity are '$', and on both sides of the second drug entity are '#'.

Encoding Sentences from Domain Knowledge. The interpretation information of the drug entity as the domain knowledge is crawled on Wikipedia and DrugBank through crawler technology. Because some words may be biased, the explanation information will be filtered. The information irrelevant to the drug entity is deleted to avoid the impact of useless information on the performance of the model. For a sentence in domain knowledge, it is expressed as $S_e = \{E_1, E_2, E_3, ..., E_N\}$, where E_i is the i-th word, and N represents the length of the sentence.

3.2 Feature Extraction

Biomedical Text Semantic Feature Extraction. For a given sentence S with drug entities e1 and e2 in the DDI corpus, the output of the final hidden layer of 'CLS' from the BioBERT model is H_0. The vector of the e1 can be represented as the average of the final hidden layer vectors from H_i to H_j. The vector of the e2 can be represented as the average of the final hidden layer vectors from H_k to H_m. These vectors are averaged to get an entity vector representation. After the activation function and the full connection layer, the output of e1 and e2 are H_1' and H_2' respectively. The calculation formulas of H_1' and H_2' are as follows:

$$H_1' = W_1 \left[\tan h \left(\frac{1}{j-i+1} \sum_{t=i}^{j} H_t \right) \right] + b_1 \tag{1}$$

$$H_2' = W_2 \left[\tan h \left(\frac{1}{m-k+1} \sum_{t=k}^{m} H_t \right) \right] + b_2 \tag{2}$$

For the final hidden layer vector of '[CLS]', the output H_0' is obtained through the activation function and the full connection layer, which is expressed as follows:

$$H_0' = W_0(\tan h(H_0)) + b_0 \tag{3}$$

where $W_0 \in R^{d \times d}$, $W_1 \in R^{d \times d}$ and $W_2 \in R^{d \times d}$ are weight matrices. d is the hidden layer size of BioBERT. b_0, b_1, b_2 are bias vectors.

The semantic feature representation of domain knowledge is obtained through the BioBERT model. Then the entity interpretation vector is fused with the entity vector. For the sentence S_e of domain knowledge is successfully matched with the entity e1. The final hidden layer vector H_{e1} of 'CLS' is obtained through BioBERT. H_{e1}, H_{e2} respectively represent the e1 and e2 entity information vectors. The final vectors H_1' and H_2' are averaged with He_1' and He_2' respectively to obtain the new entity representations. They are expressed as H_1'', H_2''.

The calculation methods are shown in formula (4) and formula (5). The representation of semantic features of the sentence is shown in formula (6).

$$He_1' = W_3(\tan h(H_{e1})) + b_3 \tag{4}$$

$$He_2' = W_4(\tan h(H_{e2})) + b_4 \tag{5}$$

$$f^b = W_5\left[concat\left(H_0', H_1'', H_2''\right)\right] + b_5 \tag{6}$$

where W_5 is the weight matrix. b_3, b_4, b_5 are bias vectors.

Biomedical Text Syntactic Feature Extraction. As shown in Fig. 3, the dependency parsing output of sentence S in the DDI dataset obtained by StanfordCoreNLP is denoted as $D = [(A_i, P_i, P_i)]$, where A_i is the attribute of the dependency tree. P_i is the position information of the dependency tree node.

The dependent parsing output is converted to adjacency matrix A, and self-connections are added to the adjacency matrix. The calculation formula is as follows:

$$\tilde{A} = A + I_N \tag{7}$$

where I_N is the identity matrix.

We send the adjacency matrix and the feature representation of the sentence in the DDI dataset into the GCN network. The hidden layer of the final sentence is represented as $H^{(l+1)}$.

$$H^{(l+1)} = \sigma\left(\tilde{D}^{-\frac{1}{2}}\tilde{A}\tilde{D}^{-\frac{1}{2}}H^{(l)}\theta^{(l)}\right) \tag{8}$$

where $\tilde{A}$ is the adjacency matrix. $\tilde{D}$ is the degree matrix. σ denotes an activation function. $H^{(l)}$ is the matrix of activations in the l-th layer. $H^{(0)} = H_0$. θ is a weight matrix.

The calculation formula of the final syntactic feature f^g is shown in formula (10):

$$\hat{A} = \tilde{D}^{-\frac{1}{2}}\tilde{A}\tilde{D}^{-\frac{1}{2}} \tag{9}$$

$$f^g = \hat{A}\sigma\left(\hat{A}H_0W_6\right)W_7 \tag{10}$$

where $W_6 \in R^{C \times H}$, $W_7 \in R^{H \times F}$ are weight matrices. C is the size of the input layer. H is the size of the hidden layer. F is the size of the output layer.

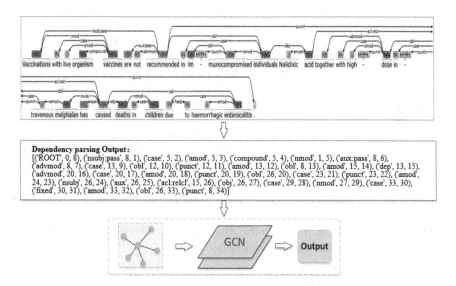

Fig. 3. The extraction process of dependency parsing.

3.3 Classification

DDI extraction is a multi-class classification task. The two drug entities in each sentence in the DDI dataset will be classified into a specific type. The probability distribution of each type is obtained by softmax. In the training process, we use the cross-entropy loss function. The result f' is obtained by fusing the feature f^b and the feature f^g. Then f' is sent to the classifier. The model selects the type with the highest probability as the classification result. The calculation formulas are as follows:

$$f' = W'\left[concat\left(f^b, f^g\right)\right] + b' \tag{11}$$

$$p = softmax\left(f'\right) \tag{12}$$

where p is the probability of each type. W' is a weight matrix. b' is a bias vector.

4 Result and Discussion

4.1 Datasets and Evaluation Metrics

We use the DDI extraction 2013 dataset [23], which is the public dataset for the DDI extraction task. It is more authoritative and representative. The five types in the dataset are as follows:

(1) Advice: This sentence describes the recommendation to use two drugs simultaneously. (e.g., "Patients who take both ezetimibe and cyclosporine should be carefully monitored").

(2) Mechanism: This type states a pharmacokinetic mechanism. (e.g., "Probenecid competes with meropenem for active tubular secretion and thus inhibits the renal excretion of meropenem.").

(3) Effect: The sentence describes the effect of the interaction between drugs or the pharmacodynamic mechanism of the interaction. (e.g., "Rifabutin: There have been reports of uveitis in patients to whom fluconazole and rifabutin were coadministered").

(4) Int: The sentence describes the drug interactions in this sentence but does not indicate any other information. (e.g., "Data from in vitro studies of alprazolam suggest a possible drug interaction with alprazolam for the following: sertraline and paroxetine.").

(5) Negative: The sentence states that there is no interaction between two target drugs.

The performance of the model in this experiment is reflected by the precision (P), recall (R), and F1 score (micro-average F-score).

4.2 Experimental Settings

We use the BioBERT model to encode the input sentence. In order to prevent over-fitting, this experiment uses the dropout mechanism. Table 1 shows the specific hyper-parameter settings.

Table 1. The setting of hyper-parameters parameter

Parameter name	Value
Sentence feature dimension	768
Max sentence length	400
Number of hidden layers of BioBERT	12
Batch size	8
Dropout rate	0.1
Epoch	10
Learning rate	2e−5
Number of hidden layers of GCN	16
Weight decay	5e−4

4.3 Experimental Results

Comparison with Other Models. We test the performance of our model on the DDI extraction 2013 test set, and Table 2 shows the comparison results of our model with other methods.

It can be seen from the comparison results that our model is better than the existing models. We use the values of P, R, and F1 score to prove the performance of our model. From the Table 2, we can see that the values of P, R, and F1 are 82.8%, 81.0%, and 81.9%, respectively. In terms of the F1 score, our model is higher than the R-BioBERT model by 1.2%. Furthermore, in terms of P and R, our model is better than the R-BioBERT model.

Table 2. Comparison with other models. The '-' denotes the value is not provided in the paper.

Model	P	R	F1
FBK-irst	65.0	66.0	65.0
KIM	-	-	67.0
CNN	75.7	64.7	69.8
DCNN	77.2	64.4	70.2
ACNN	76.3	63.3	69.1
RNN	78.6	63.8	72.1
LSTM	73.4	69.7	71.5
Two-stage LSTM	-	-	69.0
ASDP-LSTM	74.1	71.8	72.9
ATT-BLSTM	78.4	76.2	77.3
BERT	-	-	79.9
BioBERT	-	-	78.8
R-BioBERT	82.7	78.8	80.7
Our model	82.8	81.0	81.9

Table 3. Comparison of each type between other models

Model	F1 score on each DDI type			
	Advice	Mechanism	Effect	Int
FBK-irst	69.2	67.9	62.8	54.7
KIM	72.5	69.3	66.2	48.3
CNN	77.8	70.2	69.3	46.4
DCNN	78.2	70.6	69.9	46.4
LSTM	79.4	76.3	67.6	43.1
ASDP-LSTM	80.3	74.0	71.8	54.3

(*continued*)

Table 3. (*continued*)

Model	F1 score on each DDI type			
	Advice	Mechanism	Effect	Int
ATT-BLSTM	85.1	77.5	76.6	57.7
R-BioBERT	83.8	83.3	81.0	59.5
Our model	87.3	84.6	82.0	56.1

In order to evaluate the multi-class performance of our model, we evaluated each type of DDI. Table 3 shows the comparison results of the F1 score of each type between our model and other methods. The F1 score of our model in Advice, Mechanism, Effect, and Int types are 87.3%, 84.6%, 82.0%, and 56.1%, respectively. Compared with R-BioBERT, our model shows better performance in Advice, Mechanism, and Effects types.

Ablation Study. In order to prove the validity of domain knowledge and syntactic information, we conducted ablation studies.

Table 4. Comparison of the results of ablation studies.

Model	Overall performance		
	P	R	F1
R-BioBERT	82.7	78.8	80.7
Domain knowledge	82.1	80.8	81.4
Syntactic information	82.9	80.3	81.6
Our model	82.8	81.0	81.9

The ablation study is divided into four sub-experiments to verify the validity of domain knowledge and syntactic information. The results of specific ablation studies are shown in Table 4. The R-BioBERT experiment is the baseline. The domain knowledge experiment represents adding domain knowledge to the R-BioBERT model. The syntactic information experiment represents adding syntactic information to the R-BioBERT model.

It can be seen from the experimental results that after adding domain knowledge to the R-BioBERT model, the F1 score is improved by 0.7%. It can be seen that for DDI extraction, additional entity interpretation information can make the model easier to understand the semantics of DDI text. This shows that domain knowledge is effective for drug-drug relation extraction. Then we added syntactic information to the R-BioBERT model, and the F1 score increased by 0.9%. There is no doubt that the syntactic structure features extracted by GCN play a great role in DDI relation extraction. When domain knowledge and syntactic information are added to our model, the F1 score is increased by 1.2%. The results of ablation studies proved the importance of domain knowledge and syntactic information for the DDI extraction task. Moreover, it proves the powerful performance of our model in extracting drug-drug relation.

4.4 Case Study

To further demonstrate domain knowledge and syntactic information can improve the performance of the model, in Table 5, we show some cases from the DDI extraction 2013 test set.

Sentence 1 contains multiple drug entities, which may affect the model to learn the semantic information of the DDI text. After the information of drug entities is matched to the domain knowledge from the knowledge base, the model can clearly distinguish each drug entity, so the model makes the correct prediction.

In Sentence 2, probably because of the word "recommended", the prediction result from the original model is Advise types. The entity information of drugs is obtained through DrugBank. After adding domain knowledge, the model can learn the representation information of two entities. However, syntactic information may have played a more important role. After adding syntactic information, the model can learn the long-distance grammatical relation of the sentence. The model can accurately grasp the syntactic structure of the sentence.

For Sentence 3, a short sentence, the original model and our model made correct predictions.

Table 5. Examples of extraction results by different methods on the DDI dataset.

Sentence instance	Prediction results
Sentence 1 Drugs that induce hepatic enzymes such as *phenobarbital*, *phenytoin*, and **rifampin** may increase the clearance of *methylprednisolone* and may require increased in **methylprednisolone** dose to achieve the desired response	R-BioBERT: Mechanism Our model: Advise
Sentence 2 Vaccinations with live organism vaccines are not recommended in immunocompromised individuals. **Nalidixic acid** together with high-dose intravenous **melphalan** has caused deaths in children due to haemorrhagic enterocolitis	R-BioBERT: Advise Our model: Effect
Sentence 3 The findings suggest that the dosage of **S-ketamine** should be reduced in patients receiving **ticlopidine**	R-BioBERT: Advise Our model: Advise

5 Conclusion

In this paper, we propose a model that can reasonably integrate domain knowledge and syntactic information to extract DDI relation. Domain knowledge can make the model obtain an enhanced representation of the DDI text, and syntactic information can make the model better learn sentence sequence information and long-distance grammatical relation. Our model is evaluated on the DDI extraction 2013 test set, and the experimental results show that our model performs better than the existing models. In addition, from the ablation studies, we can analyze the effectiveness of our various modules on the model performance. The results of the ablation study show that domain knowledge and syntactic information can improve the performance of the model.

In future work, we will try to improve the model's performance in the type with a small amount of data and apply our model to document-level biomedical relation extraction.

Acknowledgment. This work is supported by grant from the Natural Science Foundation of China (No. 62072070 and 62106034).

References

1. Roblek, T., Vaupotic, T., Mrhar, A., et al.: Drug-drug interaction software in clinical practice: a systematic review. Eur. J. Clin. Pharmacol. **71**(2), 131–142 (2015)
2. Zhang, T., Leng, J., Liu, Y.: Deep learning for drug–drug interaction extraction from the literature: a review. Brief. Bioinform. **21**(5), 1609–1627 (2020)
3. Zhang, Y., Lin, H., Yang, Z., et al.: Neural network-based approaches for biomedical relation classification: a review. J. Biomed. Inform. **99**, 103294 (2019)
4. Hong, L., Lin, J., Li, S., et al.: A novel machine learning framework for automated biomedical relation extraction from large-scale literature repositories. Nat. Mach. Intell. **2**(6), 347–355 (2020)
5. Zhao, S., Su, C., Lu, Z., et al.: Recent advances in biomedical literature mining. Briefings Bioinform. **22**(3), bbaa057 (2021)
6. Segura-Bedmar, I., Martínez, P., de Pablo-Sánchez, C.: A linguistic rule-based approach to extract drug-drug interactions from pharmacological documents. BMC Bioinform. BioMed Central **12**(2), 1–11 (2011)
7. Chowdhury, M., Lavelli, A.: FBK-irst: a multi-phase kernel based approach for drug-drug interaction detection and classification that exploits linguistic information. In: Proceedings of the 7th International Workshop on Semantic Evaluation, pp. 351–355 (2013)
8. Kim, S., Liu, H., Yeganova, L., Wilbur, W.J.: Extracting drug–drug interactions from literature using a rich feature-based linear kernel approach. J. Biomed. Inf. **55**, 23–30 (2015)
9. Liu, S., Tang, B., Chen, Q., et al.: Drug-drug interaction extraction via convolutional neural networks. Comput. Math. Methods Med. **2016**, 6918381 (2016)
10. Zhao, Z., Yang, Z., Luo, L., et al.: Drug drug interaction extraction from biomedical literature using syntax convolutional neural network. Bioinformatics **32**(22), 3444–3453 (2016)
11. Liu, S., Chen, K., Chen, Q., et al.: Dependency-based convolutional neural network for drug-drug interaction extraction. In: 2016 IEEE International Conference on Bioinformatics and Biomedicine (BIBM), pp. 1074–1080. IEEE (2016)
12. Asada, M., Miwa, M., Sasaki, Y.: Extracting drug–drug interactions with attention CNNs. BioNLP **2017**, 9–18 (2017)
13. Kavuluru, R., Rios, A., Tran, T.: Extracting drug-drug interactions with word and character-level recurrent neural networks. In: 2017 IEEE International Conference on Healthcare Informatics (ICHI), pp. 5–12. IEEE (2017)

14. Wang, W., Yang, X., Yang, C., et al.: Dependency-based long short term memory network for drug-drug interaction extraction. BMC Bioinform. **18**(16), 99–109 (2017)

15. Sahu, S.K., Anand, A.: Drug-drug interaction extraction from biomedical texts using long short-term memory network. J. Biomed. Inform. **86**, 15–24 (2018)

16. Huang, D., Jiang, Z., Zou, L., et al.: Drug–drug interaction extraction from biomedical literature using support vector machine and long short term memory networks. Inf. Sci. **415**, 100–109 (2017)

17. Zheng, W., Lin, H., Luo, L., et al.: An attention-based effective neural model for drug-drug interactions extraction. BMC Bioinform. **18**(1), 445 (2017)

18. Zhang, Y., Zheng, W., Lin, H., et al.: Drug–drug interaction extraction via hierarchical RNNs on sequence and shortest dependency paths. Bioinformatics **34**(5), 828–835 (2018)

19. Park, C., Park, J., Park, S.: AGCN: attention-based graph convolutional net-works for drug-drug interaction extraction. Expert Syst. Appl. **159**, 113538 (2020)

20. Peng, Y., Yan, S., Lu, Z.: Transfer learning in biomedical natural language processing: an evaluation of BERT and ELMo on ten benchmarking datasets. BioNLP **2019**, 58 (2019)

21. Lee, J., Yoon, W., Kim, S., et al.: BioBERT: a pre-trained biomedical language representation model for biomedical text mining. Bioinformatics **36**(4), 1234–1240 (2020)

22. Wu, S., He, Y.: Enriching pre-trained language model with entity information for relation classification. In: Proceedings of the 28th ACM International Conference on Information and Knowledge Management, pp. 2361–2364 (2019)

23. Herrero-Zazo, M., Segura-Bedmar, I., Martínez, P., et al.: The DDI corpus: an annotated corpus with pharmacological substances and drug–drug interactions. J. Biomed. Inform. **46**(5), 914–920 (2013)

Hierarchical Modular Event Detection Based on Dependency Graph

Wei Zhang, Chunping Ouyang$^{(\boxtimes)}$, Yongbin Liu, and Yaping Wan

University of South China, Hunan, China
ouyangcp@126.com

Abstract. Event Detection (ED) is a very important sub-task in the field of information extraction, which studies how to correctly identify the trigger words that trigger event generation from unstructured text containing event information. We can regard ED as a token-based multi-classification task and sequence labeling task. However, in the previous methods, the ED task is performed for fine-grained types of events, ignoring the more abstract information of coarse-grained event types, which leads to missing conceptual semantic information about the class hierarchy of events. We propose a new ED method (Hierarchical Modular Event Detection Based on Dependency Graphs, HMED) in this paper. First, we implement dynamic modeling of multi-order dependency label information between words, which is used to generate the fine-grained representations of event types. Then we design an upper-level conceptual module based on the characteristics of the ACE corpus to compute the coarse-grained representations of event types and fuse fine-grained and coarse-grained event conceptual semantic information through global attention. On the widely used ACE2005 corpus, our hierarchical module can significantly improve the performance when compared with the most current state-of-the-art results.

Keywords: Event detection · Hierarchical · Dependency label · Upper-level concepts

1 Introduction

Event extraction (EE) is an important information extraction task that consists of two stages of tasks in a given document. Event detection (ED) is a crucial subtask of event extraction, which aims to identify event triggers and classify them into specific types from texts. Taking Fig. 1 as an example, ED is supposed to recognize the event trigger "died" and "fired", and classify them separately to the event type Die and Attack, while other words are marked as "O" for the non-event type "None".

In many ED systems, it has been shown that dependency trees [9, 17] can capture the dependency relationships between word pairs. As shown in Fig. 1, the top of the sentence shows many information about the dependency labels between entities, and these rich labels will give us additional contextual information. However, the relationships between word pairs are subject to change, and we cannot simply use this fixed dependency

M. Sun et al. (Eds.): CCKS 2022, CCIS 1669, pp. 68–80, 2022.
https://doi.org/10.1007/978-981-19-7596-7_6

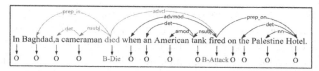

Fig. 1. A sentence from the ACE2005 corpus, the above is the result of the dependency parsing.

information. But due to the superior performance of GCNs in handling unstructured data in recent years, graphs can capture and represent more dependencies than tree structures, so more research use dependency graphs [8–10, 17] to handle diverse dependencies.

However, one of the problems is that many words can convey different meanings in different contexts, due to the existence of polysemes. In Fig. 2, the "charged" in S1 means "Charge-Indict" event, but without the previous information, the model may classify it as a "Transfer-Money" event in fine-grained event types (lower-level). Another problem is in the ED task, the event classification task is also required after the model extracts the event triggers, and the existing classification methods (call fine-grained event types) do not take into account the upper-level broad classes to which the fine-grained event types belong. In the fine-grained event classification task, the upper-class event information (called coarse-grained event types) should be fully considered. Some examples are shown in Fig. 2. Specifically, "charged", "deal" and "fired" can be classified correctly by the upper-level concept types, however, they are misclassified in the lower-level concept view.

Sentence	Lower-level Concept fine-grained event types	Upper-level Concept coarse-grained event types
S1:...was sentenced to five years in prison for being charged in court.	Transfer-Money ✗	Justice ✓
S2:A suspect was reportedly planning to deal chemicals they had produced in-house.	NA ✗	Transaction ✓
S3:The blood of soldiers scattered between the jungles became the evidence of that they were fired.	End-Position ✗	Conflict ✓

Fig. 2. In sentence S3, the "fired" is incorrectly classified as the "End-Position" in the lower-level concept frame. But its real lower-level concept type is the "Attack". If we use the upper-level concept frame, it can be classified as "Conflict" correctly in the upper-level concept.

In this paper, we propose a Hierarchical Modular Event Detection Based on Dependency Graph (HMED) to address the above problem in the ED task. We first design a multilayer graph structure based on dependency relations, which can convert the input sentences into a graph in which nodes represent words and edges represent dependency relations between words. And attention is used to score the multi-order dependencies so that the information represented by nodes and edges is dynamically updated. Finally, Hierarchical Modular Network enables the model to fully consider the higher-level information when classifying trigger words and more accurately determine the type of trigger words. We conducted an experimental study on the ACE 2005 corpora to demonstrate the advantages of our approach. Our contributions are summarized as follows:

- We introduce syntactic structure features and multi-order dependency label information in the neural network. We use attention to perform a convolution operation on the syntactic dependency graph to dynamically update the dependency label.
- For event classification, we propose a module called Hierarchical Modular Network to improve the accuracy of event classification by fusing coarse-grained and fine-grained event information.
- We analyzed the individual and compound effects of the dynamic update module and the hierarchical module on the event detection task and achieved the best performance (F1 values) on the ACE 2005 corpus.

2 Related Work

The earliest event detection studies were pattern-matching methods [1, 2]. Subsequently, some researchers have combined document-level features for event detection, [3] designed a document-level prediction model, and [4] utilized cross-document feature information. However, the performance of this method is mainly related to the accuracy of the template, so it is poorly portable and requires experienced experts to prepare it, and the preliminary work takes a lot of time. Later, machine learning and deep learning enable a good improvement in event detection performance. [20] Machine learning is applied to combine linguistic and structural information, which in turn improves the pattern-based approach to obtaining grammatical features.

Most recent event detection works are based on a deep learning architecture, and typical works such as Convolutional Neural Networks [5], Recurrent Neural Networks [6, 7], and Graph Convolutional Networks [8–10]and Transformer [11, 12]. Another type of approach enhances the ED by introducing additional information, such as an external knowledge base [13], document information [14, 15], cross-language detection [16, 21] decodes the three subtasks of entity extraction, trigger word extraction, and argument extraction completely jointly to achieve a better combination of information. Other recent research advances include combining few-shot [22] for meta-learning and combining image information [23] in news articles for ED tasks. There are also many authors who have adopted the new idea of Q&A [11, 19] for ED tasks.

Dependent syntactic analysis is one of the key techniques in natural language processing and is widely used in the ED domain to parse text and obtain interdependencies between words in a sentence. [7] proposes to use dependency trees to model syntactic information, [17] proposes to transform dependency trees into graphs for ED, and the latest study [10] adds typed dependency label information to dependency graphs.

3 Methodology

In this section, we will introduce the overall framework of HMED. The model first designs a multilayer graph convolutional network, which generates fine-grained event types by dynamically modeling multi-order dependency label information. Secondly, the global attention mechanism in the hierarchical module is used to determine the coarse-grained event type to which the trigger word belongs, and finally, the mixed representation of the two is used as the final input to the classifier. Figure 3 shows the event detection architecture of HMED, which consists of four main components: (1) Encoding Module, (2) Feature Aggregator, (3) Hierarchical Modular, (4) Classification Layer. Next, we detail all components in turn.

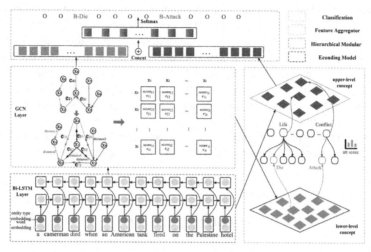

Fig. 3. The architecture of hierarchical modular event detection based on dependency graph.

3.1 Encoding Module

Given a sentence S = $\{w_1, w_2, ..., w_n\}$, where n is the length of sentence S. Then we transform each word w_i to a real-valued vector x_1. We convert the sentence into a vector sequence X = $\{x_1, x_2, ..., x_n\}$ and x_i is concatenated by two parts: 1) Word embedding vector: Same as the previous work [14], we use the word embedding pre-trained by Skip-gram model on NYT corpus; 2) Entity type embedding vector: We obtain real-valued embedding by looking up the random initialized entity type embedding table.

We use BiLSTM to capture the contextual semantic of words, and encode the forward semantic dependency and backward semantic dependency of each word w as $\overrightarrow{h_i}$ and $\overleftarrow{h_i}$. Finally, we stitch the two together as a final semantic representation h_i,

$$h_i = \left[\overrightarrow{h_i}, \overleftarrow{h_i}\right] \qquad (1)$$

3.2 Feature Aggregator

GCN is an extension of convolutional neural networks. It extends the two-dimensional convolutional space into three-dimensional, thus conveying and aggregating more information. Recently, GCN-based methods [8–10] have been widely used for ED tasks. Here we use EE-GCN [10] as a feature aggregator and optimized its update strategy.

The ordinary GCN uses a binary matrix to describe the graph structure. When we input a sentence S of length n, the adjacency matrix is represented as $A \in R^{n \times n}$. If there is a relationship between two words in the sentence, the representation of the two nodes in the corresponding graph in the matrix is 1, otherwise it is 0.

Relation Aware

According to this idea, and because the text contains rich contextual semantic information, we build a relation-aware adjacency tensor matrix $E \in R^{n \times n \times p}$, and p denotes the number of channels in the adjacency tensor. We introduce trainable embedding lookup table and then initialize the relation-aware adjacency tensor based on the dependencies between words. In the undirected graph, if there is a dependency between words x_i and x_j, E_{ij} will be initialized to the corresponding relation representation vector from the lookup table, and if there is no relation between words x_i and x_j it is initialized to a zero vector of dimension p.

The relation-aware, specifically, aggregates syntactically connected words through the relation-aware adjacency tensor E, generating a new representation for each word.

$$H^l = RA\left(E^{l-1}, H^{l-1}\right) \tag{2}$$

$$= \sigma\left(Pool\left(H_1^l, H_2^l, \ldots, H_p^l\right)\right) \tag{3}$$

each element of E represents a relational representation between words, so that relational information can be embedded in the aggregation process. Each dimension of the relational representation can be considered as a channel of the tensor E, so words from different channels can be aggregated separately by relation-awareness. In order to utilize the information of multi-order dependencies, we fill the zero vector positions in the matrix with edges whose dependency distances are greater than 2, thus allowing the multi-order distance dependency labels to participate in node updates as well. The relation-aware aggregation operation is defined as follows:

$$H_i^l = E_{:,:,i}^{l-1} H^{l-1} W \tag{4}$$

$W \in R^{d \times h}$ is a learnable filter, h denotes the hidden unit dimension of the graph neural network. $E^{l-1} \in R^{n \times n \times p}$ denotes the adjacency tensor matrix obtained after initialization or the previous layer of the graph convolutional neural network layer, $E_{:,i}^{l-1}$ denotes the i_{th} channel slice of E^{l-1}, n is the sentence length. $H^{l-1} \in R^{n \times d}$ denotes the input word representation vector, d denotes the dimension of the word vector, and σ is the ReLU activation function.

Dynamic Update

However, since the relationship between two words may change in different contexts, i.e., there are different dependency labels between words in different contexts, we need to dynamically update the dependency labels again according to the updated nodes, in addition to updating the node representation. Since multi-order distance dependencies are included, we add attention here in order to prevent semantic ambiguity. We assign different weights to the edges based on the two nodes connecting this edge. Edges useful for identifying central trigger words are enhanced, and finally the dependency labels of the edges are dynamically updated. Here we use the improved EEGCN [10] method. The operation is defined as follows.

$$E^l_{i,j,.} = W_u E^{l-1}_{i,j,.}\left[h^l_i \oplus h^l_j\right], i, j \in [1, n] \tag{5}$$

here, $W_u \in R^{(2 \times h + p) \times p}$ denotes a learnable parameter matrix, h denotes the hidden unit dimension. $\oplus$ denotes the matrix splicing operation, h^l_i and h^l_j denote the word representation vector of word x_i and word x_j in the current graph neural network layer. $E^{l-1}_{ij} \in R^p$ is the dependency representation vector between word x_i and word x_j, and p denotes the dimension of the dependency representation vector.

3.3   Hierarchical Modular

To provide an effective generalization bias at the conceptual level of event trigger word types, specifically, we designed a neural module network for each basic unit of the conceptual level to identify the upper-level broad classes of that event type. We then fuse this information with fine-grained event type information to improve the correct event classification by reducing the solving space of the classifier.

Fig. 4. Modular layering for event types in ACE2005.

The modular hierarchical design of event types is illustrated in Fig. 4, with each upper-level major class containing several lower-level minor classes, which is translated into mathematical form as a two-dimensional matrix $d^{34 \times 9}$. The corresponding One-hot vectors for each type in the matrix are shown in Table 1.

The input sentence $S = \{w_1, w_2, ..., w_n\}$ is encoded to obtain the hidden vector $h_i = \{h_1, h_2, ..., h_n\}$. By using the global attention mechanism, we take the hidden embedding and the upper-level concept module as input, and calculate the score of the upper-level module corresponding to each hidden embedding by a multi-layer perceptron, and map the correlation between the two by the score. For each upper-level concept c, we use d_c to denote semantic features, which hidden states are calculated as:

$$h^c_i = \tanh(W_a[h_i; d_c]) \tag{6}$$

w represents the trainable matrix shared between different upper modules. The score of h_i is calculated by softmax:

$$s^c_i = \frac{\exp\left(W_b h^c_i\right)}{\sum^n_{j=1} \exp\left(W_b h^c_j\right)} \tag{7}$$

Table 1. Modular hierarchical vector representation.

[1, 0, 0, 0, 0, 0, 0, 0, 0]	#B-Be_Born	Life	[1, 0, 0, 0, 0, 0, 0, 0, 0]	#I-Marry	Life
[1, 0, 0, 0, 0, 0, 0, 0, 0]	#I-Be_Born	Life	[0, 0, 0, 0, 1, 0, 0, 0, 0]	#B-Attack	Conflict
[1, 0, 0, 0, 0, 0, 0, 0, 0]	#B-Die	Life	[0, 0, 0, 0, 1, 0, 0, 0, 0]	#I-Attack	Conflict
[1, 0, 0, 0, 0, 0, 0, 0, 0]	#I-Die	Life	[0, 0, 0, 0, 1, 0, 0, 0, 0]	#B-Demonstrate	Conflict
[1, 0, 0, 0, 0, 0, 0, 0, 0]	#B-Marry	Life	[0, 0, 0, 0, 1, 0, 0, 0, 0]	#I-Demonstrate	Conflict

the final representation of the event type embedding that incorporates the upper-level concepts is as follows:

$$E^c = \sum_{i=1}^{n} s_i^c h_i^c \tag{8}$$

3.4 Classification Layer

By integrating fine-grained event types and coarse-grained event types, the fused hybrid representation of the two is fed into the classifier to predict event types. We fuse H^l with the E^c obtained from the hierarchical modular network by matrix stitching to obtain the hybrid representation p:

$$p = \left[H^l \oplus E^c \right] \tag{9}$$

we then feed p into a fully connected network and use the Softmax function to calculate the final distribution y of event types. The label with the highest probability is the final event type. The b is a bias term, and we use Adam to optimize here.

$$y = softmax(W_p + b) \tag{10}$$

4 Experiments

4.1 Data and Settings

We perform extensive experimental studies on the ACE 2005 corpora. The ACE05 contains 599 documents and defines 33 types of events. We also use the same test set with 40 documents as previous works and the same development set with 30 documents and 529 documents are used to train [9]. We use the 'BIO' tag scheme. The tags 'B-' and 'I-' represent the starting position and internal position of the word in the trigger word, respectively, and the tag 'O' represents the non-trigger word. In keeping with the previous work, we also use *Precision(P)*, *Recall(R)* and *F* measure(F_1) as an evaluation.

During preprocessing, we used the Stanford CoreNLP toolkit [24] for word separation, annotation, and syntactic analysis. We specified the maximum length of the input sentences as 30 and the word embedding dimension as 100. The number of layers of the graph convolutional neural network was set to 2, the hidden layer dimension was set to 200, and the batch size was set to 30. And the Adam optimization algorithm was used for training with a learning rate of 0.001 and a dropout setting of 0.5.

4.2 Baselines

We compare our models with various state-of-the-art baselines on ACE2005: 1) DMCNN [5], which uses a dynamic multi-pooling CNN for event detection in a sentence; 2) JRNN [6], which combines hand-designed features to detect events using bidirectional RNN; 3) GCN-ED [9], which first attempts model dependency trees using GCN; 4) HBTNGAM [14], which fuses sentence-level and document-level information for multi-event detection in a sentence; 5) JMEE [8], which uses self-attention and GCN to model event interdependencies for event detection; 6) MOGANED [17], which models syntactic representations using aggregated attention and GCN; 7) EE-GCN [10], which performs event detection using both syntactic structure and dependency label information; 8) MLBiNet [15], which proposes a multilayer network using cross-sentence semantic information and event dependencies to extract multiple events.

4.3 Overall Performance

As can be seen from Table 2, our proposed HMED model has higher classification accuracy compared to the results of the above baseline model in event classification. It even shows that our model achieves a 3.3% performance improvement over the original EE-GCN. Although the results in terms of accuracy are not ideal, the model achieves the highest value in terms of recall and F1 value, so the model's overall efficiency in event classification is the best. This indicates that the performance of event detection can be improved by combining lower-level concepts with upper-level concepts through a hierarchical modular network.

Table 2. Performance comparison of different methods on the ACE2005.

Model	P	R	F1
DMCNN	75.6	63.6	69.1
JRNN	66.0	73.0	69.3
GCN-ED	77.9	68.8	73.1

(continued)

Table 2. (*continued*)

Model	P	R	F1
HBTNGAM	77.9	69.1	73.3
JMEE	76.3	71.3	73.7
MOGANED	79.5	72.3	75.7
EE-GCN	76.7	78.6	77.6
MLBiNet	80.6	77.4	78.6
HMED (ours)	78.3	**83.7**	**80.9**

5 Analysis

5.1 Ablation Study

We conduct an ablation study of each module in this section. Table 3 shows: 1) We remove the multi-order dependency labels and use the one-order approach of EEGCN for dynamic updates with little performance degradation, which shows that although the multi-order labels are assigned lower attention, but still have an important role in expanding semantic information. 2) When we remove the dynamic update module (DUM) from the GCN, the results drop by 2.6%. It confirms our previous mention that words will represent different meanings in different contexts. 3) When the Hierarchical Modular (HM) is removed, the results drop by 1.4%, with significant performance degradation. This indicates hierarchical modular network can works well to enhance classification ability in ED tasks. 4) Removing the BiLSTM from the encoding stage leads to a 5.7% drop in results. This is because when converting sentences into sequence structures, by using BiLSTM has a more obvious advantage in capturing important sequence information over a longer distance. 5) The model drop reaches 3.1% after removing both HM and DUM, which once again indicates that combined with dynamically updated multi-order dependency label information, our proposed HM can classify trigger words more accurately.

Table 3. The table shows the effect of removing the corresponding component.

Componet	F1
HMED	80.9
-Multi-order	80.5
-DUM	78.3
-HM	79.5
-BiLSTM	75.2
-DUM&HM	77.8

5.2   Effect of Hierarchical Modular

In this section, we experimentally demonstrate the effectiveness of the hierarchical modular network. We add HM to some of the following baselines, as shown in Table 4. We have the following observations: 1) The addition of the hierarchical network module results in a subtle improvement in DMCCNN. 2) Since we are dealing with a lot of data with non-Euclidean structures, the GCN that incorporates syntactic representations improves by 2.0% by adding HM, and the MOGANED that aggregates information from multilayer GCNs by aggregating attention improves by 2.6%. 3) MLBiNet is utilized for document-level information, compared to the first two which perform extraction at the sentence level, MLBiNet iteratively propagates sentence and inter-sentence information, but we still obtain some improvement.

Table 4. Performance of different baselines with the addition of HM.

Model	P	R	F1	F1↑
DMCNN + HM	76.4	64.9	70.2	+1.1
GCN + HM	77.1	73.2	75.1	+2.0
MOGANED + HM	81.3	75.5	78.3	+2.6
MLBiNet + HM	76.7	82.3	79.4	+0.8

5.3   Effect of GCN Layers

We experimentally demonstrate the parameter selection of the GCN with specific effects as shown in Fig. 5. The model achieves the best performance at 2 layers. We consider that it may be because when the GCN is 1 layer, the dependency information is still represented in the tree structure, which is not enough to consider more contextual information. This also demonstrates the significant effect of using graph structures to represent sentences for ED tasks. The increase in the number of layers causes the nodes to gain more information, and when there are too many layers, the nodes represent redundant information and some of them become similar. This causes the model to be over-fitted and model's ability to judge trigger words is weakened.

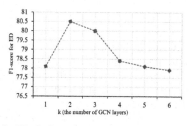

Fig. 5. The influence of GCN layers on F1 value.

5.4 Case Study

We use heat maps to verify the effectiveness of the hierarchical module. Using the previous example sentence, we use the visualized scores to map the correlation between the upper and lower strata. Figure 6 (a) shows that words with obvious connections to the upper-level concept modules correspond to higher scores and darker colors. If the word has multiple meanings, such as fired, so it may be classified as other event types when we do a direct fine-grained classification. But the upper-level concept module allows us to more easily assign it to the corresponding broad category. Then we can train it with the upper-level concept it belongs to and various information to accurately determine the type of trigger words.

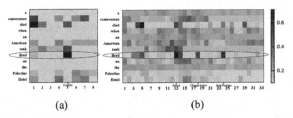

(a)   (b)

Fig. 6. The horizontal coordinates of heat map (a) are the eight coarse-grained event types of ACE05 and (b) are the 33 fine-grained event types.

6 Conclusion

In this paper, we propose Hierarchical Modular Event Detection based on Dependency Graph (HMED) in this paper. First, we design a dynamically updated dependency graph based on multi-order dependencies to obtain the representation of lower-level concepts and introduce a new representation of upper-level conceptual module to improve the classification accuracy of event detection. The effectiveness of our method is demonstrated experimentally and the start-of-the-sort was achieved in the ACE2005 dataset. In the future, we will focus on the main issues that exist at the document level, i.e., multi-event situations and co-reference resolution.

References

1. Huang, R., Riloff, E.: Modeling textual cohesion for event extraction. In: Proceedings of AAAI Conference on Artificial Intelligence, pp. 1664–1670 (2012)
2. Li, Q., Ji, H., Huang, L.: Joint event extraction via structured prediction with global features. In: Proceedings of the 51st Annual Meeting of the Association for Computational Linguistics (Volume 1: Long Papers), pp. 73–82 (2013)
3. Hong, Y., Zhang, J., Ma, B., Yao, J., Zhou, G., Zhu, Q.: Using cross-entity inference to improve event extraction. In: Proceedings of the 49th Annual Meeting of the Association for Computational Linguistics: Human Language Technologies, pp. 1127–1136 (2011)

4. Ji, H., Grishman, R.: Refining event extraction through cross-document inference. In: Proceedings of ACL-08: Hlt, pp. 254–262 (2008)

5. Chen, Y., Xu, L., Liu, K., Zeng, D., Zhao, J.: Event extraction via dynamic multi-pooling convolutional neural networks. In: Proceedings of the 53rd Annual Meeting of the Association for Computational Linguistics and the 7th International Joint Conference on Natural Language Processing (Volume 1: Long Papers), pp. 167–176 (2015)

6. Nguyen, T. H., Cho, K., Grishman, R.: Joint event extraction via recurrent neural networks. In: Proceedings of the 2016 Conference of the North American Chapter of the Association for Computational Linguistics: Human Language Technologies, pp. 300–309 (2016)

7. Sha, L., Qian, F., Chang, B., Sui, Z.: Jointly extracting event triggers and arguments by dependency-bridge RNN and tensor-based argument interaction. In: Proceedings of the AAAI Conference on Artificial Intelligence, pp. 5916–5923 (2018)

8. Liu, X., Luo, Z., Huang, H.: Jointly multiple events extraction via attention-based graph information aggregation. In: Proceedings of the 2018 Conference on Empirical Methods in Natural Language Processing, pp. 1247–1256 (2018)

9. Nguyen, T., Grishman, R.: Graph convolutional networks with argument-aware pooling for event detection. In: Proceedings of the AAAI Conference on Artificial Intelligence, pp. 5900–5907 (2018)

10. Cui, S., et al.: Edge-enhanced graph convolution networks for event detection with syntactic relation. In: Proceedings of the Association for Computational Linguistics: EMNLP 2020, pp. 2329–2339 (2020)

11. Liu, J., Chen, Y., Liu, K., Bi, W., Liu, X.: Event extraction as machine reading comprehension. In: Proceedings of the 2020 Conference on Empirical Methods in Natural Language Processing (EMNLP), pp. 1641–1651 (2020)

12. Yang, S., Feng, D., Qiao, L., Kan, Z., Li, D.: Exploring pre-trained language models for event extraction and generation. In: Proceedings of the 57th Annual Meeting of the Association for Computational Linguistics, pp. 5284–5294 (2019)

13. Liu, S., Chen, Y., He, S., Liu, K., Zhao, J.: Leveraging framenet to improve automatic event detection. In: Proceedings of the 54th Annual Meeting of the Association for Computational Linguistics (Volume 1: Long Papers), pp. 2134–2143 (2016)

14. Chen, Y., Yang, H., Liu, K., Zhao, J., Jia, Y.: Collective event detection via a hierarchical and bias tagging networks with gated multi-level attention mechanisms. In: Proceedings of the 2018 Conference on Empirical Methods in Natural Language Processing, pp. 1267–1276 (2018)

15. Lou, D., Liao, Z., Deng, S., Zhang, N., Chen, H.: MLBiNet: a cross-sentence collective event detection network. In: Proceedings of the 59th Annual Meeting of the Association for Computational Linguistics and the 11th International Joint Conference on Natural Language Processing (Volume 1: Long Papers), pp. 4829–4839 (2021)

16. Liu, J., Chen, Y., Liu, K.: Exploiting the ground-truth: an adversarial imitation based knowledge distillation approach for event detection. In: Proceedings of the AAAI Conference on Artificial Intelligence, pp. 6754–6761 (2019)

17. Yan, H., Jin, X., Meng, X., Guo, J., Cheng, X.: Event detection with multi-order graph convolution and aggregated attention. In: Proceedings of the 2019 Conference on Empirical Methods in Natural Language Processing and the 9th International Joint Conference on Natural Language Processing (EMNLP-IJCNLP), pp. 5766–5770 (2019)

18. Liu, A., Xu, N., Liu, H.: Self-attention graph residual convolutional networks for event detection with dependency relations. In: Proceedings of the Association for Computational Linguistics: EMNLP2021, pp. 302–311 (2021)

19. Li, F., et al.: Event extraction as multi-turn question answering. In: Proceedings of the Association for Computational Linguistics: EMNLP2020, pp. 829–838 (2020)

20. Westerhout, E.: Definition extraction using linguistic and structural features. In: Proceedings of the 1st Workshop on Definition Extraction, pp. 61–67 (2009)
21. Zhang, J., Qin, Y., Zhang, Y., Liu, M., Ji, D.: Extracting entities and events as a single task using a transition-based neural model. In: Proceedings of the 28th International Joint Conference on Artificial Intelligence, pp. 5422–5428. AAAI Press (2019)
22. Shen, S., Wu, T., Qi, G., Li, Y.F., Haffari, G., Bi, S.: Adaptive knowledge-enhanced bayesian meta-learning for few-shot event detection. In: Proceedings of the Association for Computational Linguistics: ACL-IJCNLP 2021, pp. 2417–2429 (2021)
23. Tong, M., et al.: Image enhanced event detection in news articles. In: Proceedings of the AAAI Conference on Artificial Intelligence, pp. 9040–9047 (2020)
24. Manning, C. D., Surdeanu, M., Bauer, J., Finkel, J. R., Bethard, S., McClosky, D.: The stanford CoreNLP natural language processing toolkit. In: Proceedings of 52nd Annual Meeting of the Association for Computational Linguistics: System Demonstrations, pp. 55–60 (2014)

Linked Data, Knowledge Integration, and Knowledge Graph Storage Management

Explicit Sparse Attention Network
for Multimodal Named Entity Recognition

Yunfei Liu[1,2] , Shengyang Li[1,2(✉)], Feihu Hu[1], Anqi Liu[1], and Yanan Liu[1]

[1] Key Laboratory of Space Utilization, Technology and Engineering Center for Space Utilization, Chinese Academy of Sciences, Beijing, China
{liuyunfei,shyli,hufeihu,liuaq,ynliu}@csu.ac.cn
[2] University of Chinese Academy of Sciences, Beijing, China

Abstract. Multi-modal named entity recognition (MNER) is a multi-modal task aim to discover named entities in text with visual information. Existing MNER approaches model dense interactions between visual objects and textual words by designing co-attention mechanisms to achieve better accuracy. However, mapping interactions between each semantic unit (visual object and textual word) will force the model to calculate irrelevant information, which results in the model's attention to be distracted. In this paper, to tackle the problem, we propose a novel model which concentrates the model's attention by explicitly selecting the most relevant segments to predict entities. This method based on top-k selection can reduce the interference caused by irrelevant information and ultimately help the model to achieve better performance. Experimental results on benchmark dataset demonstrate the effectiveness of our MNER model.

Keywords: Multimodal named entity recognition · Attention mechanism · Sparse attention

1 Introduction

Multimodal Named Entity Recognition (MNER) has become an important research direction of Named Entity Recognition (NER) [1], Due to its research significance in multimodal deep learning and wide-ranging applications, such as structure extraction from massive multimedia news and web product information. The assumption behind this is that structured extraction is expected to be more accurate than pure text-based NER because visual context helps resolve ambiguous polysemy [2, 3].

Obviously, how to make full use of visual information is one of the core issues of MNER, which directly affects model performance. To this end, many efforts have been made, roughly including: (1) Encoding the entire image into a global feature vector (Fig. 1(a)), which can be used to enhance the representation of each word [4], or to guide word learning visual perception representation based on RNN framework [1, 5]; (2) Based on Transformer framework [6], the entire image is evenly divided into multiple regions (Fig. 1(b)) and interacts with text sequences. (3) (Fig. 1(c)) Object-level features can reflect the mapping relationship between visual objects and text words. These mapping relationships help the model to distinguish different types of entities and extract entities accurately [7].

M. Sun et al. (Eds.): CCKS 2022, CCIS 1669, pp. 83–94, 2022.
https://doi.org/10.1007/978-981-19-7596-7_7

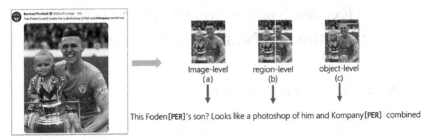

Fig. 1. An example for multi-modal named entity recognition with (a) the whole image, (b) segmented regions, (c) targeted objects.

However, modular co-attention models like [5, 6, 7], which model the interaction between each image region and each text word, force the model to compute irrelevant information, thus causes the model's attention to be distracted. This distraction hinders the NER process, so NER models require an effective attention mechanism.

In this paper. Inspired by the Explicit Sparse Transformer [8], we propose a new model called Multimodal Sparse Co-Attention Network (MSCAN), which employs explicit selection based on top-k selection and only focuses on a specified number of texts word and image objects that most relevant to MNER. We believe that this approach can reduce the interference caused by irrelevant information and ultimately help the model achieve better performance.

The main contributions of this paper can be summarized as follows:

- We introduce a multimodal sparse co-attention network to fuse visual and textual representations. Our multimodal sparse co-attention module can model the correlations between visual objects and textual entities as well as the internal connections of objects or entities, which facilitates precise entity extraction.
- We conduct experiments on the multimodal social media NER dataset, and the experimental results show that our model outperforms previous state-of-the-art methods.

2   Related Work

2.1   Multi-modal NER

As multimodal data becomes more popular across many media platforms, several recent studies have focused on the MNER task, which aims to leverage associated images to better identify named entities contained in text. Specifically, [4] proposed a multimodal NER network with modal attention to fuse textual and visual information. To model interactions between modalities and filter out noise in visual context, [1, 5] proposed an adaptive co-attention network and a gated visual attention mechanism for MNER, respectively. [6] utilize Transformers to model text sequences and evenly divide images for many and many cross-modal interactions. Furthermore, they introduce the auxiliary task of entity span detection to further improve the performance.

In this work, we follow this line of work. But unlike them, our goal is to propose an efficient multimodal approach based on the recent Transformer architecture [9].

2.2 Attention Mechanism

Attention mechanisms are widely used in various deep learning tasks [5, 10–12] mentioned visual objects as a more natural basis for attention and proposed a bottom-up attention model for the visual question answering task [11]. Object-level features are considered as fine-grained visual features that may help to extract entities related to different visual objects in multimodal NER tasks. For the multimodal NER task, a modal attention focusing on image, word and character level representations is proposed in [4]. Their method only considers text span and single image attention. [5] proposed an adaptive co-attention model in which both text and image attention are captured simultaneously. Variants of co-attention networks have emerged in recent years [13, 14]. However, these co-attention methods use separate attention distributions for each modality, ignoring the interactions between modalities. In contrast, we propose a co-attention mechanism to establish complete interactions between visual objects and textual entities, leading to improved NER performance.

3 Methodology

In this section, we present a novel multimodal named entities recognition model which combines object-level image features and textual features. we first introduce how we extract the image features and text features. For each input image, we extract objects with an object detector. Fine-grained image object-level features are utilized to help identify different types of entities. Then we describe the explicit sparse attention used in our model, and employ a fusion mechanism to obtain the joint embedding of the attended image features and attended text features, After that, An explicit selection is implemented to filter out completely irrelevant information and outputs the multimodal representations. Finally, the conditional random field (CRF) layer takes the multimodal representations as input to predict a NER label sequence. The overall architecture is given in Fig. 2.

3.1 Feature Extractor

Word Representations. We employ the recent contextualized representations from BERT [15] as our sentence encoder, which can give different representations for the same word in different contexts. Following [15], Each input sentence is preprocessed by inserting two special tokens: [CLS] to the beginning and [SEP] to the end, respectively. Formally, Given an input sentence with n words let $S = (w_1, w_2, \ldots, w_n)$, let $S' = (w_0, w_1, \ldots, w_{n+1})$ be the modified input sentence, where w_0 and w_{n+1} denote the two inserted tokens, we represent each word in a sentence by combining the sum of word, segment, and position embeddings for each token w_i. Let $X = (x_0, x_1, \ldots, x_{n+1})$ be the word representations of S'. As shown in the bottom left of Fig. 2, X is then fed to the pre-trained BERT encoder to obtain $A = (a_0, a_1, \ldots, a_{n+1})$, where $a_i \in \mathbb{R}^d$ is the generated contextualized representation for x_i.

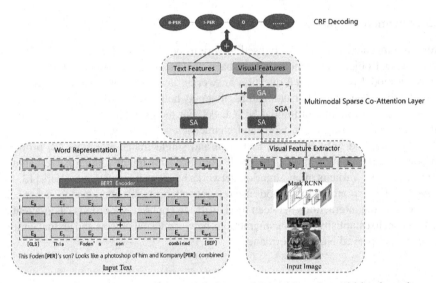

Fig. 2. The overall architecture of our model. Our model combines the multi-level word representations and object-level visual features to predict entities. A multimodal sparse co-attention module is applied to find relevant objects and entities and filter out irrelevant visual information

Visual Feature Extractor. As one of the state-of-the-art CNN models for image recognition, Mask RCNN [16] has demonstrated its ability to extract meaningful feature representations of input images in its deep layers. Unlike previous work on multimodal named entity recognition [1, 4, 5], we leverage Mask RCNN [16], an object detection model pretrained on the COCO dataset [17], to identify objects in images. We choose the output of the last pooling layer of Mask RCNN as visual object features, which contains the discriminative information describing the semantics of each object. In most cases, only salient objects are related to the entities mentioned in a sentence. Therefore, we consider the top k objects with the highest object classification probabilities, denoted by $U = (u_1, u_2, \ldots, u_k) \in R^{1024 \times k}$, where u_i is the 1024-dimensional vector representation for the i-th visual object.

To project the visual representations into the same space of the word representations and make sure that the feature projector has sufficient representation capacity to capture a large number of statistical properties between image and text modalities, we choose a feedforward network as the feature projector, denoted as W_u, The visual feature projector maps object features from the Mask RCNN to new vectors with the same dimensions as the projected text features:

$$B = W_u^T U \tag{1}$$

The projected features of object set can be denoted as $B = (b_1, b_2, \ldots, b_k) \in \mathbb{R}^{k \times d}$, where $b_i \in \mathbb{R}^d$ is the i-th object projected visual features.

3.2 Multimodal Sparse Co-attention Layer

In this subsection, we propose our proposed multimodal sparse co-attention layer for MNER. We design a multimodal sparse co-attention layer module that combines visual and textual features into predicted entities. The multimodal sparse co-attention layer module learns to model self-attention to objects or entities and guided attention between objects and entities, and generates vector representations with aggregated knowledge between image and text. As shown in Fig. 2, our multimodal sparse co-attention layer module takes input from the visual object representations and textual representations mentioned in the previous section.

Our model is composed of the SA (self-attention) units that can learn self-attention for textual words, and the SGA (self & guided-attention) units that can learn self-attention of image objects and textual-guided attention for input images. The SA and SGA units are inspired by the scaled dot-product attention proposed in [9], and the difference is that we implement an explicit selection [8] based on top-k selection to obtain more concentrated attention.

The attention function consists of a query and a set of key-value pairs, where query, key and value are all vectors. As shown in Fig. 3(a), it first measures the similarity score between query and key, and then reduces the score by $\sqrt{d_k}$, where d_k is usually the dimension of query and key. Then it applies a softmax function to get the weights of the values. The final output of the matrix can be calculated as:

$$A_{tt}(q, k, v) = softmax(\frac{qK^{\mathrm{T}}}{\sqrt{d_k}})v \tag{2}$$

where q, k, v represent query, key and value, respectively, In Fig. 3(b), we integrate our sparse module between the scale function and the softmax function to convergent attention by selecting the items with higher numerical value and ignoring the elements with smaller numerical values, since softmax function is dominated by the largest elements.

As shown in Fig. 3(c), based on the assumption that elements with higher values in matrix P represent closer correlations, we select the element with the largest contribution in each row of matrix P to aggregate the focus, where P is the multiplication matrix in the query and key.

$$P = \frac{qK^{\mathrm{T}}}{\sqrt{d}} \tag{3}$$

Specifically, it first selects the k-th largest value of row i and mark it as t_i. If the value of the j-th element is larger than t_i, the position (i, j) is recorded. The sparse module masking function $M(\cdot)$ is as follows:

$$M(P, k) = \begin{cases} P_{ij}, & P_{ij} \geq t_i \\ -\infty, & P_{ij} < t_i \end{cases} \tag{4}$$

The elements smaller than the k-th largest value are set to negative infinity, then we apply the softmax function to get the weight of this value, those elements with negative infinity will close to zero, thus avoiding the influence of negative noise. It should be noted

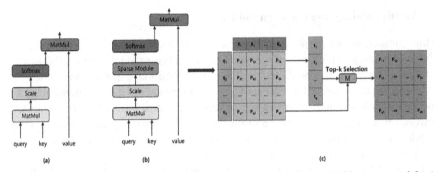

Fig. 3. (a) Original scaled dot-product attention. (b) Attention integrated with sparse module. (c) Top-k selection sparse module

that our proposed sparse module borrows from previous methods and can effectively filter noisy information. Finally, the participation feature F is given by:

$$F = softmax(M(P, k))V \tag{5}$$

We apply multi-head attention [22] to jointly pay attention to information from different representation subspaces from different locations to improve the representation ability of attention features. Using the same idea, our multi-head sparse attention has n parallel attention heads, each corresponding to an independent sparse scaled dot-product attention function. Multi-head sparse attention is formulated as:

$$Multihead(Q, K, V) = Concat(head_1, head_2, \ldots, head_n)W^o \tag{6}$$

$$head_j = A\left(QW_j^Q, KW_j^K, VW_j^V\right) \tag{7}$$

where W^o, W_j^Q, W_j^K, W_j^V are the projection matrices.

Then, we use the SA and SGA attention units to build the multimodal sparse co-attention layer module:

The self-attention (SA) unit has two sublayers: the first sublayer is a multi-head sparse attention layer, and the second sublayer is a feed-forward layer. First, the multi-head attention layer takes a set of input text features $A \in \mathbb{R}^{n \times d_n}$ as query, key and value. Then, the output features of the multi-head attention layer are transformed by two fully connected layers with ReLU activation and dropout (FC-RELU-Dropout-FC). Furthermore, to facilitate optimization, we apply a residual connection [11] with a normalization layer [3] to the outputs of both layers.

The SGA (self & guided-attention) unit is composed of three sub-layers and outputs the attended image features. The first and the second sub-layers are both a multi-head sparse attention layer with sparse scaled dot-product attention. The first sub-layer of the first SGA unit takes image features $B \in \mathbb{R}^{k \times d_v}$ obtained by Eq. (1) as input and each other SGA unit takes the output attended image features of its previous SGA unit as input to its first sub-layer for capturing the intra connections of objects. The second sub-layer takes the attended image features obtained from its previous sub-layer and the output of the SA, i.e., the attended textual features as input to learn textual-guided attention for the input image features to capture the inner relationship between the each paired word and object. The last sublayer is a feedforward layer, the same as in SA, which also takes as input the output of its previous sublayer.

$$A_{SA} = SA(A, A, A) \tag{8}$$

$$B_{SGA} = SGA(A_{SA}, B, B) \tag{9}$$

where $B_{SGA} \in R^{n \times dv}$ is the output features of SGA unit, which contain the attended object features for each word in the sentence. Figure 4 shows the details of SA and SGA units. Finally we add the textual representation from BERT and the output features of SGA unit to generate the multimodal representation:

$$C = A + B_{SGA} \tag{10}$$

where C denotes the multimodal representation of the input sentence.

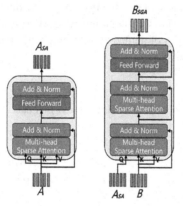

Fig. 4. The details of SA (self-attention) and SGA (self & guided-attention) units.

3.3 CRF Decoding

Label dependencies are helpful for named entity recognition tasks. After obtaining the multimodal representation from the Multimodal Sparse Co-attention Layer, we apply a Conditional Random Field (CRF) layer to model label dependencies and predict NER label sequences.

To integrate the word and the visual representations, we concatenate A and B to obtain the final hidden representations $C = (c_0, c_1, \ldots, c_n)$, where $c_i \in \mathbb{R}^{2d}$. Following [18], we then feed C to a standard CRF layer, which defines the probability of the label sequence y given the input sentence S and its associated image V:

$$P(y|S, V) = \frac{exp(score(\mathbf{C}, \mathbf{y}))}{\sum_{\mathbf{y}'} exp(score(\mathbf{C}, \mathbf{y}'))} \tag{11}$$

$$score(\mathbf{C}, \mathbf{y}) = \sum_{i=0}^{n-1} T_{y_i, y_{i+1}} + \sum_{i=1}^{n-1} E_{c_i, y_i} \tag{12}$$

$$E_{c_i, y_i} = W_{MNER}^{y_i} \cdot c_i \tag{13}$$

where $T_{y_i, y_{i+1}}$ is the transition score from the label y_i to the label y_{i+1}, E_{c_i, y_i} is the emission score of the label y_i for the i-th word, and $W_{MNER}^{y_i} \in \mathbb{R}^{2d}$ is the weight parameter specific to y_i.

4   Experimentation

4.1   Experimental Settings

Dataset. We evaluate our model on the multimodal social media dataset [5] from Twitter. It contains 8257 tweets. The dataset contains four different types of entities: Person, Location, Organization, Misc. We utilize the standard BIO2 labeling scheme, as most previous NER works [5, 19] label non-entities with label O. The total number of entities is 12784. Following the same setup as Zhang et al. [5], we divide the dataset into training set, development set and testing set containing 4000, 1000 and 3257 tweets, respectively. The statistics of various types of named entities in the training set, development set and testing set are shown in Table 1.

Table 1. Statistics of the twitter dataset

Entity type	Train	Dev	Test	Total
Person	2217	552	1816	4583
Location	2091	522	1697	4308
Organization	928	247	839	2012
Misc	940	225	726	1881
Total entity	6176	1546	5078	12784

Experimental Setup. For each unimodal and multimodal approach compared in the experiments, the maximum length of the sentence input and the batch size are respectively set to 128 and 16. For our approach, (1) the word representations A are initialized with the cased BERT-base model pre-trained by [15], and fine-tuned during training. (2) The visual embeddings are initialized by Mask RCNN with dimension of 1024 and fine-tuned during training, The number of objects is tuned from 1 to 5. (3) The number of attention heads in multi-head attention set to 2. (4) Our model is trained with an SGD optimizer, where we set the learning rate for 0.008. Our dropout rate is 0.5 and the learning rate decay is 0.05.

4.2 Result and Discussion

Results and Ablation Studies. We conduct extensive experiments and ablation studies on the Twitter dataset to explore the performance of our models. In order to limit the size of the models and save computing time, we set the appropriate stacked layers N of attention units and the number of head h of multi-head sparse attention, according to the experience of AdapCoAtt [5] and UMT [6]. Therefore, we only need to explore the effectiveness of sparse attention networks with different variants and choose the appropriate k to make the models achieve the best performance. The results are shown in Table 2, Table 3. And the best results in the tables are bold.

MSCA-SA: MSCA-SA means that only the SA units for learning textual features self-attention adopt explicit sparse attention, while the SGA units adopt the ordinary scaled dot-product attention. The length of the input textual words is 128, thus we need to select $k_1 \in [1, 128]$ most relevant textual key words for subsequent experiments. During ablation studies, we evaluate the performance of $k_1 \in \{10, 30, 50, 70, 90, 110\}$. From Table 2, we can see that the accuracy of the model roughly increases first and then decreases with the increase of k_1. When $k_1 = 70$, the model achieves the highest accuracy, 71.68%.

Table 2. Ablation results of MSCA-SA on Different textual words

k_1	Overall	PER.	LOC.	ORG.	MISC
10	67.28	79.23	74.25	51.33	28.35
30	68.32	84.71	79.92	58.26	38.82
50	69.24	84.75	80.52	60.29	37.30
70	**71.68**	85.23	**81.57**	**63.04**	**39.45**
90	70.47	**85.32**	81.22	61.11	37.96
110	69.89	85.29	80.65	59.39	38.90

MSCA-SA & SGA: MSCA-SA & SGA means that both the SA units and the first sub-layer for learning image self-attention in SGA adopt explicit sparse attention, while the second sub-layer for learning textual-guided attention in SGA adopts the ordinary scaled dot-product attention. Considering that the input features of the second sub-layer in SGA are selected by top-k selection, we no longer use sparse attention in it. The number of objects is tuned from 1 to 5, During ablation studies, we set the parameter k_1 of top-k selection used in SA to 70 and evaluate the performance of different $k_2 \in \{1, 2, 3, 4, 5\}$ of top-k selection used in SGA. From Table 3, we can see that the performance of the model rises first and then falls as k_2 increases. When $k_2 = 3$, the model achieves the highest accuracy, 74.86%.

Comparison With Existing Models. We compare our methods with several state-of-the-art methods. Table 4 Shows the testing results of compared models and our models. Our MSCA-SA & SGA ($k_1 = 70, k_2 = 3$) achieve better results than AdapCoAtt and other

Table 3. Ablation results of MSCA-SA&SGA on Different object number

k_2	Overall	PER.	LOC.	ORG.	MISC
1	71.03	82.64	77.46	55.14	35.17
2	72.68	83.82	78.93	57.04	38.87
3	**74.86**	84.76	**79.43**	**59.32**	**41.73**
4	72.85	**85.09**	79.21	57.17	38.61
5	72.81	84.46	79.26	56.25	39.03

models in Table 4. Our MSCA-SA & SGA model outperforms the compared models in F1 value. CNN + BiLSTM + CRF [20] is a textual baseline of our models without the visual information. HBiLSTM-CRF [19], which is an improvement of CNN-BiLSTM-CRF, replacing the bottom CNN layer with LSTM to build the hierarchical structure. BERT [15], which is most competitive baseline for NER with multi-layer bidirectional Transformer encoder and followed by stacking a softmax layer for entity prediction.

The state-of-the-art multimodal NER methods: MNERMA [4], VAM [1] and Adap-CoAtt Model [6], outperform the textual baseline by considering the image-level features. However, we show that when incorporating the object-level features, the model performance is improved from 70.69% to 74.86%. We also compare our model with the most recent approach UMT [6]. Our proposed MSCA-SA&SGA gains comparable results against UMT, our model can outperform the UMT in Precision and F1 values from 71.67% to 74.50%, and 73.41% to 74.86% respectively. This is a good proof of the robustness of our method that using explicit sparse attention on the task of MNER. All the above experimental results, including ablation experiments, prove the effectiveness of our models.

Table 4. The overall performance of our models and other state-of-the-art methods.

Modality	Model	Prec.	Recall	F1
Text	CNN + BiLSTM + CRF [20]	66.24	68.09	67.15
	HBiLSTM-CRF [19]	70.32	68.05	69.17
	BERT [15]	68.30	**74.61**	**71.32**
Text + Image	MNERMA [4]	72.33	63.51	67.63
	VAM [1]	69.09	65.79	67.40
	AdapCoAtt [5]	72.75	68.74	70.69
	UMT [6]	71.67	**75.23**	73.41
	MSCA-SA & SGA ($k_1 = 70, k_2 = 3$)	**74.50**	75.21	**74.86**

5 Conclusion

In this paper, we propose a novel model called Multimodal Sparse Co-Attention Network (MSCAN) for MNER. Considering that many existing co-attention-based MNER methods model dense interactions between each image region and each text word, which would force the model to compute irrelevant information and negatively affect the performance of the model, MSCAN reduces interference from irrelevant information and focuses the model's attention by using explicit selection based on top-k selection. The experimental results demonstrate the effectiveness of our model.

In future research, we will focus on exploring methods that can adaptively learn the optimal value of parameter k, and strive to explore more effective attention mechanisms, not only for MNER, but also for more multi-modal Tasks.

Acknowledgements. This work was supported by the National Defense Science and Technology Key Laboratory Fund Project of the Chinese Academy of Sciences: Space Science and Application of Big Data Knowledge Graph Construction and Intelligent Application Research and Manned Space Engineering Project: Research on Technology and Method of Engineering Big Data Knowledge Mining.

References

1. Lu, D., Neves, L., Carvalho, V., Zhang, N., Ji, H.: Visual attention model for name tagging in multimodal social media. In: Proceedings of ACL 2018, pp. 1990–1999 (2018)
2. Zhang, D., Ju, X., Li, J., Li, S., Zhu, Q., Zhou, G.: Multi-modal multi-label emotion detection with modality and label dependence. In: Proceedings of EMNLP 2020, pp. 3584–3593 (2020)
3. Ju, X., Zhang, D., Li, J., Zhou, G.: Transformer based label set generation for multi-modal multi-label emotion detection. In: Proceedings of ACMMM2020, pp. 512–520 (2020)
4. Moon, S., Neves, L., Carvalho, V.: Multimodal named entity recognition for short social media posts. In: Proceedings of NAACL-HLT 2018, 852–860 (2018)
5. Zhang, Q., Fu, J., Liu, X., Huang, X.: Adaptive co-attention network for named entity recognition in tweets. In: Proceedings of AAAI 2018, pp. 5674–5681 (2018)
6. Yu, J., Jiang, J., Yang, L., Xia, R.: Improving multimodal named entity recognition via entity span detection with unified multimodal transformer. In: Proceedings of ACL 2020, pp. 3342–3352 (2020)
7. Tang, Y., Wu, X.: Salient object detection using cascaded convolutional neural networks and adversarial learning. IEEE Trans. Multimedia **23**, 2520–2532 (2021)
8. Zhao, G., Lin, J., Zhang, Z., Ren, X., Su, Q., Sun, X.: Explicit sparse transformer: concentrated attention through explicit selection. In: Proceedings of the 8th International Conference on Learning Representations (ICLR 2020), Addis Ababa, Ethiopia, 26–30 April 2020
9. Vaswani, A., et al.: Attention is all you need. In: Proceedings of NIPS, pp. 5998–6008 (2017)
10. Sukhbaatar, S., et al.: End-to-end memory networks. In: Proceeding Advances Neural Information Processing System, pp. 2440–2448 (2015)
11. Anderson, P., et al.: Bottom-up and top-down attention for image captioning and visual question answering. In: Proceeding IEEE Conference Computer Vision Pattern Recognition, pp. 6077–6086 (2018)
12. Egly, R., Driver, J., Rafal, R.D.: Shifting visual attention between objects and locations: evidence from normal and parietal lesion subjects. J. Exp. Psychol. General **123**(2), 161–177 (1994)

13. Lu, J., Yang, J., Batra, D., Parikh, D.: Hierarchical question-image co-attention for visual question answering. In: Proceeding Advances Neural Information Processing System, pp. 289–297 (2016)

14. Nam, H., Ha, J.W., Kim, J.: Dual attention networks for multimodal reasoning and matching. In: Proceedings of the IEEE Conference on Computer Vision and Pattern Recognition, pp. 299-307 (2017)

15. Devlin, J., Chang, M.W., Lee, K., Toutanova, K.: Bert: Pre-training of deep bidirectional transformers for language understanding (2018). arXiv preprint arXiv:1810.04805

16. He, K., Gkioxari, G., Dollár, P., Girshick, R.: Mask R-CNN. In: Proceedings of the IEEE International Conference on Computer Vision, pp. 2961-2969 (2017)

17. Lin, T.-Y., et al.: Microsoft COCO: common objects in context. In: Proceeding European Conference on Computer Vision, pp. 740–755 (2014). https://doi.org/10.1007/978-3-319-10602-1_48

18. Lample, G., Ballesteros, M., Subramanian, S., Kawakami, K., Dyer, C.: Neural architectures for named entity recognition. In: Proceedings of NAACL-HLT (2016)

19. Lample, G., Ballesteros, M., Subramanian, S., Kawakami, K., Dyer, C.: Neural architectures for named entity recognition. In: Proceeding Conference North America Chapter Assocation Computer Linguistics: Human Language Technology, pp. 260–270 (2016)

20. Ma, X., Hovy, E.: End-to-end sequence labeling via bi-directional LSTM-CNNS-CRF. In: Proceeding 54th Annual Meeting Assocation Computer Linguistics (Volume 1: Long Papers), pp. 1064–1074 (2016)

Optimization of Bit Matrix Index for Temporal RDF

Tianyi Zhou[1,2], Yu Liu[1,2(✉)], Hang Zhang[1,2], Feng Gao[1,2], and Xiaolong Zhang[1,2]

[1] Department of Computer Science and Technology, Wuhan University of Science and Technology, Wuhan 430072, Hubei, China
liuyu@wust.edu.cn
[2] Hubei Province Key Laboratory of Intelligent Information Processing and Real-Time Industrial, Wuhan 430072, Hubei, China

Abstract. Temporal knowledge is crucial in many knowledge-based systems. A common approach for expressing temporal knowledge on the syntactical level is to add temporal triples as metadata for triples, called RDF reification. However, this will increase the volume and complexity of data, and leads to a decrease in the storage and retrieval performance for temporal RDF. In the field of RDF storage, the bit matrix is a simple yet highly efficient structure for indexing RDF data. In this paper, we provide an extension to bit matrix architecture (TBitStore) to support the indexing of temporal RDF. To begin with, TBitStore constructs an index over both Subject-Object key and temporal information. Then, it uses a time-bound matching mechanism to accelerate subquery execution. Moreover, it leverages a temporal statistics-based index to optimize the query plans. The experimental results show that TBitStore can reduce the storage space compared to the original bit matrix database for temporal RDF data, as well as improve the performance of querying temporal RDF.

Keywords: Temporal RDF · Bit Matrix · Temporal index · Query optimization

1 Introduction

Knowledge graphs have been a key technology for enabling AI in many domains [1, 2]. However, the conventional RDF structure does not cater to time-sensitive scenarios in the volatile domain (e.g., finance). Despite many efforts, storing and querying temporal knowledge is still challenging.

Handling temporal knowledge requires both time-oriented representation and storage/querying mechanisms. Most existing temporal RDF storage systems build on top of the conventional RDF database, which can be divided into two categories: relational databases that use relational tables to organize RDF data and native databases designed specifically for knowledge graphs that use models such as the graph or the bit matrix to represent and manage RDF data. For example, Chen et al. [3] and Huang et al. [4] extend the relational and graph database to satisfy the need to manage temporal RDF data, respectively.

© The Author(s), under exclusive license to Springer Nature Singapore Pte Ltd. 2022
M. Sun et al. (Eds.): CCKS 2022, CCIS 1669, pp. 95–107, 2022.
https://doi.org/10.1007/978-981-19-7596-7_8

Compared to the relational and graph model, the bit matrix [5–7] was proposed to cope with the growth of RDF data and achieve efficient management of large-scale RDF data. It is a simple but expressive structure for RDF data with good compressibility for modeling billion-level RDF data. Such a storage structure facilitates the widespread use of merge joins for join processing. In summary, considering that the temporal RDF data contains more information and therefore has more data volume compared with the conventional RDF data, the bit matrix database has advantages over other storage models in handling temporal RDF data.

However, since the current bit matrix database can only parse and store RDF data in regular triple format. There are also some problems in managing temporal RDF data directly using the bit matrix database. As shown in Fig. 1, adding time information to the data will lead to complications of the original triple relationships as well as additional reasoning steps for querying and answering. Moreover, the existing indexing and query plan optimization would fail to efficiently locate sub-graphs, because one predicate may relate to an enormous amount of temporal-related triples. All the above will reduce the efficiency of the bit matrix database for managing data.

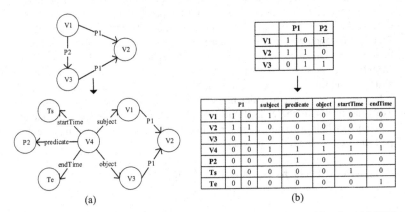

Fig. 1. Adding valid time to the relationship (V1, P2, V3) using RDF Reification. (a) RDF graph. (b) The bit matrix corresponding to the RDF graph

In this regard, we present a temporal RDF database (TBitStore) as a tension of bit matrix database TripleBit [6], to improve the storage and query efficiency of temporal RDF data. The main contributions of this paper are 2-fold:

1) we propose a novel storage structure on top of TripleBit that constructs SO (Subject-Object) keys by combining the subject and object of each predicate, and associating SO keys with the temporal information, to store and retrieve temporal information.
2) we propose a time-oriented statistics index that divided the statistical information related to the predicate into multiple components which have different temporal intervals, and a 2-dimensional K-D tree is employed to enable the time-bounded search of all components.

The rest of this paper is organized as follows. Section 2 provides a brief overview of the work related to temporal RDF and the TripleBit system. Section 3 presents our storage and indexing structure for temporal RDF. Section 4 describes the flow of the TBitStore for handling temporal queries. Section 5 presents the experimental evaluation of our approach. Section 6 concludes the paper and outlines our future work.

2 Related Work

2.1 Temporal RDF

Temporal RDF Representation. Existing temporal RDF representation usually uses two kinds of method: 1) extending RDF vocabularies by a set of temporal predicates, such as RDF reification, OWL-Time; 2) adding timestamps to the predicate of a triple or to the triple itself, such as extending a triple into a quadruple [3]. For the first method, Gutierrez et al. [8] proposed a temporal RDF model to represent the syntax and semantics of temporal RDF by using RDF vocabularies and temporal tags. Gao et al. [9] developed a set of temporal hypergraph representation models for financial domain knowledge and defined inference rules for temporal and polynary relations in the financial domain.

For the second method, Bellamy-McIntyre [10] used a representation of the temporal RDF data model stRDF in the form of a quaternion (s, p, o, i) to represent the effective time using the time-dependent mathematical formula. Zimmermann et al. [11] described a generic framework for semantic Web data representation and inference, capable of handling multiple annotation information such as time, authenticity, or provenance.

Temporal RDF Storage. Nowadays, there are various techniques to store temporal RDF data, including the use of well-known relational databases, and some special systems such as graph databases.

In the relational database part, Pugliese et al. [12] built the tGRIN index based on the GRIN index. tGRIN introduces the consideration of the temporal spacing factor in the nodal distance calculation. In [13], the KDTree index and the combined bitmap index are used for fast indexing temporal information globally and locally, respectively. Although the relational-based temporal storage scheme is mature, it cannot reflect the graph characteristics of RDF data and has drawbacks in coping with data growth and handling large-scale RDF data.

In the graph database part, Huang et al. [4] presented the TGraph system which applies the Neo4j database to store static data in the temporal graph, while constructing a multi-layer file structure to store dynamic attributes and relate them to static data. However, in the case of gradually increasing data size, since the TGraph records all changes in memory, many data are repeatedly recorded resulting in redundant space occupation.

2.2 TripleBit

The TripleBit system uses the bit matrix model and is designed as a storage structure that allows direct and efficient querying of compressed data. In the bit matrix model of TripleBit, each row of the matrix represents an entity, and each column represents a triple. For a column in the matrix, 1 and 0 are used to mark whether the corresponding entity row exists in the triple represented by that column. Only two positions in each matrix column are 1, and the rest are 0.

TripleBit lexicographically sorts the columns by predicates and vertically partitions the matrix into multiple disjoint buckets, one for each predicate. In addition, TripleBit designs three auxiliary index structures to speed up the retrieval operations on the data: (1) ID-Chunk Index, which is used to quickly locate the position of a subject or object in the data chunks corresponding to the predicate; (2) ID-Predicate Index, which provides a mapping from a subject or object to its associated predicate and is used to speed up queries in the case of unknown predicates; (3) Statistics Index(Aggregate Indexes), which contains four tables recording information on the number of associated subjects, objects, subject-predicate pairs, and object-predicate pairs in the dataset, and is used to estimate the selectivity of query pattern, which reflects the number of triples that match the pattern [14].

The execution time of a query is heavily influenced by the number and execution order of join operations and the means to find the results of the query [6], TripleBit uses the selectivity estimation to generate query plans to optimize the query process. The lower the selectivity, the smaller the result sets, the fewer subsequent searches and joins, and hence the higher the priority of the operation's execution.

3   Temporal RDF Storage and Indexing

3.1   Temporal Data Model

To improve the efficiency of handling temporal data, as shown in Fig. 2, TBitStore transforms the temporal RDF data modeled using RDF reification into a quadruple form model for parsing and representation i.e., (s,p,o):[t], where s, p, and o are the subject, predicate, and object in the triple, and t represents the time information.

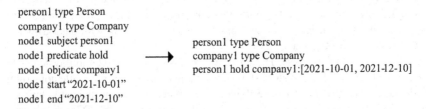

Fig. 2. Converting RDF data containing temporal information into the temporal data model

In addition, we use three different time types to describe the time information corresponding to the triples:

1) CONSTANT: This type does not contain time information, and is mainly used to describe triples that are always valid throughout the RDF database's life cycle;

2) POINT: This type includes only a time point and can describe the triple valid at a certain moment in the dataset;

3) PERIOD: This type includes both start time and end time, and is used to describe triples that are valid for a period.

3.2 Storage Structure

In terms of temporal RDF data storage, TBitStore applies the bit matrix model to manage the subject, predicate, and object data in temporal RDF data and adopts the key-value mapping approach to store and manage the temporal information of the triple.

TripleBit uses a prefix-suffix mapping table to transform entity URIs and strings into corresponding entity IDs for compression and representation. Here we use sid, pid, and oid to denote the entity ID of subject, predicate, and object respectively.

As shown in the solid line part of Fig. 3, the subjects and objects corresponding to each predicate will be stored as two copies using the structure of chunk list (bucket), sorted by sid as well as oid, respectively [6]. In addition, <x, y> pairs are used in the chunk to record the sid and oid, where x denotes the ID with the smaller value and y is the difference between the larger ID and the smaller ID. Obviously, within the predicate bucket, the combination of sid as well as oid can uniquely specify a certain triple. Therefore, sid, oid can be used to construct the SO(Subject-Object) key(soid) to represent the triple and link it to its time information.

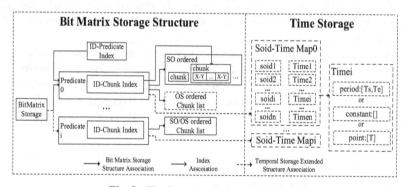

Fig. 3. The Storage scheme of TBitStore

Definition 1 (soid). For an RDF dataset, let S_p be the set of triples whose predicate is P. For any triple $r \in S_p$, there exists the function G and a unique integer n satisfying n $= G(s_r, o_r)$. Where s_r and o_r are the IDs of the subject and object in the r, respectively. The integer n is called the subject-object key of the r, soid.

TBitStore constructs soid by shifting the sid left and performing the binary-and operation with oid. For the time information, as shown in the dashed part of Fig. 3, TBitStore no longer stores it as an entity in the chunk, but extracts and stores it in the mapping table of SO keys and time information corresponding to the predicate (Soid-Time Map). To save space, the system converts the time information into integers for storage and comparison. For example, "2020–10-01T12:30:00" will be coded as 20201001123000. Especially, CONSTANT type of time data will be recorded as 0.

To further speed up the efficiency of temporal query, based on the original sorting by sid and oid, TBitStore executes a secondary non-decreasing sorting according to the start time code of the time information belonging to each triple. If the end time of the time constraint is less than the start time of the matching item during the scanning process, the subsequent matching can be interrupted directly.

3.3 Temporal Statistics Index

TripleBit's Statistics Index does not consider the effect of time when estimating the selectivity and thus can lead to errors between the estimated value and the true value of the selectivity when handling temporal queries, which will lead to incorrect judgments about the execution order of each pattern. Therefore, we design the Temporal Statistics Index (TSI) to estimate the selectivity of temporal query patterns. The index divides the predicate statistics into multiple temporal components based on time, which is used to record the statistical information related to predicates at different periods and applies a two-dimensional K-D tree to achieve range retrieval of all temporal components.

Definition 2 (Temporal Component). For an RDF dataset, Tp is the set of valid times of all triples associated with the predicate P. By integrating the time in Tp into n mutually distinct time intervals Ti, the predicate P can be divided into n components. Each component P_{Ti} has different temporal information. These components can be called the temporal components of the predicate P.

The temporal component of the predicate records the temporal triples associated with the predicate. Each component counts the triples with the same time information. As for the triple whose time intersects with, contains, or is contained by the existing component, a new temporal component will be constructed for recording. In the following, we describe the index structure with the time information in years as an example.

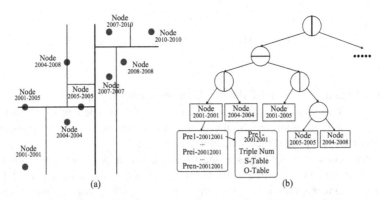

(a)   (b)

Fig. 4. K-D tree partitioning and structure of predicate temporal components

Since the temporal data has two-dimensional attributes, start time and end time. As shown in Fig. 4, a two-dimensional K-D tree structure is used to implement the range query for all predicate temporal components, and the K-D tree is constructed based on temporal nodes with start and end time, and each node stores components with the same start and end time as the node. Especially, for the CONSTANT type of components, a temporal node of the CONSTANT type is constructed for storing, which is not involved in the K-D tree construction but will be added to the K-D tree range retrieval result. As shown in Fig. 4(a), the K-D tree divides the region in which the temporal node is located until only one node remains in each region. Then, as shown in Fig. 4(b), the only remaining node in each region are stored in the leaf node of the K-D tree.

4 Temporal Query Processing

TBitStore uses τ-SPARQL [15] as the temporal query syntax, which extends the FROM keyword in SPARQL to add a FROM τ expression, where τ is the time constraint for this query.

Definition 3 (Time Constraint, TC). TC is used to describe the time constraints of query patterns in the query graph. Let S be the result set of a subquery pattern in the query graph, r be a triple in the S, and t_r be the time of r. Then $\forall r \in S$, $t_r \subseteq TC$.

For example, for the query statement SELECT * FROM T1 WHERE {pattern1. Pattern2.}, pattern1 and pattern2 have the same TC, i.e., T1. The time information of each triple in the result set is in the time range specified by T1.

Table 1. Calculation of selectivity estimates for temporal query patterns

Temporal query pattern	Calculation of selectivity estimation
(S ?P ?O):TC	KDTree.range(TC).forEach().count(S)
(S P ?O):TC	KDTree.range(TC).forEach().check(P).count(S)
(?S ?P O):TC	KDTree.range(TC).forEach().count(O)
(?S P O):TC	KDTree.range(TC).forEach().check(P).count(S)
(?S ?P ?O):TC	KDTree.range(TC).forEach().count(Triple)
(?S P ?O):TC	KDTree.range(TC).forEach().check(P).count(Triple)
(S ?P O):TC	Constant: 2
(S P O):TC	Constant: 1

4.1 Selectivity Estimation

As described in Sect. 3.3, the TSI is mainly used to optimize temporal queries, while TBitStore also retains the Statistics Index of TripleBit for non-temporal queries.

Query plan generation is based on the estimation of the triple pattern selectivity and the join selectivity. For a triple pattern, it can be calculated using the TSI. The selectivity of the join operation is computed by the estimated result of two triple patterns involved in the join [7]. In total, there are eight triple query patterns, each pattern in the temporal query is bounded by a temporal constraint TC, such as (S ?P O):TC.

Table 1 shows the calculation of the estimated selectivity of eight temporal query patterns by the TSI. As shown in the table, *KDTree.range(TC)* means K-D tree range query the temporal nodes that match the temporal constraints TC; *forEach()* iterates through all temporal components in the temporal nodes of the K-D Tree range query results; *check(P)* determines whether the temporal component belongs to the predicate P; *count(S/O/Triple)* is used to calculate the subject S, object O or the total number of triples in the predicate temporal component, and return the final calculated sum as the estimates of selectivity. Finally, the system generates the query plan based on the selectivity estimates of each pattern. Especially, for the triple pattern (S P O):TC and (S ?P O):TC, since the relationship between the two entities is finite, their selectivity estimates are set as the constant, 1 and 2, respectively, just like in TripleBit.

4.2 Query Execution

After generating a query plan, the system begins querying and joining each pattern. As described in Sect. 4.1, there are eight query patterns in total, and TripleBit responds to the query requirements of different patterns by applying ID-Chunk Index and ID-Predicate Index. Based on this, TBitStore extends the temporal-constrained filtering step by combining Soid-Time Map in the original pattern query process. Due to space limitation, we focus on describing the query process of two representative temporal triple patterns, (S P ?O):TC and (S ?P ?O):TC.

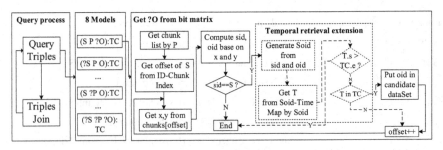

Fig. 5. (S P ? O):TC query process

For the temporal triple pattern shaped as (S P ?O):TC, as shown in Fig. 5, TBitStore obtains the chunk list based on the known P and S, then locates the corresponding offsets of S according to the ID-Chunk Index. Then, the program scans the chunk list starting from the offset position and reads <x, y> pairs to calculate the sid and oid for query pattern matching. After that, the program constructs soid from the sid and oid and uses soid to get time information for temporal filtering. For the pattern like (S ?P ?O):TC, the set Ps of all predicates related to S can be obtained from the ID-Predicate Index. And then, for traversing all predicates in Ps, each traversal query pattern is (S Pi ?O):TC, where Pi ∈ Ps and the query process are the same as Fig. 5.

5   Evaluation

To verify the effectiveness of TBitStore, we compare and analyze it with the TripleBit system in terms of storage space occupation, selectivity estimation accuracy, and temporal query efficiency, respectively. Both systems are implemented in C++ and deployed on the same server with CentOS 7.7 operating system, Intel(R) Xeon(R) CPU E5–2660 v4 @ 2.00 GHz, and 128 GB of RAM.

Table 2. Dataset characteristics

Dataset source	Dataset name	Number of triples
LUBM	LUBM-1M	1316700
	LUBM-5M	5358624
	LUBM-10M	11108166
	LUBM-50M	53845210
FIN	FIN-50K	54200
	FIN-100K	106000
	FIN-300K	363216
	FIN-1M	1089604

The experiments use LUBM as well as the financial equity dataset (referred to below as FIN) as the test dataset. As shown in Table 2, four sets of temporal test datasets of different sizes are constructed based on LUBM and the financial equity data, respectively. For the LUBM dataset, we add CONSTANT, POINT, and PERIOD types of time information to the triple according to the semantics of each triple predicate. Both LUBM after adding time information and FIN are represented using RDF reification.

5.1   Storage Space

TBitStore converts temporal data represented using RDF reification into a temporal data model shown in Fig. 2, and the storage structure for handling temporal RDF data is optimized. The different handling methods for temporal RDF data make some differences in the space occupied by the two in storing the same dataset.

As shown in Fig. 6(a), (b), for the same temporal dataset, the space occupied by TripleBit is larger than that of TBitStore. In the simulated dataset LUBM, the space occupied by TripleBit storage is 3–4 times larger than that of TBitStore. In FIN, for FIN-50K, the smallest data set, TripleBit storage occupies 3 times more space than TBitStore, while for FIN-1M, the largest data set, this ratio is 4.42.

This is because TBitStore reduces the complexity of handling temporal RDF data from the underlying storage model level, it constructs the association of triples with their time information and extracts the time information to store in the Soid-Time Map. In contrast, Triplebit combines RDF reification to represent and manage temporal RDF data, which in turn increases the number of nodes and relations in the dataset. For example, for LUBM-1M, the number of relations increases by 274.96%, and the number of nodes increases by 69.57% after adding the time information. Therefore, TripleBit needs to construct more chunk lists to store the extra entity data.

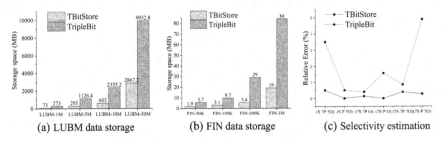

Fig. 6. Storage space and selectivity estimation comparison: TBitStore vs. TripleBit

5.2 Selectivity Estimation

Here we take the relative error approach to compare the selectivity estimation results of TBitStore and TripleBit. As shown in Eq. 1, m is the query pattern, E_m is the estimated selectivity of m, and S_m is the actual selectivity of m. The relative error δ is calculated as the ratio of the absolute error of E_m and S_m to S_m.

$$\delta = |E_m - S_m| / S_m \tag{1}$$

The experiments are based on the LUBM-1M dataset. As described in Sect. 4.1, only the first six patterns are compared, since the estimates for the latter two models selectively were the same for both. Figure 6(c) shows the results, because time constraints are taken into account, the estimation accuracy of temporal triple pattern selectivity is often higher in TBitStore with TSI than in Triplebit.

5.3 Query Performance

To evaluate the performance of TBitStore in handling temporal queries, we define three different types of queries:

1) The Simple query, which contains only one triple pattern;
2) The Path query, which consists of two triple patterns connected through one common node;
3) The Star query, consisting of two Path queries, includes four triple patterns and two common nodes.

Each type of query contains five query statements with different temporal constraints. For TBitStore, all three types of queries are written using τ-SPARQL syntax. Meanwhile, for TripleBit, the temporal query statements are converted into standard SPARQL statements, and the time is filtered using the FILTER keyword.

$$S_T = T_f/T_t \tag{2}$$

In this paper, we use the geometric mean to record the elapsed time for each query type. The use of geometric mean is less affected by extreme values than the arithmetic mean [16], so individual queries with longer and shorter elapsed time have little impact on the overall performance evaluation. To compare the performance of the two systems more obviously, as shown in Eq. 2, we use the speedup ratio S_T to show the comparison of the retrieval efficiency of the two systems. Where T_f is the elapsed time of retrieval by TripleBit using FILTER keywords and T_t is the elapsed time of retrieval by TBitStore.

The experimental results are shown in Fig. 7. The query efficiency is improved by tens of times in the LUBM dataset, and the improvement becomes progressively larger as the size of the dataset increases. TBitStore outperforms TripleBit in terms of temporal queries, and has a large improvement, reaching 2 orders of magnitude faster. In the FIN dataset, the efficiency of all three queries is also improved by several times. Since the key-value mapping-based indexing structure of TBitStore can obtain the time information of the triples in constant time, this makes it possible to add temporal-constrained matching to the original execution process without much additional overhead, and reducing the size of the candidate dataset, thus further reducing the time consuming of subsequent join operations.

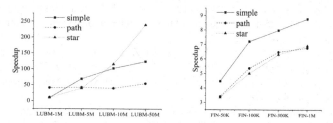

Fig. 7. Speedup ratios for different query types on different datasets

6 Conclusions

To achieve efficient management of temporal RDF data, we propose a temporal RDF-oriented indexing architecture TBitStore in combination with an existing bit matrix RDF database, which adopts key-value mapping to store and index temporal information, and introduces time factor consideration in query plan generation. Compared to the existing bit matrix database, the storage space usage is reduced by 50%–80%, while the time retrieval efficiency is improved by several times, up to two orders of magnitude.

At the same time, the key-value mapping-based association method in this study suffers from hash conflicts, which will lead to unstable retrieval efficiency. In the future, we will further test TBitStore using more datasets such as YAGO2 [17], etc., and compare it with other temporal RDF databases to optimize and improve the system. In addition, the existing knowledge graph representation mechanism is mostly based on dual relationships of ordinary graphs, which simplifies the complexity of data relations. In contrast, the hyperedge that can connect any number of nodes in the hypergraph can more accurately describe the relations between multiple associated entities. TBitStore currently does not support the management of polynary relationships in hypergraphs, and we will further investigate the management of temporal hypergraph data.

Acknowledgments. This work is supported by the Science and Technology Innovation 2030 - "New Generation Artificial Intelligence" (2020AAA0108501).

References

1. Auer, S., Bizer, C., Kobilarov, G., Lehmann, J., Cyganiak, R., Ives, Z.: DBpedia: a nucleus for a web of open data. In: Aberer, K., et al. (eds.) ASWC/ISWC -2007. LNCS, vol. 4825, pp. 722–735. Springer, Heidelberg (2007). https://doi.org/10.1007/978-3-540-76298-0_52
2. Huakui, L., Liang, H., Feicheng, M.: Constructing knowledge graph for financial equities. Data Anal. Knowl. Discov. **4**(5), 27–37 (2020)
3. Yuan-yuan, C., Li, Y., Zheqing, Z., Zongmin, M.: Temporal RDF model and index method based on neighborhood structure. Computer Science **48**(10), 167–176 (2021)
4. Huang, H., Song, J., Lin, X., et al.: TGraph: a temporal graph data management system. In: Proceedings of the 25th ACM International on Conference on Information and Knowledge Management, pp. 2469–2472 (2016)
5. Atre, M., Chaoji, V., Zaki, M.J., et al.: Matrix "Bit" loaded: a scalable lightweight join query processor for RDF data. In: Proceedings of the 19th International Conference on World Wide Web, pp. 41–50 (2010)
6. Pingpeng, Y., Liu, P., Buwen, W., Hai, J., Wenya, Z., Ling, L.: TripleBit: a fast and compact system for large scale RDF data. Proc. VLDB Endowment **6**(7), 517–528 (2013)
7. Liu, P.: Research on Highly Scalable RDF Data Storage System. Huazhong University of Science & Technology (2012)
8. Gutierrez, C., Hurtado, C., Vaisman, A.: Temporal RDF. In: Gómez-Pérez, A., Euzenat, J. (eds.) ESWC 2005. LNCS, vol. 3532, pp. 93–107. Springer, Heidelberg (2005). https://doi.org/10.1007/11431053_7
9. Gao, F., Zheng, L., Gu, J.: Hypergraph based knowledge representation and construction for Polynary and temporal relations in financial domain. J. Shanxi Univ. (Nat. Sci. Ed), **45**(4), 1–12 (2022)
10. Bellamy-McIntyre, J.: Modeling and querying versioned source code in rdf. In: Gangemi, A., et al. (eds.) The Semantic Web: ESWC 2018 Satellite Events: ESWC 2018 Satellite Events, Heraklion, Crete, Greece, June 3–7, 2018, Revised Selected Papers, pp. 251–261. Springer International Publishing, Cham (2018). https://doi.org/10.1007/978-3-319-98192-5_44
11. Zimmermann, A., Lopes, N., Polleres, A., et al.: A general framework for representing, reasoning and querying with annotated semantic web data. J. Web Semant. **11**, 72–95 (2012)
12. Pugliese, A., Udrea, O., Subrahmanian, V.S.: Scaling RDF with time. In: Proceeding of the 17th International Conference on World Wide Web. New York: ACM, pp. 605–614 (2008)
13. Zhao, P., Yan, L.: A methodology for indexing temporal RDF data. J. Inf. Sci. Eng. **35**(4), 923–934 (2019)

14. Stocker, M., Seaborne, A., Bernstein, A., et al.: SPARQL basic graph pattern optimization using selectivity estimation. In: Proceedings of the 17th international conference on World Wide Web, pp. 595–604 (2008)
15. Tappolet, J., Bernstein, A.: Applied temporal RDF: efficient temporal querying of RDF data with SPARQL. In: Aroyo, L., et al. (eds.) The Semantic Web: Research and Applications, pp. 308–322. Springer Berlin Heidelberg, Berlin, Heidelberg (2009). https://doi.org/10.1007/978-3-642-02121-3_25
16. Broekstra, J., Kampman, A., van Harmelen, F.: Sesame: a generic architecture for storing and querying rdf and rdf schema. In: Horrocks, I., Hendler, J. (eds.) The Semantic Web—ISWC 2002, pp. 54–68. Springer Berlin Heidelberg, Berlin, Heidelberg (2002). https://doi.org/10.1007/3-540-48005-6_7
17. Hoffart, J., Suchanek, F.M., Berberich, K., et al.: YAGO2: a spatially and temporally enhanced knowledge base from wikipedia. Artif. Intell. **194**, 28–61 (2013)

Natural Language Understanding and Semantic Computing

CSKE: Commonsense Knowledge Enhanced Text Extension Framework for Text-Based Logical Reasoning

Yirong Zeng, Xiao Ding$^{(\boxtimes)}$, Li Du, Ting Liu, and Bing Qin

Research Center for Social Computing and Information Retrieval, Harbin Institute of Technology, Harbin, China
{yrzeng,xding,tliu,qinb}@ir.hit.edu.cn

Abstract. Text-based logical reasoning requires the model to understand the semantics of input text, and then understand the complex logical relationships within the text. Previous works equip pre-trained language models with the logical reasoning ability by training these models on datasets obtained by logical-driven text extension. However, these methods only generate instances based on logical expressions entailed within the input text. And we argue that external commonsense knowledge is still necessary for restoring the complete reasoning chains for generating more reasonable and abundant instances. To address this issue, in this paper, we propose CSKE, a commonsense knowledge enhanced text extension framework. CSKE incorporates abundant commonsense from an external knowledge base to restore the potentially missing logical expressions and encodes more logical relationships to then extend them through logical equivalence laws. Experiments on the benchmark datasets show that our method can improve the performance of logical reasoning, especially on the instances containing complex logical relationships.

Keywords: Logical expression · Logical reasoning · Commonsense knowledge

1 Introduction

The text-based logic reasoning task requires a model to understand the semantics of text and then underlying the logical relationship within a text. Figure 1 provides a typical example for illustrating the text-based logical reasoning task. Given an input text and a corresponding question, to choose the correct answer, a model should recognize the logic expressions embedded in the input question and candidate options, such as $\alpha \rightarrow \beta$ and $\delta \rightarrow \neg\gamma$, and then combine them with the necessary commonsense knowledge to find the most plausible answer.

This ability is a core cognitive ability of human beings, and developing models with such ability has been a long-perused yet still challenging goal for researchers. Primary Artificial Intelligence systems exploit symbolic reasoning methods to model the logical relationship between the symbolized proposition, which are too rigid to generalize to complex natural languages. In recent years, the neural network-based methods, especially large-scale pre-trained models have expressed impressive performance on natural language processing (NLP) tasks [2–7]. However, analyses have demonstrated that the pre-trained language models may struggle in understanding the logical relationships within input text, especially when the underlying logical relationships are complex. They prefer the bias that selects correct answers without knowing the context and question, and thus they hardly capture logical relationships and only use word-level semantic information [8].

Context:
(α)Any sale item that is purchased can be (β) returned for store credit but ($\neg$) not for (γ) a refund of the purchase price.

Question:
If the statements above are true, which one of the following must also be true?

Options:
A. ($\neg\alpha$) An item is not on sale (r_1)causes it ($\neg\beta$) cannot be returned for store credit. ($\neg\alpha \rightarrow \neg\beta$)
B. (δ) Every piece of gardening equipment ($\neg$) is not (γ) returnable for a refund. ($\delta \rightarrow \neg\gamma$)

Answer: B

- -

Logical expressions in context: $\{(\alpha \rightarrow \beta), (\alpha \rightarrow \neg\gamma)\}$
A failed reasoning without commonsense option B: $\delta \rightarrow \neg\gamma \nLeftarrow (\delta\,?\,\alpha) \wedge (\alpha \rightarrow \neg\gamma)$ ✗
Necessary commonsense knowledge:
- gardening equipment is a sale item. $(\delta \rightarrow \alpha)$
A successful reasoning with commonsense: $(\delta \rightarrow \alpha) \wedge (\alpha \rightarrow \neg\gamma) \Rightarrow (\delta \rightarrow \neg\gamma)$ ✓

Fig. 1. An example for illustrating the text-based logical reasoning task. Given an input context, a corresponding question, and candidate options, to choose the correct answer, a model should understand the logic relationships $(\neg, r_1)$ between logic symbols $(\alpha, \beta,\ etc\ ...)$, necessary commonsense knowledge described in yellow. (Color figure online)

To derive models with both strong logical understanding ability and logical reasoning ability, recently, works propose to combine the strength of these two lines of previous works. Specifically, Jiao et al. [12] proposed a self-supervised contrastive learning approach to enhance the understanding of the logical information ability of neural models, while it cannot leverage underlying logical information in the input text directly and still struggle to solve complex logical reasoning task. Wang et al. [8] proposed to understand logical information in the text and extend logical expressions in context to cover implicit logical expressions following logical equivalence laws, while the logical expressions that can be used in their work are limited and struggle to cover the necessary underlying logical expressions due to intermediate logic relationships and commonsense knowledge missing, such as commonsense $\delta \rightarrow \alpha$ missing in Fig. 1. Although lead to certain progress on benchmark datasets, however, they cannot make full use of logical information in the text and thus suffer from complex logical reasoning problems.

To address these issues, we propose a logical CommonSense Knowledge Enhanced text extension framework (CSKE). In our framework, we introduce logical commonsense knowledge and encode multiple logical relationships, such as causal relationships, timing relationships, and conditional relationships, to not only restore potentially missing logical propositions but also get more logical expressions, which contribute to our approach to understanding more complex logical information and uncover the underlying logic structure. We extend our logical expression by logical equivalence laws to enhance the logical reasoning ability of the model. Through contrastive learning based on data augmentation in our framework, a richer negative sample can be generated, and it facilitates the model's full understanding of logical relationships.

The experimental results show that our approach outperforms strong baselines methods on the widely adopted benchmark dataset ReClor, especially on the samples which require complex logical reasoning. We also conduct an ablation experiment, which shows that each component helps promote the logical reasoning ability of the model.

2 Related Work

Textual-based logical reasoning requires a model for understanding the logical information of input text and has attracted increasing research attention recently.

Early approaches to logical reasoning focused on modeling the relationship between atomized propositions [11–15], but they cannot adapt to NLP. To promote the development of logical reasoning methods based on natural language, researchers focus on multiple-choice question-answer tasks because it requires strong logical reasoning capabilities. For example, LigiQA [1] dataset has been proposed and is collected from the National Civil Servants Examination of China. ReClor [8] dataset has been proposed. It comes from Law School Admission Test (LSAT) [16] and Graduate Management Admission Test (GMAT) [17] and requires more logical reasoning skills to solve.

In the beginning, researchers prefer to devise a specific model architecture suited to logical reasoning and viewing symbolic knowledge as prior knowledge of graphs, such as Focal Reasoner [18] and DAGN [19]. Recently, Betz et al. [20] and Clark et al. [21] demonstrated that large-scale pre-training models based on mass training data also had the potential to solve complex reasoning tasks. Built on top of the pre-trained model, Jiao et al. proposed a self-supervised contrastive learning approach to enhance the logical reasoning ability of neural models [12]. Wang et al.proposed LReasoner [8], a context extension framework and data augmentation algorithm. It extends logical expression in context to cover implicit logical expressions following logical equivalence laws. However, they cannot make full use of logical information and suffer from complex logical reasoning problems.

In this paper, we propose a logical commonsense knowledge enhanced text extension framework. It restores potentially missing logical propositions and get more logical expressions by introducing common sense knowledge and multiple logical relationships. Furthermore, it is better to understand logical information in input text by contrastive learning based on data augmentation.

3 Methodology

In this paper, we devise a logical commonsense knowledge enhanced text extension framework and it is illustrated in Fig. 2. The framework can be divided into five steps as follow. First, logic extraction, it extracts logical symbols and their relationships to obtain logical expressions of text. Second, commonsense enhanced logic extension, it introduces commonsense relationships between logical symbols, restoring potentially missing logical expressions and increasing the number of logical expressions, and uncovering underlying logical relationships by logic laws. Third, logic verbalization, it converts logical expressions into text described in natural language and feeds them as an extended context into a pre-trained model to match the options and find the answer. Finally, contrastive learning, it generates negative samples by modifying the existing logical expressions in the context to better understand logical information in the input text.

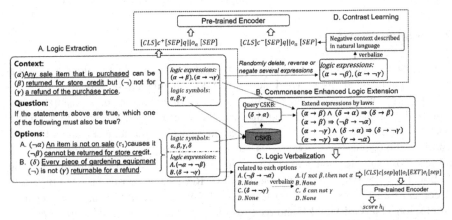

Fig. 2. The overall architecture of logical commonsense knowledge enhanced text extension framework. c, q, o_i, and e_i are the context, question, i-th option, and the extended context for the i-th option, respectively. {α, β, γ, ···}denote the logical symbols, { ¬, r_1 }denote the logical relationships. {(α→β), ···}denote the logical expressions, logical commonsense expressions are shown in yellow. (Color figure online)

3.1 Problem Formulization

Before introducing our approach in detail, we first formalize the text-based logical reasoning task. In this paper, we study logical reasoning on multiple-choice question answering. Specifically, given a context c, a question q, and K associated options $\{o_1, o_2, \ldots o_k\}$, the model is required to select a correct option as the answer o_a.

3.2 Logic Extraction

Logic extraction is the first step in this approach. It extracts logical symbols and logical expressions explicitly mentioned in context and options.

We first employ a constituency parser to extract constituents including noun phrases and gerundial phrases as basic symbols. We define a set of negative words, such as "*unable*", "*not*", "*hardly*", and "*neither*". If any negative word is related to a logical symbol α. , we add a negative tag ¬ before it, such as ¬α. Then we determine if there is a logical relationship between the logical symbols for cause, purpose, result, condition, and time. If there is a logical relationship or a close connection between two logical symbols in a sentence, then we can construct a logical expression based on them. We define a set of logical relationship words that contains multiple logical relationships, which is illustrated in Table 1. If there is a logical relationship word between two adjacent logical symbols in a sentence, it can be determined that there is a corresponding logical relationship between them, such as "α *in order to* β", "α *after* β" and "α *resulting in* β". Here, we define five group logical relationships and they can be described as follows.

Table 1. Logical relationships words for purpose, cause, result, condition, time

Purpose	In order to, thus, in order for
Cause	Due to, owing to, thanks to, according to, attributed to, since, because
Result	Resulting in, leading to, causing
Condition	If, unless, on condition that, as long as
Time	Before, after

3.3   Commonsense Enhanced Logic Extension

Commonsense introduction addresses the need to restore the missing logical relationships in context and options from common sense while increasing the number of logical relationships. But not all common sense is necessary, so we limit the number of commonsense by only considering the commonsense relationship between candidate options and context, commonsense knowledge is introduced when commonsense is needed. Specifically, the model starts with logic extraction, and then extends logical expressions existing in the context, then tries to match the most appropriate logical expression for each option, we introduce common sense when all options cannot match the logical expression. Since in most cases common sense knowledge is missing between context and options, we consider the common sense between them.

As the example in Fig. 2, a logical expression set $\{\alpha \rightarrow \beta, \beta \rightarrow \neg\gamma\}$ and a logical symbol set $\{\alpha\beta\gamma\}$ in context, a logical expression set $\{ (\delta \rightarrow \neg\gamma), \}(\neg\alpha \rightarrow \neg\beta)\}$ and logical symbols $\{\alpha, \beta, \gamma, \delta\}$ in option A and B. We cannot match an appropriate logical expression for options A and B, so query the Common Sense Knowledge Base (CSKB) for commonsense relationships by matching the logical symbols between context and options. For example, there is a commonsense triplet Is (gardening equipment, a sale item) in CSKB, we query the relationship of logical symbol α (gardening equipment) and β (a sale item) by trying to match a triplet and take them as subject and object in CSKB. Based on this, we introduce a new commonsense logical expression $(\alpha \rightarrow \beta)$. The Common Sense Knowledge Base (CSKB) we use is ConceptNet [22].

In addition to the logical expressions explicitly mentioned in the context, there are still some other underlying ones that we need to logically infer and extend. We combine the extracted logical expressions existing in the context with introduced commonsense logical expressions as a logical expression set S and perform logical inference over them to further extend the underlying logical expressions according to logical equivalence laws. Here we follow two logical equivalence laws s including contraposition [23] and transitive law [24]:

Contraposition:

$$(\alpha \rightarrow \beta) \Rightarrow (\neg\beta \rightarrow \neg\alpha) \tag{1}$$

Transitive Law:

$$(\alpha \rightarrow \beta) \wedge (\beta \rightarrow \gamma) \Rightarrow (\alpha \rightarrow \gamma) \tag{2}$$

Then the extended underlying logical expressions form an extensive set of the current logical expression set S as S_E.

3.4   Logic Verbalization

After a logical extension, we need to try to match the most appropriate logical expressions for each option and verbalize them into natural language for better utilization in the pre-trained model. Different from previous work, we select the related expressions from both S. and S_E for each option. We calculate the cosine similarity between logical expressions by word vectors of logical symbols. A logical expression is regarded as related to an option if their cosine similarity is more than a threshold and we set the threshold to 0.9, then we select the logical expression with the highest cosine similarity as a result. We transform all logical expressions related to the option as symbolic space into natural language by filling them into a predefined template [8]. For example, $(\neg\alpha \rightarrow \neg\gamma)$ can be converted to "if do not α, then it will not γ".

Pre-trained models for multiple-choice question answering concatenate the context, the question, and each option as the input and encode the sequence to calculate its score. Specifically, the concatenated sequence is formulated as $[CLS]c[SEP]q||o[SEP]$, in which c is the context and $q||o$ is the concatenation of the question and each option. We take an extended context as sentence e, and introduce a special token [EXT], and then we reformulate the input sequence as $[CLS]c[SEP]q||o[EXT]e[SEP]$ for encoding and feed the [CLS] representation into a classification layer to get each option's score and select the correct answer. The cross-entropy loss is calculated as:

$$\mathcal{L}_A = -\sum \log P(o_a \,|\, c, q) \tag{3}$$

where o_a is the correct answer.

3.5   Contrastive Learning

In order to make the model more sensitive to logical relationships to better solve the logical reasoning problem, we propose a logic-driven data augment for contrastive learning, and it enhances the ability of the model to identify logical symbols and logical relationships [25].

Background. Contrastive learning, as an unsupervised technique, focuses on learning common features between samples in the same class and distinguishes differences between samples in different classes. It is illustrated in Fig. 3, it starts with the original data. Positive and negative samples are obtained by data augmentation. The encoder encodes the positive and negative samples respectively. Representations of the same samples are drawn closer, while different samples are further away in the encoding space by loss functions.

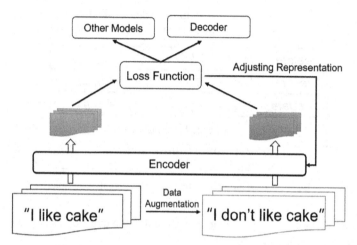

Fig. 3. A general framework for contrastive learning

The goal can be described as follows.

$$s\bigl(f(x), f(x^+)\bigr) \ll s\bigl(f(x), f(x^-)\bigr) \tag{4}$$

x^+ is a positive sample and x^- is a negative sample, $f(\cdot)$ is an encoder to learn a representation and the $s(\cdot)$ is a metric function that measures the similarity between two representations.

Our Application. Inspired by [8, 26], we use a similar data augment to build contrastive learning. We construct positive and negative samples in the following way. For negative samples, we simply take the original context and the correct option as the positive sample, which is formalized as (c^+, q, o_a), where c^+ represents the positive context, q represents the question, o_a represents the correct option. For negative samples, we construct literally similar but logically different contexts based on logical expression, which are formalized as (c^-, q, o_a), c^- is the negative context.

Specifically, we generate a negative sample by modifying the existing logical expressions in the context and verbalizing the modified logical expressions into a negative context and it is illustrated in Fig. 4. Inspired by previous work, we randomly delete, reverse, and negate logical expressions to build negative context. The deletion operation is used to remove several logical expressions in the context, the reverse operation is used to reverse the relationship between logical symbols, and the negative operation is used to mark the logical symbol negatively.

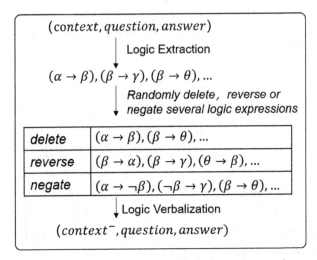

Fig. 4. Procedure to construct a logical negative sample

In this task, our goal is to calculate the score that the question can be solved by the correct answer under a given context:

$$s'(c^+, q, o_a) \gg s'(c^-, q, o_a) \tag{5}$$

where (c^+, q, o_a) and (c^-, q, o_a) are the positive and negative sample, and s' is the score function. The contrastive loss can be formalized as follows:

$$\mathcal{L}_C = -log \sum (\frac{\exp(s'(c^+,q,o_a))}{\exp(s'(c^+,q,o_a))+\exp(s'(c^-,q,o_a))}) \tag{6}$$

where $\mathcal{L}_C$ denotes the contrastive loss. Our method is trained with a combined loss as $\mathcal{L} = \mathcal{L}_A + \mathcal{L}_C$.

4   Experiments

Dataset. We evaluated our method on a challenging logical reasoning benchmark ReClor. It is extracted from the logical reasoning question of the standardized graduate admission exam. The held-out test set is further divided into EASY and HARD subsets, denoted as Test-Easy and Test-Hard, respectively. The instances in Test-Easy are biased and can be solved even without knowing contexts and question by neural models.

Baseline. We compare our method with not only basic baselines, including GPT [2], GPT-2 [3], BERT [4], Xlnet [5], but also several strong baselines, including DAGN [19], Focal Reasoner [18], MERIt [12] and LReasoner [8]. Besides, we add an extra baseline model, named Random, which means no training, and a random selection of answers.

Implementation Detail. We take RoBERTa-large as our backbone models and implement them using Huggingface [27]. We use a batch size of 8 and fine-tune on ReClor for 8 epochs and the learning rate is set to 1e–5. In negative sample construction, we select one or two logical expressions to modify depending on the number of logical expressions. We set the random seed to 10086 to guarantee the reproducibility of the result. We get the experimental results on an NVIDIA a100 with 80 G memory.

5 Result and Analysis

5.1 Overall Results

The overall results on ReClor are shown in Table 2.

Table 2. The overall results on ReClor. * denotes the average under 5 different random seeds.

Model	Test	Test-Easy	Test-Hard
Random	25.0	25.0	25.0
GPT	45.4	73.0	23.8
GPT-2	47.2	73.0	27.0
BERT	49.8	72.0	32.3
Xlnet	56.0	75.7	40.5
DAGN	58.2	76.1	44.1
Focal Reasoner	58.9	77.1	44.6
RoBERTa	55.6	75.5	40.0
MERIt (RoBERTa)	59.6	78.1	45.2
LReasoner (RoBERTa)*	58.3	**78.8**	42.1
CSKE (our)	**60.2**	77.3	**46.8**

It can be observed that:

1. A simple pre-training model, such as GPT, does not perform well on the current dataset, especially their performance is similar to Random on Test-Hard, indicating that they are not capable of complex reasoning. Strong baselines, such as Xlnet, DAGN and Focal Reasoner, have improved their performance significantly compared to simple pre-training models.
2. Built on top of RoBERTa, our model exceeds all baselines and delivers the best performance on Test sets and Test-Hard sets, including MERIt and LReasoner. This shows that our logical commonsense knowledge enhanced text extension framework can enhance the logical reasoning ability of the model. This is because, introducing commonsense knowledge and encoding multiple logical relationships can capture more logical information and make better use of logical information than baselines.

3. Our model is comparable to the strong baseline LReasoner and MERIt on Test-Easy sets. While it outperforms all baseline on Test-Hard evidently, which shows our approach makes better use of underlying logical information and it has an advantage in solving complex logical reasoning problems. This is because, by introducing external commonsense knowledge and encoding multiple logical relationships, our approach can restore the complete logical reasoning chain to support for reasoning process.

5.2 Ablation Study

To investigate the specific effect of each component of our approach, we conduct an ablation study. And the results are shown in Table 3. To observe the impacts brought by commonsense knowledge and multiple logical relationships, we built three baseline models by not using commonsense knowledge -(CSK), multiple logical relationships -(MLR), and both -(CSK + MLR).

From Table 3, it can be observed that:

1. Commonsense knowledge (CSK) and multiple logical relationships (MLR) can improve the performance of the model respectively.
2. CSK and MLR work better when added all than a single one, indicating that their promotion to the model is not entirely overlapping but independent.
3. MLR can improve performance on Test-Hard evidently, which shows that it can promisingly enhance the ability of models to solve complex logical reasoning.

Table 3. Ablation study of our method built on top of RoBERTa.

Model	Dev	Test	Test-Easy	Test-Hard
CSKE (our)	66.6	60.2	77.3	46.8
- (CSK)	66.8	59.6	76.6	46.2
- (MLR)	66.6	58.7	78.9	42.9
- (CSK + MLR)	64.7	58.3	78.8	42.1

To visualize the impact of commonsense knowledge and multiple logical relationships on the results, we calculated their impact on the number of matched options which means an option can match an appropriate logical expression for itself and this is a measure of logical information injected into the pre-trained model. The results are shown in Table 4, and from it, we can observe evidently that CSK and MLR can significantly increase the number of matched options.

Table 4. Impaction of CSK and MLR on the number of matched options.

Model	Sample size	Matched options	CSK	Logic expressions
CSKE (our)	4638	7851	1021	1993
- (CSK + MLR)	4638	1989	0	1007

6 Conclusion

In this paper, we focus on text-based logical reasoning on multiple-choice question answering. we propose a logical commonsense knowledge enhanced text extension framework CSKE. In our framework, we introduce logical commonsense knowledge and encode multiple logical relationships which not only restore underlying missing logical propositions but also get more logical expressions. We extend our logical expression by logical equivalence laws to cover implicit ones. Through contrastive learning based on data augmentation in our framework, a richer negative sample can be generated, and it facilitates the model's full understanding of logical relationships. Experimental results on the ReClor dataset show that our model exceeds all baselines and delivers the best performance on Test sets and Test-Hard sets. About the further work, we plan to encode full logical relationships directly and optimize data augment to capture more logical information.

Acknowledgements. We thank the anonymous reviewers for their constructive comments, and gratefully acknowledge the support of the Technological Innovation "2030 Megaproject" - New Generation Artificial Intelligence of China (2018AAA0101901), and the National Natural Science Foundation of China (62176079, 61976073).

References

1. Liu, J., et al.: LogiQA: A Challenge Dataset for Machine Reading Comprehension with Logical Reasoning
2. Radford, A., et al.: Improving language understanding by generative pre-training (2018)
3. Radford, A., et al.: Language models are unsupervised multitask learners. OpenAI blog 1.8, p. 9 (2019)
4. Devlin, J., et al.: Bert: Pre-training of deep bidirectional transformers for language understanding. arXiv preprint arXiv:1810.04805 (2018)
5. Yang, Z., et al.: Xlnet: generalized autoregressive pretraining for language understanding. In: Advances in Neural Information Processing Systems 32 (2019)
6. Liu, Y., et al.: Roberta: A robustly optimized bert pretraining approach. arXiv preprint arXiv: 1907.11692 (2019)
7. Lan, Z., et al.: Albert: a lite bert for self-supervised learning of language representations. arXiv preprint arXiv:1909.11942 (2019)
8. Yu, W., et al.: ReClor: a reading comprehension dataset requiring logical reasoning. In: International Conference on Learning Representations (2019)
9. Wang, S., et al.: Logic-driven context extension and data augmentation for logical reasoning of text. arXiv preprint arXiv:2105.03659 (2021)

10. Jiao, F., et al.: MERIt: meta-path guided contrastive learning for logical reasoning. In: Findings of the Association for Computational Linguistics: ACL 2022 (2022)

11. Bowman, S., et al.: A large annotated corpus for learning natural language inference. In: Proceedings of the 2015 Conference on Empirical Methods in Natural Language Processing (2015)

12. Williams, A., Nikita N., Samuel B.: A broad-coverage challenge corpus for sentence understanding through inference. In: Proceedings of the 2018 Conference of the North American Chapter of the Association for Computational Linguistics: Human Language Technologies, Volume 1 (Long Papers) (2018)

13. Wang, A., et al.: GLUE: a multi-task benchmark and analysis platform for natural language understanding. In: Proceedings of the 2018 EMNLP Workshop BlackboxNLP: Analyzing and Interpreting Neural Networks for NLP (2018)

14. Khot, T., Ashish S., Peter C.: Scitail: a textual entailment dataset from science question answering. In: Thirty-Second AAAI Conference on Artificial Intelligence (2018)

15. Liu, H., et al.: Natural language inference in context-investigating contextual reasoning over long texts. In: Proceedings of the AAAI Conference on Artificial Intelligence, vol. 35, no. 15 (2021)

16. LSAT Homepage. https://www.lsac.org/lsat/taking-lsat/test-format/logical-reasoning/log ical-reasoning-sample-questions

17. GMAT Homepage. https://www.mba.com/exams/gmat/about-the-gmat-exam/gmat-exam-str ucture/verbal

18. Ouyang, S., Zhuosheng, Z., Hai Z.: Fact-driven logical reasoning. arXiv preprint arXiv:2105. 10334 (2021)

19. Huang, Y., et al.: DAGN: discourse-aware graph network for logical reasoning. In: Proceedings of the 2021 Conference of the North American Chapter of the Association for Computational Linguistics: Human Language Technologies (2021)

20. Betz, G., Christian, V., Kyle, R.: Critical thinking for language models. In: Proceedings of the 14th International Conference on Computational Semantics (IWCS) (2021)

21. Clark, P., Oyvind, T., Kyle R.: Transformers as soft reasoners over language.In: Proceedings of the Twenty-Ninth International Conference on International Joint Conferences on Artificial Intelligence (2021)

22. ConceptNet Homepage. https://conceptnet.io/

23. Russell, S.J.: Artificial intelligence a modern approach. Pearson Education, Inc. (2010)

24. Zhao, J-K., Rudnick, E.M., Patel, J.H.: Static logic implication with application to redundancy identification. In: Proceedings. 15th IEEE VLSI Test Symposium (Cat. No. 97TB100125). IEEE (1997)

25. Ye, M., et al.: Unsupervised embedding learning via invariant and spreading instance feature. In: Proceedings of the IEEE/CVF Conference on Computer Vision and Pattern Recognition (2019)

26. Chen, T., et al.: A simple framework for contrastive learning of visual representations. In: International conference on machine learning. PMLR (2020)

27. Wolf, T., et al.: Transformers: state-of-the-art natural language processing. In: Proceedings of the 2020 Conference on Empirical Methods in Natural Language Processing: System Demonstrations (2020)

A Survey on Causal Discovery

Wenxiu Zhou and QingCai Chen[✉]

Harbin Institute of Technology, Shenzhen, Shenzhen, China
qingcai.chen@hit.edu.cn

Abstract. Discovering and understanding the causal relationships underlying natural phenomena is important for many scientific disciplines, such as economics, computer science, education, medicine and biology. Meanwhile, new knowledge is revealed by discovering causal relationships from data. The causal discovery approach can be characterized as causal structure learning, where variables and their conditional dependencies are represented by a directed acyclic graph. Hence, causal structure discovery methods are necessary for discovering causal relationships from data. In this survey, we review the background knowledge and the causal discovery methods comprehensively. These methods are isolated into four categories, including constraint-based methods, score-based methods, functional causal models based methods and continuous optimization based methods. We mainly focus on the advanced methods which leverage continuous optimization. In addition, we introduce commonly utilized benchmark datasets and open source codes for researchers to evaluate and apply causal discovery methods.

Keywords: Causal discovery · Causal structure learning · Directed acyclic graphs · Continuous optimization

1 Introduction

Learning causality is considered as the foundation of human intelligence and an essential component of artificial intelligence [26]. Note that causality is different from correlation. Correlation refers to when two variables show a trend of increasing or decreasing, they are related [1]. However, Causality is usually manifested as cause and effect, where the cause contributes to the occurrence of the effect and the effect partially depends on it. Causality is widely applied in numerous fields, such as advertisement [4], biology [39], psychological science [15], medical treatments [28]. Therefore, in recent years, causal discovery methods have been a significant research topic for inferring causal relationships from data [25,27].

The causal relationship between one thing and another seems obvious in many cases. Nevertheless, in many real-world situations, it is hard to discover and determine causal relationships. Therefore, learning causal relationships is a very challenging task. Conducting a randomized controlled experiment is a

© The Author(s), under exclusive license to Springer Nature Singapore Pte Ltd. 2022
M. Sun et al. (Eds.): CCKS 2022, CCIS 1669, pp. 123–135, 2022.
https://doi.org/10.1007/978-981-19-7596-7_10

traditional and effective method of discovering causality, but in real life, such experiments may not be possible due to prohibitive cost and ethics. For example, in the medical field, conducting the randomized controlled experiments to verify the effectiveness of drug treatment is likely to delay the optimal treatment time for patients. Therefore, researchers often get non-experimental observation data. Without intervention and manipulation, observation data presents researchers with many challenges: Firstly, observed datasets may not contain all relevant variables, and there may be unobservable variables, which are often referred to as unmeasured confounding variables [41]. Secondly, learning causality from real observation data can be challenging due to selection bias. For example, in a dataset, samples are collected from people with a bachelor's or higher degree, not randomly from the general population. Thirdly, there are potential causal relationships in the data that may not be known in advance. These are three problems that exist in the causal discovery.

To solve these problems, researchers develop various frameworks, including the structural causal model [25] and the potential outcome framework [32]. The structural causal model aims to learn a causal graphical structure among variables form observation data. While the potential outcome framework estimates potential outcomes and calculates the treatment effect, known as causal inference. Under these frameworks and some assumptions, these methods are capable of inferring causal structure and causal effects using relatively abundant observation data.

In this paper, we comprehensively review the causal discovery methods under structural causal model. There are a number of surveys are already available, such as [42]. Different from previous work, this survey provides a clearer summary of current causal discovery methods, focuses more on continuous optimization based methods and more advanced methods. Additionally, we provide an introduction to some important and basic knowledge of causal discovery. Besides, we introduce some commonly utilized benchmark datasets and open-source code packages are summarized for researchers evaluate and apply causal discovery methods.

2   Background

In this section, we introduce the background knowledge about causal discovery, involving the task description and the structural causal model used in causal discovery.

Generally speaking, the causal discovery task entails learning the relationships between causal variables between variables from observation data, and causal graph are often used to represent the causal relationship between variables.

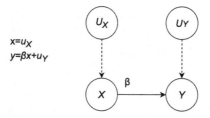

Fig. 1. A simple structural equation model, and its correlative diagrams

2.1   Structural Causal Model

The Structural Causal Model (SCM) provides a thorough theory of causality [24], which combines the structural equation models (SEM) [25] and the causal graphical models for causal analysis and inference based on probabilities.

Causal Graph. The causal graph is a particular type of Bayesian network whose edges represent causal effects and satisfy the conditional independence criterion. A causal graph is a directed graph that demonstrates the causal relationships between variables, indicated as $G = (V, E)$, where V and E represent the node set and edge set, respectively. And each node indicates a variable and $x \rightarrow y$ represents a directed edge that indicates a causal relationship from x to y. In this paper, we only take into account *directed acyclic graphs* (DAGs) which are directed graphs without cycles.

Structural Equation Models. How people use mathematics to express causal relationships between diseases and symptoms? The geneticist Sewall Wright [44] first attempts to express this relationship mathematically and the causal relationship is conveyed by combining equations and graphs. For example, a linear equation would be derived if X denotes a disease and Y denotes a symptom:

$$y = \beta x + U_Y, \tag{1}$$

where x denotes the disease severity, y denotes the symptom severity, and U_Y represents all other factors except x that affect the Y. In a similar way, if U_X represents all factors affecting X, then $x = U_X$. Due to the symmetry of algebraic equations, Eq. (1) still unable to accurately reflect the causal relationship between the disease X and the symptom Y, if (1) is rewritten as follows:

$$x = (y - U_Y)/\beta, \tag{2}$$

it can be misunderstood as indicating that the symptom has an influence on the disease. Wright proposed the equation with a diagram to illustrate the directionality. For example, as shown in Fig. 1, symptom Y does not affect the disease X because there is no arrow from Y to X. Thus, the complete causal model of a symptom and a disease is shown in the Fig. 1: The graph represents that X

has causal effect on Y and the equations describe the quantitative relationships among the variables which are determined from the data. In the equation, the parameter β is the path coefficient which quantifies the causal effect of X on Y.

3   Methods

In this section, we introduce the four categories methods on Causal Discovery which are list in the Table 1.

Table 1. This table contains four categories of causal discovery methods

Category	Methods
Constraint-based	SGS [36], PC [37], FCI [9,38], CIT [31]
Score-based	GES [8], FGES [30], hybrid [40]
Functional causal models based	LiNGAM [34,35], ANM [16,27], CGNNs [13]
Continuous optimization based	NOTEARS [47], DAG-GNN [45], GAE [23], Gran-DAG [19], RL-BIC [49], LEAST [48], CORL [43], BCD Nets [10], DAG-GAN [11], DAG-WGAN [29]

3.1   Traditional Methods

Constraint-based Methods discover a number of causal graphs that imply the conditional independence found in data by performing hypothesis tests [20]. Statistical tests are used to confirm that the candidate graphs satisfy the independence based on the faithfulness assumption. And faithfulness means that all conditional independences in the data underlying distribution are represented by the causal graph G. The SGS algorithm [36] is a common constraint-based method that starts from a completely undirected causal graph and removes redundant edges in the graph through a conditional independent decision method. In practice, the number of candidate causal graphs increases exponentially as the number of nodes increases. So the PC algorithm [37] use an effective schedule of tests to explore the whole space of possible causal graph. But there may be unmeasured variables in the data which are the common cause of two or more measured variables. The Fast Causal Inference(FCI) algorithm and a set of extensions [9,38] are designed to search across a larger causal graph space that includes unobserved common causes. Furthermore, Gaussian or multinomial distributions are required for most standard statistical tests. New statistical tests of conditional independence are constantly being exploited, which provide constraint-based algorithms for nonlinear and non-Gaussian data [31].

However, constraint-based methods have two major drawbacks. First, the faithfulness assumption can be countered. Second, due to the inability to distinguish graphs that belong to the same Markov equivalence class, the causal direction between the two variables may still undetermined.

Score-based Methods assign each directed acyclic graph (DAG) $\mathcal{G}$ a score calculated from the observed data via a scoring function $\mathcal{F}$, and then searches the space of all DAGs for $\hat{\mathcal{G}}$ with the best score. [27] set the goal as

$$\hat{\mathcal{G}} = argmax_{\mathcal{G} \ over \ X}\mathcal{F}(\mathcal{D}, \mathcal{G}), \tag{3}$$

where D denotes the observed data of variables X. There are many common scoring functions such as Bayesian Information Criterion [33], Bayesian Gaussian equivalent score [12], Minimum Description Length [8] and so on. Due to its combination of acyclic constraints and the number of possible DAGs growing exponentially as the number of nodes growing, Problem (3) is a NP-hard problem. In order to handle it, Greedy Equivalence Search (GES) [8] and the faster and optimized Fast GES (FGES) [30] are proposed which search in a local and heuristic manner but converge to the global optimal scoring model under the constraints of infinite data. There are also hybrid methods, such as the max-min hill-climbing method [40], which uses a constraint-based approach to reduce the search space before applying a score-based method. But there is a lack of principled methods to combining scoring functions and search strategies.

The score-based methods also have two disadvantages, one is that the search space is large and the time complexity is high, and the other is that the solution may be local optimal.

Functional Causal Models Based Methods. A Functional Causal Model (FCM) upon a variable vector $X = (X_1, ..., X_d)$ is a triplet $C = (\mathcal{G}, f, \mathcal{E})$, representing a set of equations [13]:

$$X \leftarrow f_i(X_{Pa(i;\mathcal{G})}, E_i), E_i \sim \mathcal{E}, for \ i = 1, ..., d. \tag{4}$$

Each equation describes the direct causal relationship within a set of causes $X_{Pa(i;\mathcal{G})} \subset \{X_1, ..., X_d\}$ to observed variable X_i, described by some causal function f_i up to the effects of noise variable E_i in distribution $\mathcal{E}$. FCMs-based methods are different from constraint-based methods which are assumed faithfulness and only identify Markov equivalence classes. FCMs-based methods can distinguish distinct DAGs within the same equivalence class due to supplementary assumptions about data distribution and functional classes. There are many methods based on FCMs, for example, Linear Non-Gaussian Acyclic Model (LiNGAM) [34, 35] and nonlinear additive noise model [16, 27]. And the Causal Generative Neural Networks (CGNNs) [13] learn FCMs as generative neural networks, trained by backpropagation to minimize the Maximum Mean Discrepancy (MMD) [14] between the observational data and the generated data.

3.2   Continuous Optimization Based Methods

DAGs with NOTEARS (2018). The method NOTEARS [47] is a new approach for learning DAGs based on score by firstly turning the traditional combinatorial optimization problem into a continuous problem:

$$\min_{\mathbf{A} \in R^{d \times d}} F(\mathbf{A}) \qquad \min_{\mathbf{A} \in R^{d \times d}} F(\mathbf{A}) \tag{5}$$
$$subject\ to\ \mathcal{G}(A) \in \text{DAGs}\quad subject\ to\ h(\mathbf{A}) = 0,$$

where $\mathcal{G}(A)$ denotes a d-node graph that is induced by a weighted adjacency matrix A, and h is a smooth function for enforcing acyclicity:

$$h(\mathbf{A}) = tr\left(e^{\mathbf{A} \circ \mathbf{A}}\right) - d = 0. \tag{6}$$

NOTEARS demonstrates on the linear SEM by $X_j = a_j^T \mathbf{X} + U_j$, where a_j is the weight of the edge pointing to X_j in the adjacency matrix. And it utilizes a least-squares loss with a $l1$ penalty and an enhanced Lagrangian method [22] with L-BFGS [5] to optimize the objective.

NOTEARS transforms the combinatorial constraint problem into a continuous constraint problem, which can be solved more efficiently. And they demonstrate that the approximation algorithm is close to the optimal solution. But there are also two disadvantages, one is that it only focuses on linear SEM, and the other is that the time complexity of acyclic constraint is $O(d^3)$, which is not suitable for large-scale causal graphs.

DAG with Graph Neural Networks (DAG-GNN, 2019). To capture complex nonlinear mappings, DAG-GNN [45] uses deep generative models (specifically, variational autoencoders [17]) to learn the DAG and uses Evidence Lower BOund (ELBO) [3] as the score function. The method assumes faithfulness and utilizes an encoder to encode $\mathbf{X}$ into the potential posterior $\mathbf{Z}$:

$$\mathbf{Z} = f_4\left(\left(\mathbf{I} - \mathbf{A}^T\right) f_3(\mathbf{X})\right), \tag{7}$$

where f_3, f_4 are parameterized function and A is a weighted adjacency matrix of the DAG and $\mathbf{X}$ is a sample of a joint distribution of variables and a variable is a scalar or vector. DAG-GNN uses the decoder to recover observations:

$$\mathbf{X} = f_2\left(\left(\mathbf{I} - \mathbf{A}^T\right)^{-1} f_1(\mathbf{Z})\right). \tag{8}$$

If f_2 is invertible, then (8) is equivalent to

$$f_2^{-1}(\mathbf{X}) = \mathbf{A}^T f_2^{-1}(\mathbf{X}) + f_1(\mathbf{Z}), \tag{9}$$

a generalized version of the linear SEM model and better captures nonlinearity. Acyclicity constraint is derived from NOTEARS [47]:

$$tr\left[(\mathbf{I} + \alpha \mathbf{A} \circ \mathbf{A})^d\right] - d = 0, \tag{10}$$

where α is a hyperparameter. Similar to NOTEARS, they also utilize the Augmented Lagrangian methods for optimization.

Graph AutoEncoder (GAE, 2019). GAE [23] proposes a graph autoencoder framework that supports nonlinear SEM and is readily applicable to vector-valued variables. They handle the more complex nonlinear model by drawing a connection with GAE and use the message passing operation which is similar to the graph convolutional layer used in [18]:

$$f\left(X_j, \mathbf{A}\right) = g_2\left(\mathbf{A}^T g_1\left(X_j\right)\right), \tag{11}$$

where g_1 and g_2 are multilayer perceptrons (MLPs). To solve the constrained optimization, they utilize the Augmented Lagrangian method and acyclicity constraint used in NOTEARS. They demonstrate that GAE outperforms NOTEARS and DAG-GNN especially on large causal graphs.

Gradient Based Neural DAG Learning (Gran-DAG, 2020). Gran-DAG [19] extends NOTEARS to deal with nonlinear causal relationships between variables by using neural networks and follows a nonlinear additive noise structure: $X_j = f_j\left(Pa_j + U_j\right)$, where the nonlinear function f_j is simulated by a fully-connected neural network. They use the *neural network path* and *neural network connectivity matrix* C to maintain mechanism independence corresponding to the independence implied by adjacency matrix. Then redefine the weighted adjacency matrix A_ϕ with C and adapt the acyclicity constraint as follows:

$$h(\phi) = tr(e^{A_\phi}) - d = 0. \tag{12}$$

They propose solving the maximum likelihood optimization problem:

$$\max_{\phi} E_{X \sim P_X} \sum_{j=1}^{d} \log p_j\left(X_j \mid X_{Pa_j^\phi}; \phi_{(j)}\right) \quad s.t. \quad tr(e^{A_\phi}) - d = 0, \tag{13}$$

and utilize the augmented Lagrangian method to achieve an approximate solution to problem (13). They show GraN-DAG outperforms other gradient-based approaches including NOTEARS and DAG-GNN.

Causal Discovery with Reinforcement Learning (RL-BIC, 2020). RL-BIC [49] applies Reinforcement Learning (RL) to discover causal structure, which uses a encoder-decoder model as *actor* to generate directed graphs from the observed data and computing a reward consisting of a predefined scoring function BIC together with two penalty terms to enforce acyclicity. They assume the model in [16] for data generating procedure. Furthermore, they prune the generated edges in a greedy approach based on regression performance or score function. They show the effectiveness of RL-BIC with causal graphs of 30 nodes, but it is still challenging to deal with large graphs exceeding 50 nodes.

Scalable Learning for Bayesian Networks (LEAST, 2021). LEAST [48] formulates the structure learning into an optimization problem with a continuous constraint and enforces graph acyclicity by using an upper bound of the graph spectral radius, as follows:

$$\bar{\delta}^{(j)} = \sum_{i=1}^{d} b^{(j)}[i],$$
$$where \quad b^{(j)} = \left(r\left(F^{(j)}\right)\right)^{\alpha} \odot \left(c\left(F^{(j)}\right)\right)^{1-\alpha} \quad and$$
$$F^{(j+1)} = \left(D^{(j)}\right)^{-1} F^{(j)} D^{(j)} \quad and \tag{14}$$
$$D^{(j)} = Diag\left(b^{(j)}\right).$$

Combing Eq. (14) with the least squares loss and l_1-regularization, the time complexity is close to $O(d)$ and the training time is 5 to 15 times faster than NOTEARS and can solve 100k-level node problems.

Ordering-Based Causal Discovery with RL (CORL, 2021). In order to solve existing RL-based methods limited to small-scale problems, a novel RL-based approach for causal discovery CORL [43] is proposed, which incorporates RL into the ordering-based paradigm. Specifically, they define the variable ordering search problem as a multi-step Markov decision process, use an encoder-decoder architecture to implement the ordering generating process, and finally use RL to optimize objective based on the reward mechanisms designed for each ordering. And in this work, variable selection methods are used. For linear data, they apply linear regression to the obtained fully-connected DAG and then prune edges by using thresholding. While for the non-linear model, they adopt the CAM pruning used in [19]. They validate that CORL performs fewer episodes than RL-BIC2 [49] before the episode reward converges and improves the performance of existing RL-based causal discovery methods.

Bayesian Causal Discovery Nets (BCD Nets, 2021). BCD Nets [10] estimate a distribution over DAGs that characterizes a linear-Gaussian SEM by using a variational inference [3] framework. They use the deep neural network to express a variational family of decomposed posterior distributions over the SEM parameters. Further, they achieve low-variance stochastic optimization of variational objective via continuous relaxations [21]. Moreover, on the edge weights, they apply a horseshoe prior [6] to promote sparsity. They demonstrate that BCD Nets outperform the maximum likelihood method on low-dimensional data.

DAG Learning with Generative Adversarial Nets (DAG-GAN, 2021). DAG-GAN [11] considers causal structure learning from a distribution optimization perspective and proposes an adversarial framework to discover the causal structure from data. In terms of distributional optimization, score-based learning can be formulated as follows:

$$\min_{\mathcal{G}} M\left(p_d, p_c\right) \ subject \ to \ \mathcal{G} \in \text{DAGs}, \tag{15}$$

where p_d and p_c respectively represent the real distribution and the generated distribution and M denotes a probability measure. Furthermore, they propose a score function based on Maximum mean discrepancy as M, which is a common probability measure defined on a unit ball ($\|f\|_{\mathcal{H}<1}$) in Reproducible Kernel Hilbert Space $\mathcal{H}$ [14] as

$$M(p_d, p_c) = sup_{f \in \mathcal{H}, \|f\|_{\mathcal{H}<1}} E_{p_d} f(x) - E_{p_c} f(x). \tag{16}$$

DAG-GAN is composed of two parts: a *generator* and a *discriminator*. They utilize a h-layer MLP as generator to simulate the causal generative mechanism. And the output is a collection of fake samples that shares the same DAG as the real data in order to fool the discriminator. In contrast to the generator, the objective of the discriminator is to distinguish whether a sample is from the generator or not. And DAG-GAN is extensively tested to demonstrate its superiority over other advanced methods.

DAG-WGAN (2022). DAG-WGAN [29] proposes an auto-encoder architecture and uses the Wasserstein-based adversarial loss together with an acyclicity constraint. Similar to [45], DAG-WGAN uses SCM to simulate the causal structure by the encoder and decoder. The encoder produces latent representations of the data as

$$Enc \equiv \mathbf{Z} = \left(\mathbf{I} - \mathbf{A}^T\right) f_1(\mathbf{X}). \tag{17}$$

The corresponding decoder Dec is as

$$Dec \equiv \tilde{\mathbf{X}} = f_2\left(\left(\mathbf{I} - \mathbf{A}^T\right)^{-1} \mathbf{Z}\right). \tag{18}$$

The auto-encoder calculates the latent representations through a reconstruction loss and a regularizer loss to avoid over-fitting. DAG-WGAN utilizes the decoder of the auto-encoder as the generator. Additionally, they use critics to provide gradient penalties for adversarial losses which is based on the popular PacGAN [7] framework and is implemented as follows:

$$\hat{\mathbf{X}} = MLP(\tilde{\mathbf{X}}, \mathbf{X}, leaky - ReLU, Dropout, GP, pac), \tag{19}$$

where GP stands for Gradient Penalty [2] and pac is a notion coming from PacGAN. DAG-WGAN shows that generalizing the current auto-encoder architecture with Wasserstein-based adversarial loss can further improve the performance. But the model can not support vectors or mixed-typed data.

4   Guideline About Experiments

In this section, we introduce the related experimental information, containing the available datasets and the open-source code packages.

4.1   Available Datasets

Bayesian Network Repository (Bnlearn)[1] provides a variety of datasets as well as their ground truth graphs including Gaussian Bayesian Networks, Conditional Linear Gaussian Bayesian Networks, Discrete Bayesian Networks and so on.

4.2   Open-Source Code Packages

Causal Discovery for Python (Causal-Learn)[2] is a python package for causal discovery that implements both classical and state-of-the-art causal discovery algorithms, which is implemented based on Python. Further, it provides visualization and evaluation.

gCastle. [46] is a toolbox developed by Huawei Noah's Ark Lab for causal structure learning, which includes various causal learning functions and evaluation tool, including data generation and processing, causal structure learning methods containing classic and advanced methods, especially gradient-based methods and evaluation metrics (F1, SHD, FDR, etc.).

5   Conclusion

Causal discovery has become a significant and popular research topic in recent years. We provide a thorough review of the causal discovery methods under structural causal model and present the relevant background in this survey. We introduce both classic and advanced causal discovery methods based on continuous optimization. Additionally, we list the available benchmark datasets and open-source code packages for experiments.

Continuous optimization based methods greatly reduce the time complexity of causal discovery, but the acyclic constraint is still a limitation. In addition, in the future, the accuracy of learning causality can be improved from the perspective of solving confounding factors and selection bias.

Acknowledgement. We thank all reviewers for their valuable suggestions to make the paper more comprehensive. This work is supported by the Natural Science Foundation of China (Grant No. 61872113).

References

1. Altman, N., Krzywinski, M.: Points of significance: association, correlation and causation. Nat. Methods **12**(10), 899–900 (2015)
2. Arjovsky, M., Chintala, S., Bottou, L.: Wasserstein generative adversarial networks. In: International Conference on Machine Learning, pp. 214–223. PMLR (2017)

---

[1] https://www.bnlearn.com/bnrepository/.
[2] https://github.com/cmu-phil/causal-learn.

3. Blei, D.M., Kucukelbir, A., McAuliffe, J.D.: Variational inference: a review for statisticians. J. Am. Stat. Assoc. **112**(518), 859–877 (2017)
4. Bottou, L., et al.: Counterfactual reasoning and learning systems: the example of computational advertising. J. Mach. Learn. Res. **14**(11), 3207–3260 (2013)
5. Byrd, R.H., Lu, P., Nocedal, J., Zhu, C.: A limited memory algorithm for bound constrained optimization. SIAM J. Sci. Comput. **16**(5), 1190–1208 (1995)
6. Carvalho, C.M., Polson, N.G., Scott, J.G.: Handling sparsity via the horseshoe. In: Artificial Intelligence and Statistics, pp. 73–80. PMLR (2009)
7. Cheng, A.: PAC-GAN: packet generation of network traffic using generative adversarial networks. In: 2019 IEEE 10th Annual Information Technology, Electronics and Mobile Communication Conference (IEMCON), pp. 0728–0734. IEEE (2019)
8. Chickering, D.M.: Optimal structure identification with greedy search. J. Mach. Learn. Res. **3**(Nov), 507–554 (2002)
9. Colombo, D., Maathuis, M.H., Kalisch, M., Richardson, T.S.: Learning high-dimensional directed acyclic graphs with latent and selection variables. Ann. Stat. **40**, 294–321 (2012)
10. Cundy, C., Grover, A., Ermon, S.: BCD Nets: scalable variational approaches for Bayesian causal discovery. In: Advances in Neural Information Processing Systems 34 (2021)
11. Gao, Y., Shen, L., Xia, S.T.: DAG-GAN: causal structure learning with generative adversarial nets. In: 2021 IEEE International Conference on Acoustics, Speech and Signal Processing (ICASSP), ICASSP 2021, pp. 3320–3324 (2021)
12. Geiger, D., Heckerman, D.: Learning Gaussian networks. In: Uncertainty Proceedings 1994, pp. 235–243. Elsevier (1994)
13. Goudet, O., Kalainathan, D., Caillou, P., Guyon, I., Lopez-Paz, D., Sebag, M.: Causal generative neural networks. arXiv preprint arXiv:1711.08936 (2017)
14. Gretton, A., Borgwardt, K., Rasch, M., Schölkopf, B., Smola, A.: A kernel method for the two-sample-problem. In: Advances in Neural Information Processing Systems 19 (2006)
15. Grosz, M.P., Rohrer, J.M., Thoemmes, F.: The taboo against explicit causal inference in nonexperimental psychology. Perspect. Psychol. Sci. **15**(5), 1243–1255 (2020)
16. Hoyer, P., Janzing, D., Mooij, J.M., Peters, J., Schölkopf, B.: Nonlinear causal discovery with additive noise models. In: Advances in Neural Information Processing Systems 21 (2008)
17. Kingma, D.P., Welling, M.: Auto-encoding variational Bayes. arXiv preprint arXiv:1312.6114 (2013)
18. Kipf, T.N., Welling, M.: Semi-supervised classification with graph convolutional networks. In: International Conference on Learning Representations (2017)
19. Lachapelle, S., Brouillard, P., Deleu, T., Lacoste-Julien, S.: Gradient-based neural DAG learning. In: International Conference on Learning Representations (2020)
20. Malinsky, D., Danks, D.: Causal discovery algorithms: a practical guide. Philos Compass **13**(1), e12470 (2018)
21. Mena, G., Belanger, D., Linderman, S., Snoek, J.: Learning latent permutations with Gumbel-Sinkhorn networks. In: International Conference on Learning Representations (2018)
22. Nemirovsky, A.: Optimization II. Numerical methods for nonlinear continuous optimization. Israel Institute of Technology (1999)
23. Ng, I., Zhu, S., Chen, Z., Fang, Z.: A graph autoencoder approach to causal structure learning. arXiv preprint arXiv:1911.07420 (2019)

24. Pearl, J.: Causal inference in statistics: an overview. Stat. Surv. **3**, 96–146 (2009)
25. Pearl, J.: Causality. Cambridge University Press, Cambridge (2009)
26. Pearl, J.: Theoretical impediments to machine learning with seven sparks from the causal revolution. In: Proceedings of the Eleventh ACM International Conference on Web Search and Data Mining, p. 3 (2018)
27. Peters, J., Janzing, D., Schölkopf, B.: Elements of Causal Inference: Foundations and Learning Algorithms. The MIT Press, Cambridge (2017)
28. Petersen, M., et al.: Association of implementation of a universal testing and treatment intervention with HIV diagnosis, receipt of antiretroviral therapy, and viral suppression in East Africa. JAMA **317**(21), 2196–2206 (2017)
29. Petkov, H., Hanley, C., Dong, F.: DAG-WGAN: causal structure learning with Wasserstein generative adversarial networks. arXiv preprint arXiv:2204.00387 (2022)
30. Ramsey, J., Glymour, M., Sanchez-Romero, R., Glymour, C.: A million variables and more: the fast greedy equivalence search algorithm for learning high-dimensional graphical causal models, with an application to functional magnetic resonance images. Int. J. Data Sci. Anal. **3**(2), 121–129 (2017)
31. Ramsey, J.D.: A scalable conditional independence test for nonlinear, non-gaussian data. arXiv:1401.5031 (2014)
32. Rubin, D.B.: Estimating causal effects of treatments in randomized and nonrandomized studies. J. Educ. Psychol. **66**(5), 688 (1974)
33. Schwarz, G.: Estimating the dimension of a model. Ann. Stat. **6**, 461–464 (1978)
34. Shimizu, S., Hoyer, P.O., Hyvärinen, A., Kerminen, A., Jordan, M.: A linear non-gaussian acyclic model for causal discovery. J. Mach. Learn. Res. **7**(10), 2003–2030 (2006)
35. Shimizu, S., et al.: DirectLiNGAM: a direct method for learning a linear non-gaussian structural equation model. J. Mach. Learn. Res. **12**, 1225–1248 (2011)
36. Spirtes, P., Glymour, C., Scheines, R.: Causality from probability. Evolving Knowledge in Natural and Artificial Intelligence (1989)
37. Spirtes, P., Glymour, C.N., Scheines, R., Heckerman, D.: Causation, Prediction, and Search. MIT Press, Cambridge (2000)
38. Spirtes, P.L., Meek, C., Richardson, T.S.: Causal inference in the presence of latent variables and selection bias. arXiv preprint arXiv:1302.4983 (2013)
39. Triantafillou, S., Lagani, V., Heinze-Deml, C., Schmidt, A., Tegner, J., Tsamardinos, I.: Predicting causal relationships from biological data: applying automated causal discovery on mass cytometry data of human immune cells. Sci. Rep. **7**(1), 1–11 (2017)
40. Tsamardinos, I., Brown, L.E., Aliferis, C.F.: The max-min hill-climbing Bayesian network structure learning algorithm. Mach. Learn. **65**(1), 31–78 (2006)
41. Tu, R., Zhang, K., Bertilson, B., Kjellstrom, H., Zhang, C.: Neuropathic pain diagnosis simulator for causal discovery algorithm evaluation. In: Advances in Neural Information Processing Systems 32 (2019)
42. Vowels, M.J., Camgoz, N.C., Bowden, R.: D'ya like DAGs? A survey on structure learning and causal discovery. arXiv preprint arXiv:2103.02582 (2021)
43. Wang, X., et al.: Ordering-based causal discovery with reinforcement learning. In: International Joint Conference on Artificial Intelligence (2021)
44. Wright, S.: Correlation and causation. J. Agric. Res. **20**, 557–585 (1921)
45. Yu, Y., Chen, J., Gao, T., Yu, M.: DAG-GNN: DAG structure learning with graph neural networks. In: International Conference on Machine Learning, pp. 7154–7163. PMLR (2019)

46. Zhang, K., et al.: gCastle: a Python toolbox for causal discovery. arXiv preprint arXiv:2111.15155 (2021)
47. Zheng, X., Aragam, B., Ravikumar, P.K., Xing, E.P.: DAGs with no tears: continuous optimization for structure learning. In: Advances in Neural Information Processing Systems 31 (2018)
48. Zhu, R., et al.: Efficient and scalable structure learning for Bayesian networks: algorithms and applications. In: 2021 IEEE 37th International Conference on Data Engineering (ICDE), pp. 2613–2624. IEEE (2021)
49. Zhu, S., Ng, I., Chen, Z.: Causal discovery with reinforcement learning. In: International Conference on Learning Representations (2020)

EK-BERT: An Enhanced K-BERT Model for Chinese Sentiment Analysis

Huan Bai, Daling Wang$^{(\boxtimes)}$, Shi Feng, and Yifei Zhang

School of Computer Science and Engineering, Northeastern University, Shenyang, China
2101688@stu.neu.edu.cn, {wangdaling,fengshi,
zhangyifei}@cse.neu.edu.cn

Abstract. Pre-trained language models (PLMs), such as BERT, have achieved good results on many natural language processing (NLP) tasks. Recently, some studies have attempted to integrate factual knowledge into PLMs for adapting to various downstream tasks. For sentiment analysis task, sentiment knowledge largely helps determine the sentiment tendencies of texts, such as sentiment words. For Chinese sentiment analysis, historical stories and fables give richer connotations and more complex emotions to words, which makes sentiment knowledge injection more necessary. But clearly, this knowledge has not been fully considered. In this paper, we propose EK-BERT, an **Enhanced K-BERT** model for Chinese sentiment analysis, which is based on the K-BERT model and utilizes sentiment knowledge graph to achieve better results on sentiment analysis task. In order to construct a high-quality sentiment knowledge graph, we collect a large number of emotional words by combining several existing emotional dictionaries. Moreover, in order to understand texts better, we enhance local attention through syntactic analysis to make EK-BERT pay more attention to syntactically relevant words. EK-BERT is compatible with BERT and existing structural knowledge. Experimental results show that our proposed EK-BERT achieves better performance on Chinese sentiment analysis task.

Keywords: Chinese sentiment analysis · Sentiment knowledge graph · Local attention

1 Introduction

Pre-trained language models (PLMs), such as BERT [1], RoBERTa [2], and Transformor [3] have achieved remarkable improvement on various NLP tasks. However, due to the domain difference between pre-training and downstream tasks, these models cannot be fully effective in specific domains.

Sentiment analysis refers to the use of NLP, text analysis and computational linguistics to identify and extract subjective information from source materials, and to mine the sentiment tendencies expressed in user-generated content [4]. Polysemy and metaphor add some difficulty to sentiment analysis task. For Chinese sentiment analysis, historical stories and fables give rich connotations to words. For example, the word "chicken rib"

M. Sun et al. (Eds.): CCKS 2022, CCIS 1669, pp. 136–147, 2022.
https://doi.org/10.1007/978-981-19-7596-7_11

originally refers to the ribs of a chicken and does not contain sentiment tendency. But now the word is used to describe the things of little value or interest and often carries negative sentiment. This kind of information is hard to get from a simple text itself without external knowledge. Therefore, it is more necessary to inject related knowledge to help models understand texts.

Recently, many researches have been devoted to linking knowledge with PLMs. One approach is to treat the PLM as a database [5] and use the knowledge in it for downstream tasks. A more popular approach is to inject external knowledge into PLMs. K-BERT [6], K-Adapter [7] and KEPLER [8] have made use of structured knowledge in different ways. But these models do not take emotional knowledge further. SKEP [9] injects sentiment knowledge into the model, but it needs to retrain a model, which consumes a lot of time and resources.

Meanwhile, many studies have proved that improving local attention can help models understand natural language better. LISA [10] and SG-Net [11] have achieved remarkable results on different downstream tasks by modifying the attention mechanism. Inspired by these studies, in this work, we use syntactic dependency analysis to enhance local attention and apply it to sentiment analysis task.

In this paper, we propose an enhanced K-BERT model (dubbed EK-BERT) for Chinese sentiment analysis, to improve the K-BERT model which is compatible with existing PLMs. Our proposed EK-BERT uses sentiment knowledge graph to acquire domain knowledge related to Chinese sentiment analysis. The model also uses type-embedding to learn knowledge more effectively and adds local attention mechanism to improve the understanding ability of natural language. The experimental results show EK-BERT achieves better performance on Chinese sentiment analysis task.

Our main contributions in this paper can be summarized as the follows:

- We construct a sentiment knowledge graph Sen-Graph and uses it to fine-tune the model. As a result, EK-BERT can learn more domain knowledge and achieve better effect on sentiment analysis task.
- We add type embedding to the embedding layer of K-BERT, so EK-BERT can better learn text and knowledge differently.
- We use grammar knowledge to enhance local attention, which makes EK-BERT pay more attention to syntactically relevant words and their knowledge.

2 Related Work

Recently, in addition to applying PLMs, many researches have begun to improve their performance from other aspects, such as the injection of external knowledge introduced in Sect. 2.2 and the modification of attention mechanism introduced in Sect. 2.3.

2.1 Sentiment Analysis

Sentiment analysis methods can be divided into three categories. (1) Based on emotional dictionary. The core is the construction of the emotional dictionary. Hatzivassiloglu et al. [12], Tsai et al. [13], Yang Xiaoping et al. [14] use different methods to try to build a better emotional dictionary. (2) Based on traditional machine learning. Wang et al. [15] implement the sentiment analysis task based on support vector machine (SVM). Cloud machine learning (CML) techniques offer contemporary machine learning services. Arulmurugan et al. [16] implement an emotional modeling methodology based on cloud-based approach. (3) Based on deep learning. The core is the use of neural network. Kim et al. [17] use convolutional neural networks on text classification task for the first time and achieve good results.

PLMs also show strong capabilities on sentiment analysis task. However, the input of only text or word sequences will result in the ignorance of external knowledge and the failure to consider that the semantic information of words will change with the context, which affects the accuracy of the sentiment analysis task. Therefore, there have been some researches linking knowledge with PLMs.

2.2 Knowledge-Enhanced PLMs

Knowledge has been shown to facilitate NLP tasks. ERNIE [18] enhances the language representation of text through external knowledge. K-BERT [6] combines each sentence with knowledge triples to form a sentence tree as the input of the model. CoLAKE [19] uses word-knowledge graph to connect text and knowledge. K-Adapter [7] uses a component to learn knowledge. Each adapter learns a new kind of knowledge, which is thought to solve the catastrophic forgetting phenomenon. KEPLER [8] does knowledge injection without adding new parameters. SKEP [9] mines sentiment knowledge from unlabeled data and uses this knowledge to pre-train language models.

Although these researches have achieved good results on their respective tasks, most do not consider sentiment knowledge. SKEP combines sentiment knowledge, but it is only for English sentiment analysis and requires retraining a model.

Different above researches, our proposed EK-BERT model is based on the K-BERT and does not require retraining. Moreover, we build a sentiment knowledge graph SenGraph and utilize it to achieve better results on Chinese sentiment analysis task.

2.3 Local Attention

Local attention can enhance the influence of some words and make the model focus on more important areas. LISA [10] uses syntax to train one attention head for semantic role labeling task. SG-Net [11] incorporates explicit syntactic constraints into attention mechanism to obtain better word representation. Nguyen et al. [20] propose differentiable windows to enhance the local attention. All of these attempts demonstrate that the use of local attention enables the model to focus on more important areas, thereby improving performance on various downstream tasks.

Text comprehension is an important step for sentiment analysis, and correct grammatical analysis is obviously beneficial. Therefore, it can be concluded that enhancing local attention based on grammatical structure and making each word pay more attention to grammatically related words can improve the language comprehension ability of the model and thus improve the performance of the model on sentiment analysis task. Inspired by this, in EK-BERT model, we use grammar knowledge to enhance local attention so that the model pays more attention to syntactically relevant words and their knowledge.

3 Approach

The overall framework of EK-BERT is shown in Fig. 1. In this section, we detail its implementation.

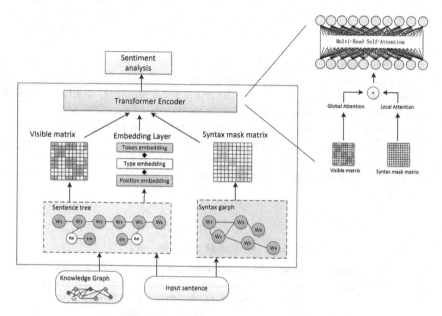

Fig. 1. Overall structure of EK-BERT.

3.1 Sentiment Knowledge Graph

The knowledge graph in Fig. 1 includes general knowledge graph and sentiment knowledge graph. The general knowledge graph provides factual knowledge for EK-BERT. There are many perfect Chinese general knowledge graphs that we can use directly. Sentiment knowledge graph provides domain knowledge for EK-BERT and it needs to be constructed. Here we construct a sentiment knowledge graph based on existing Chinese emotional dictionaries.

In this work, we combine four emotional dictionaries: Affective Lexicon Ontology [21], NTUSD (The NTU Sentiment dictionary) [22], HowNet [23] and a sentiment dictionary labeled by Tsinghua University [24], to ensure the accuracy and completeness of the emotional words contained in the sentiment knowledge graph. The construction of sentiment knowledge graph can be divided into three steps:

(1) Combine emotional dictionaries. We deduplicate sentiment words and evaluate their quality to obtain a high-quality sentiment word set. For example, NTUSD contains traditional characters, which need to be converted into simplified characters. In addition, there are many redundant emotional words in NTUSD such as "stupid", "stupid person" and "stupid thing", which need to be further generalized;

(2) Classify emotional words. Different emotional dictionaries use different rules to classify emotional words, and make these words have different labels. For example, the dictionary labeled by Tsinghua University divides words into praise and derogatory, while Affective Lexicon Ontology subdivides words into seven emotions. Therefore, we summarize the sentiment tendency categories of all words, and reclassify these words to get the last available sentiment word set. Table 1 shows some of them;

(3) Construct a sentiment knowledge graph using the sentiment word set. Figure 2 shows the sentiment knowledge graph constructed in this paper, and we call it as Sen-Graph. In Sen-Graph, there are 20,290 positive sentiment words and 23,938 negative sentiment words, including nouns, verbs, adjectives, idiom and slang. Sen-Graph contains three types of nodes: word node, sentiment tendency node and part of speech node. Each word node is connected with the corresponding sentiment tendency node and part of speech node. We also use common knowledge to supplement other attributes of emotional words such as meaning and store them as node attributes.

Table 1. Some examples of sentiment word set.

Classes	Words
Positive	行云流水 (Floating clouds and flowing water)， 行之有效 (Effective)， 胸怀坦荡 (Magnanimous mind)， 柳暗花明 (Dense willow trees and bright flowers).
Negative	满腹疑云 (Full of doubt)， 煽风点火 (Stir up trouble)， 疑神疑鬼 (Be suspicious)， 精疲力竭 (Exhausted).

3.2 Embedding Layer

The embedding layer of BERT [1] consists of token embedding, segment embedding and position embedding. K-BERT [6] proposes soft position and modifies position embedding. In EK-BERT, the token embedding and position embedding are consistent with K-BERT. For the segment embedding, since sentiment analysis task involves only one sentence, there is no need to distinguish different sentences. Moreover, the input contains

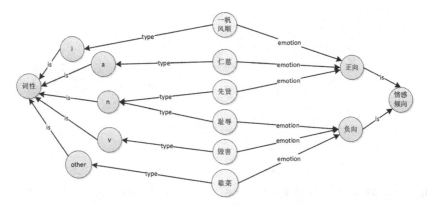

Fig. 2. Part of sentiment knowledge graph Sen-Graph.

both text and knowledge triples. Inspired by CoLAKE [19], our EK-BERT uses type embedding instead of segment embedding and divides the input into two types: word and knowledge, as shown in Fig. 3. In summary, the embedding layer of EK-BERT consists of token embedding, type embedding and position embedding.

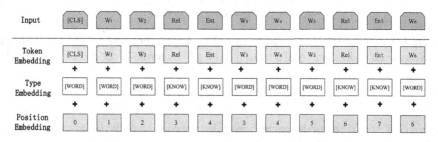

Fig. 3. Embedding layer of EK-BERT.

3.3 Local Attention

Analyzing grammatical structure contributes to natural language comprehension. Due to the complexity of Chinese grammar, correct analysis of grammatical structure is more important for Chinese sentiment analysis. In addition to global attention, when there is some grammatical correlation between words, the attention between them should increase accordingly, that is, the model should focus on more relevant words. Therefore, we use SLA [25] to modify attention mechanism of EK-BERT to combine syntax-based local attention with global attention, which is shown in Fig. 4.

The syntactic structure of the input text is obtained by using Chinese syntactic analysis tool and treated as an undirected graph. Words are considered to care about each other when they have dependencies. In order to make the model learn more semantic information, we not only make the directly connected words visible, but determine whether

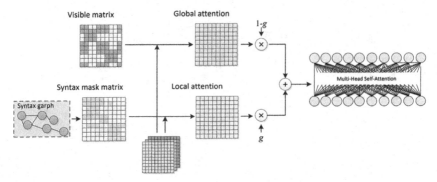

Fig. 4. The attention mechanism of EK-BERT: combining local attention and global attention.

a word w_i can pay attention to another word w_j according to the distance between the two word nodes in the grammar diagram. In global attention, knowledge is visible only with corresponding vocabularies. In local attention, the knowledge of one word can also be seen by another if words are visible to each other. The syntax mask matrix M^{syn} is defined as Formula (1):

$$M_{ij}^{syn} = \begin{cases} 1 & D(i,j) \leq m \\ -\infty & D(i,j) > m \end{cases} \tag{1}$$

where $D(i, j)$ is the distance between w_i and w_j, m is a threshold to limit the distance between word nodes. The local attention score S^{loc} is formally defined as Formula (2):

$$S^{loc} = softmax\left(\frac{QK^T}{\sqrt{d}} + M^{syn}\right) \tag{2}$$

where Q, K and V are model parameters trained according to the hidden vector, and d is the scaling factor.

The final attention Att is expressed as Formula (3):

$$Att = \left(gS^{loc} + (1 - g)S^{glb}\right)V \tag{3}$$

where g is a decimal between 0 and 1 from the hidden vector, and S^{glb} is used to represent global attention score. When the correctness of syntactic dependency analysis cannot be guaranteed, g can be set small enough to reduce the weight of local attention.

4 Experiments

4.1 Experimental Setup

4.1.1 Datasets

We conduct experiments on two Chinese sentiment classification datasets. Each of them is divided into three parts: train, dev and test. We use the train and dev parts to fine-tune the model and then evaluate its performance on the test part.

- Chinese_metaphor[1]: The dataset contains more than 4,000 sentences, published by DUTIR (the Information Retrieval Laboratory of Dalian University of Technology). We split it into three sets: 60% train, 20% dev and 20% test. This dataset classifies sentences into seven categories of emotion: joy, good, anger, sadness, fear, evil and shock. In order to adapt to the sentiment knowledge graph constructed in this work, we reclassify it into positive and negative. Joy and good are positive emotions. Others are negative emotions.
- Book_excerpet[2]: The sentences in this dataset are from books, online articles, novels, etc. We filter these sentences to obtain a dataset with uniform length distribution, including 3500 positive samples and 3500 negative samples. We split it into three sets: 80% train, 10% dev and 10% test.

4.1.2 Knowledge Graph

We employ two general knowledge graphs and one sentiment knowledge graph.

- HowNet [26]: HowNet is a large language knowledge base, and each word is described by smaller semantic units, which are called sememes. Following K-BERT, we regard HowNet as a knowledge graph and take {word, contain, sememes} as a triplet.
- CN-DBpedia [27]: CN-DBpedia is a large-scale open-domain structured encyclopedia developed by the Knowledge Works Laboratory of Fudan University. It is the earliest and currently the largest Chinese knowledge graph of open encyclopedia launched in China.
- Sen-Graph: Sen-Graph is the sentiment knowledge graph constructed in this paper. As mentioned above, its construction combines four emotional dictionaries.

4.1.3 Baselines

We compare the performance of EK-BERT to four models. BERT [1] and RoBERTa [2] are general PLMs. ERNIE [18] and K-BERT [6] are PLMs with open-domain knowledge.

- BERT: The PLM published by Google, which employs new pre-training tasks (MLM and NSP). BERT achieved new SOTA results on 11 NLP tasks when it was published.
- RoBERTa: The enhanced version of BERT. RoBERTa achieves better and more stable performance.
- ERNIE: The model is proposed by Baidu in 2019. ERNIE adds external knowledge during pre-training and gets SOTA results on Chinese NLP tasks.
- K-BERT: The model combines the knowledge graph with BERT, which does not require pre-training.

4.2 Results and Analysis

4.2.1 Main Results

We compare the results of multiple models on two datasets. For BERT, RoBERTa and ERNIE, we use the official release. For K-BERT and EK-BERT, we initialize them using

---

[1] https://github.com/DUTIR-Emotion-Group/CCL2018-Chinese-Metaphor-Analysis.

[2] https://blog.csdn.net/u013733326/article/details/105621880.

Google BERT and conduct experiment using two different general knowledge graphs. For EK-BERT, we add the sentiment knowledge graph Sen-Graph, to inject domain knowledge.

During the experiment, it is found that for the local attention mechanism, the distance limit between word nodes is very important. We have tried different distance limits and find that the performance of EK-BERT deteriorates when the distance limit is inappropriate. If it is too short, important words with dependencies cannot be seen; if it is too long, the words will notice too much irrelevant knowledge, resulting in knowledge noise. It should also be noted that for short texts, we can choose a small distance limit. Besides, there are many conjunctions and prepositions with no real meaning in Chinese. In this case, the local attention mechanism is likely to enhance the attention of these words and reduce the weight of semantic information. At this point, we can lower the weight of the local attention, as we do on Chinese_metaphor dataset.

Table 2. Results of various models on Chinese sentiment analysis task. We use the abbreviations "HN", "CN", and "Sen" to represent the HowNet, CN-DBpedia, and Sen-Graph knowledge graphs respectively.

Model\Datasets	Chinese_metaphor		Book_excerpet	
	Acc	F1	Acc	F1
BERT	87.24%	88.74%	87.90%	87.77%
RoBERTa	**88.12%**	89.47%	87.50%	87.26%
ERNIE	87.02%	88.86%	85.69%	85.28%
K-BERT(HN)	86.47%	87.76%	89.30%	89.33%
K-BERT(CN)	86.25%	87.90%	89.60%	89.28%
K-BERT(HN + Sen)	87.90%	88.96%	90.10%	90.03%
K-BERT(CN + Sen)	87.02%	88.54%	89.60%	89.52%
EK-BERT(HN + Sen)	**88.12%**	**89.72%**	**90.80%**	**90.89%**
EK-BERT(CN + Sen)	87.35%	88.78%	**90.80%**	90.78%
EK-BERT (HN + CN + Sen)	87.46%	89.10%	89.50%	89.45%

The experimental results are shown in Table 2. It can be seen from the results that: EK-BERT does achieve better performance. On dataset Chinese_metaphor, the performance of K-BERT deteriorates. We analyze the reason is the incorrect knowledge injection. Compared with K-BERT, EK-BERT adds the sentiment tendency of words, which can largely determine the sentiment of sentences. Although a word can have different sentiment tendencies, they are in the minority. This ensures that EK-BERT can use the correct sentiment knowledge most of the time. Thus, EK-BERT achieves a more stable performance on sentiment analysis task and gets the best results on both datasets.

4.2.2 Ablation Experiments

We perform ablation study on three important parts of EK-BERT and the results are shown in Table 3. EK-BERT still uses above two general knowledge graphs and one sentiment knowledge graph.

Table 3. Results of ablation experiments. We use the abbreviations "HN", "CN", and "Sen" to represent the HowNet, CN-DBpedia, and Sen-Graph knowledge graphs respectively. Moreover, we use "-x" to represent the EK-BERT model without x.

Model\Datasets	Chinese_metaphor		Book_excerpet	
	Acc	F1	Acc	F1
EK-BERT(HN + Sen)	**88.12%**	**89.72%**	90.80%	90.89%
-Local attention	86.25%	87.92%	90.40%	90.30%
-Type embedding	84.93%	86.50%	**90.90%**	**90.91%**
-Sen	87.02%	88.50%	88.80%	88.93%
EK-BERT(CN + Sen)	**87.35%**	**88.78%**	**90.80%**	**90.78%**
- Local attention	86.03%	87.63%	89.40%	89.31%
-Type embedding	85.59%	87.37%	89.30%	89.46%
-Sen	86.25%	88.13%	89.70%	89.56%

From the results, we can observe that: (1) Note that after removing sentiment knowledge graph, the performance of EK-BERT has great decline. This demonstrates Sen-Graph injects sentiment knowledge into EK-BERT and sentiment knowledge is effective for sentiment analysis task. (2) Type embedding promotes the performance of EK-BERT most of time. (3) Local attention mechanism does improve the language comprehension ability of the model. Compared with others, local attention mechanism makes EK-BERT achieve better performance.

There is an accident about the results on the Book_excerpet dataset, that is the performance increases after type embedding is removed. We analyze the phenomenon. Type embedding can make EK-BERT treat knowledge and text differently. This difference can make the influence between texts different from the influence of knowledge on texts, so the influence of wrong knowledge can be reduced to a certain extent. When type embedding removed, the model treats knowledge and text equally. If the knowledge is well matched to the text, the model does improve. But this is just an occasional phenomenon and we cannot guarantee that knowledge is always beneficial. But on the whole, type embedding is still needed.

5 Conclusion

In this paper, we propose EK-BERT model, which is more suitable for Chinese sentiment analysis task. Specifically, we use sentiment knowledge and local attention mechanism to improve the ability of the model to understand Chinese texts with sentiment tendencies. We also add type embedding hoping to help the model differentiated learning knowledge and ordinary text. The experimental results show that EK-BERT achieves better performance results than baseline models on Chinese sentiment analysis task and does not require retraining like RoBERTa and ERNIE. In future work, we will further investigate the influence of sentiment knowledge on other PLMs.

Acknowledgement. We thank the anonymous reviewers. The work is supported by Natural Science Foundation of China (62172086, 61872074, 62272092).

References

1. Devlin, J., Chang, M. W., Lee, K., Toutanova, K.: BERT: pre-training of deep bidirectional transformers for language understanding. NAACL-HLT, 4171–4186 (2019)
2. Liu, Y., et al.: RoBERTa: a robustly optimized BERT pretraining approach. CoRR abs/1907.11692 (2019)
3. Ashish, V., eta l.: Attention is all you need. In: NIPS, pp. 5998–6008 (2017)
4. Tejwani, R.: Sentiment analysis: a survey. CoRR abs/1405.2584 (2014)
5. Petroni, F., et al.: Language models as knowledge bases? In: EMNLP/IJCNLP, vol. 1, pp. 2463–2473 (2019)
6. Liu, W., et al.: K-BERT: enabling language representation with knowledge graph. In: AAAI, pp. 2901–2908 (2020)
7. Wang, R.: K-Adapter: infusing knowledge into pre-trained models with adapters. In: ACL/IJCNLP (Findings), pp. 1405–1418 (2021)
8. Wang, X.: KEPLER: a unified model for knowledge embedding and pre-trained language representation. Trans. Assoc. Comput. Linguist. **9**, 176–194 (2021)
9. Tian, H., et al.: SKEP: sentiment knowledge enhanced pre-training for sentiment analysis. In: ACL, pp. 4067–4076 (2020)
10. Strubell, E., Verga, P., Andor, D., Weiss, D., McCallum, A.: Linguistically-informed self-attention for semantic role labeling. In: EMNLP, pp. 5027–5038 (2018)
11. Zhang, Z., Wu, Y., Zhou, J., Duan, S., Zhao, H., Wang, R.: SG-Net: syntax-guided machine reading comprehension. In: AAAI, pp. 9636–9643 (2020)
12. Hatzivassiloglou, V., McKeown, K.R.: Predicting the semantic orientation of adjectives. In: ACL, pp. 174–181 (1997)
13. Tsai, A.C.R., Wu, C.E., Tsai, R.T.H., Hsu, J.Y.J.: Building a concept-level sentiment dictionary based on commonsense knowledge. IEEE Intell. Syst. **28**(2), 22–30 (2013)
14. Yang, X.P., et al.: Automatic construction and optimization of sentiment lexicon based on Word2Vec. Comput. Sci. **44**(1), 42–47 (2017)
15. Wang, S., Manning, C.D.: Baselines and bigrams: simple, good sentiment and topic classification. In: ACL, vol. 2, pp. 90–946 (2012)
16. Arulmurugan, R., Sabarmathi, K.R., Anandakumar, H.: Classification of sentence level sentiment analysis using cloud machine learning techniques. Clust. Comput. **22**(1), 1199–1209 (2017). https://doi.org/10.1007/s10586-017-1200-1
17. Kim, J., Kim, M.H.: An evaluation of passage-based text categorization. J. Intell. Inf. Sys. **23**, 47–65 (2004). https://doi.org/10.1023/B:JIIS.0000029670.53363.d0
18. Zhang, Z., Han, X., Liu, Z., Jiang, X., Sun, M., Liu, Q.: ERNIE: enhanced language representation with informative entities. In: ACL, pp. 1441–1451 (2019)

19. Sun, T.: CoLAKE: contextualized language and knowledge embedding. In: COLING, pp. 3660–3670 (2020)
20. Nguyen, T.T., Nguyen, X.P., Joty, S., Li, X.: Differentiable window for dynamic local attention. In: ACL, pp. 6589–6599 (2020)
21. Xu, L., Lin, H., Pan, Y., Ren, H., Chen, J.: Constructing the affective lexicon ontology. J. China Soc. Sci. Techn. Inf. **27**(2), 180–185 (2008)
22. Ku, L.W., Liang, Y.-T., Chen, H.-H.: Opinion extraction, summarization and tracking in news and blog corpora. In: AAAI Spring Symposium: Computational Approaches to Analyzing Weblogs, pp. 100–107 (2006)
23. Dong, Z., Dong, Q.: HowNet and the Computation of Meaning. World Scientific, Singapore (2006)
24. THUNLP Group Homepage. http://114.215.64.60:8094/site2/index.php/. Accessed 4 May 2022
25. Li, Z., Zhou, Q., Li, C., Xu, K., Cao, Y.: Improving BERT with syntax-aware local attention. In: ACL/IJCNLP (Findings), pp. 645–653 (2021)
26. Dong, Z., Dong, Q., Hao, C.: HowNet and its computation of meaning. In: COLING (Demos), pp. 53–56 (2010)
27. Xu, B., et al.: CN-DBpedia: a never-ending chinese knowledge extraction system. In: Benferhat, S., Tabia, K., Ali, M. (eds.) Advances in Artificial Intelligence: From Theory to Practice. Lecture Notes in Computer Science (Lecture Notes in Artificial Intelligence), vol. 10351, pp. 428–438. Springer, Cham (2017). https://doi.org/10.1007/978-3-319-60045-1_44

Incorporating Multilingual Knowledge Distillation into Machine Translation Evaluation

Min Zhang$^{(\boxtimes)}$, Hao Yang, Shimin Tao, Yanqing Zhao, Xiaosong Qiao,
Yinlu Li, Chang Su, Minghan Wang, Jiaxin Guo, Yilun Liu, and Ying Qin

Huawei Translation Services Center, Beijing, China
{zhangmin186,yanghao30,taoshimin,zhaoyanqing,qiaoxiaosong,liyinglu,
suchang8,wangminghan,guojiaxin1,liuyilun3,qinying}@huawei.com

Abstract. Multilingual knowledge distillation is proposed for multilingual sentence embedding alignment. In this paper, it is found out that multilingual knowledge distillation could implicitly achieve cross-lingual word embedding alignment, which is critically important for reference-free machine translation evaluation (where source texts are directly compared with system translations). Then with the framework of BERTScore, we propose a metric BERTScore-MKD for reference-free machine translation evaluation. From the experimental results on the into-English language pairs of WMT17-19, the reference-free metric BERTScore-MKD is very competitive (not only best mean scores, but also better than BLEU on WMT17-18) when the current state-of-the-art (SOTA) metrics that we know are chosen for comparison. Moreover, the results on WMT19 demonstrate that BERTScore-MKD is also suitable for reference-based machine translation evaluation (where reference texts are used to be compared with system translations).

Keywords: Multilingual knowledge distillation · Machine translation evaluation · BERTScore-MKD

1 Introduction

In traditional machine translation (MT) evaluation (also referred to as *reference-based* MT evaluation), reference texts are provided and compared with system translations. The common metrics for such evaluation include the word-based metrics BLEU [1] and METEOR [2], and the word embedding-based metrics BERTScore [3] and BLEURT [4].

However, reference sentences could only cover a tiny fraction of input source sentences, and non-professional translators can not yield high-quality human reference translations [5]. Recently, with the rapid progress of deep learning in multilingual language processing [6,7], there has been a growing interest in

---

M. Zhang and H. Yang—Equally contributed.

M. Sun et al. (Eds.): CCKS 2022, CCIS 1669, pp. 148–160, 2022.
https://doi.org/10.1007/978-981-19-7596-7_12

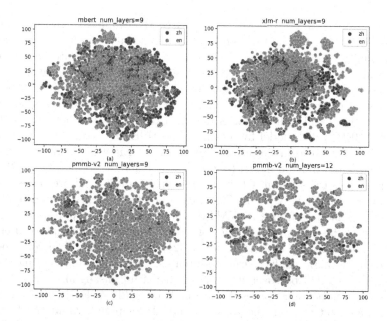

Fig. 1. First two principle components of contextual token embeddings of mBERT, XLM-R and pmmb-v2 for 100 zh-en parallel sentences in WMT19 by t-SNE (The more areas that do not cover each other, the worse the word embedding alignment effectiveness)

reference-free MT evaluation [8], which is also referred to as "quality estimation" (QE) in the MT community. In QE, evaluation metrics compare system translations with source sentences directly. And lots of methods have been proposed to approach this task. Popović et al. [9] exploited a bag-of-word translation model for quality estimation, which sums over the likelihoods of aligned word pairs between source and translation texts. Specia et al. [10] used language-agnostic linguistic features extracted from source texts and system translations to estimate quality. YiSi-2 [11] evaluates system translations by summing similarity scores over words pairs which are best-aligned mutual translations. Prism-src [12] frames the task of MT evaluation as one of scoring machine translation output with a sequence-to-sequence paraphraser, conditioned on source text. COMET-QE [13,14] encodes segment-level representations of source text and translation text as the input to a feed forward regressor. To mitigate the misalignment of cross-lingual word embedding spaces, Zhao et al. [15] proposed post-hoc re-alignment strategies which integrate a target-side GPT [16] language model. Song et al. [17] proposed an unsupervised metric SentSim by incorporating a notion of sentence semantic similarity. Wan et al. [18] proposed a unified framework (UniTE) with monotonic regional attention and unified pretraining for reference-only, source-only and source-reference-combined MT evaluations.

In a word, most of the above mentioned methods try to directly achieve cross-lingual alignment on lexical, word embedding or sentence embedding levels, which is critically important for reference-free MT evaluation. In this paper, we find out that cross-lingual word embedding alignment could be achieved implicitly by multilingual knowledge distillation (MKD) [19] for sentence embedding alignment, of which the training procedure is to map the sentence embeddings of source and target sentences in parallel data that are obtained through a multilingual pretrained model to the same location in the vector space as the source sentence embedding that is obtained through a monolingual Sentence-BERT (SBERT) [20] model by means of the MSE loss. To illustrate the alignment effect intuitively, a simple example shown in Fig. 1 is designed to compare the distilled multilingual model (paraphrase-multilingual-mpnet-base-v2[1], hereinafter referred to as pmmb-v2) with the classic multilingual pretrained models mBERT [6] and XLM-R [7]. In Fig. 1, each point represents a word in 100 zh-en parallel sentences from the WMT19 news translation shared task [8] and is composed of the first two principle components of the contextual word embeddings of the respective models by t-SNE [21]. Because each word could be well aligned in the high-quality parallel sentences, the points representing the two language words will be covered by each other if no misalignment exists in the cross-lingual embedding spaces. From Fig. 1, it could be clearly discovered that the misalignment areas in the parts (c) and (d) for pmmb-v2 are much smaller than the parts (a) and (b) for mBERT and XLM-R. This show that multilingual knowledge distillation benefits cross-lingual word embedding alignment.

In this paper, with the framework of BERTScore, we incorporate multilingual knowledge distillation into MT evaluation and propose a reference-free metric BERTScore-MKD. And then we test the performance of BERTScore-MKD on the into-English language pairs of WMT17-19 for both system-level and segment-level evaluations. The experimental results show that BERTScore-MKD is very competitive when compared with the current SOTA reference-free metrics that we know. Furthermore, from the comparison results on WMT19, it is interesting to find that BERTScore-MKD is also suitable for reference-based MT evaluation.

2   Method

In this section, the metric BERTScore-MKD will be given after the descriptions of multilingual knowledge distillation and BERTScore.

2.1   Multilingual Knowledge Distillation

The procedure of multilingual knowledge distillation (MKD) proposed by Reimers and Gurevych [19] for sentence embedding alignment is described in Fig. 2, where the teacher model is monolingual SBERT [20] which achieves state-of-the-art performance for various sentence embedding tasks, and the student model is a multilingual pretrained model like mBERT or XLM-R before distillation. From Fig. 2, it could be seen that MKD achieves the alignment of paired

---

[1] Distilled from XLM-R, more details in https://www.sbert.net/docs/pretrained_models.html.

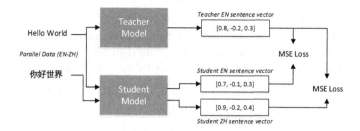

Fig. 2. Multilingual knowledge distillation [19]

sentence embedding directly. And the effectiveness of the student model's sentence embedding after distillation is demonstrated for over 50 languages from various language families [19].

2.2   BERTScore

BERTScore[2] [3] is an effective and robust automatic evaluation metric for text generation, which computes a similarity score for each token in the candidate sentence $\hat{x}$ with each token in the reference sentence x by using contextual embedding instead of exact matches. In the absence of token importance weighting, the recall R, precision P and $F1$ score are defined as:

$$R = \frac{1}{|\boldsymbol{x}|} \sum_{x_i \in \boldsymbol{x}} \max_{\hat{x}_j \in \hat{\boldsymbol{x}}} E(x_i \mid \boldsymbol{x})^\top E(\hat{x}_j \mid \hat{\boldsymbol{x}}), \tag{1}$$

$$P = \frac{1}{|\hat{\boldsymbol{x}}|} \sum_{\hat{x}_j \in \hat{\boldsymbol{x}}} \max_{x_i \in \boldsymbol{x}} E(\hat{x}_j \mid \hat{\boldsymbol{x}})^\top E(x_i \mid \boldsymbol{x}), \tag{2}$$

$$F1 = 2 \cdot \frac{P \cdot R}{P + R}, \tag{3}$$

where E is a contextual word embedding function, the outputs of E are normalized to reduce similarity computation, and x_i and $\hat{x}_j$ denote the i-th and j-th tokens in $\boldsymbol{x}$ and $\hat{\boldsymbol{x}}$ respectively. For MT evaluation, BERTScore with a pretrained model is usually used as a reference-based metric which demonstrates stronger correlations with human judgments than BLEU, and we will show that BERTScore using the distilled student model in Sect. 2.1 is suitable for both reference-free and reference-based MT evaluations.

2.3   BERTScore-MKD

Suppose $\boldsymbol{s}$ and $\boldsymbol{r}$ are two parallel sentences, which could be denoted as:

$$\boldsymbol{s} = (s_1, \ldots, s_i, \ldots, s_m), \tag{4}$$

---

[2] https://github.com/Tiiiger/bert_score.

$$r = (r_1, \ldots, r_j, \ldots, r_n), \tag{5}$$

where s_i and r_j denote the i-th and j-th tokens in s and r respectively.

According to the mean pooling strategy used in SBERT and MKD [19,20], the sentence embedding is the average of all token embeddings in the last layer of the given model. So the two sentence embeddings of s and r for the student model could be represented as:

$$SE(s) = \frac{1}{m} \sum_{i=1}^{m} E_{LL}(s_i \mid s), \tag{6}$$

$$SE(r) = \frac{1}{n} \sum_{j=1}^{n} E_{LL}(r_j \mid s), \tag{7}$$

where SE denotes the sentence embedding of the given sentence, and E_{LL} stands for the contextual word embedding function in the last layer (LL).

As illustrated in Fig. 2, after distillation with MSE loss for the student model, we could have $SE(s) \approx SE(r)$, i.e.,

$$\frac{1}{m} \sum_{i=1}^{m} E_{LL}(s_i \mid s) \approx \frac{1}{n} \sum_{j=1}^{n} E_{LL}(r_j \mid r). \tag{8}$$

Therefore, from the above equation, it could be intuitively seen that the token embeddings in the last layer of the student model could have some degree of alignment effect (if m and n are close to 1). And for the paired sentences of normal length, the word embedding alignment could also be maintained, as shown in the parts (c) and (d) of Fig. 1. However, it is not obvious that part (d) (last layer) has a better alignment effect than part (c) (9th layer). We will show that the last layer is the best choice for cross-lingual word embedding alignment in Sect. 3.4, and denote BERTScore using the last layer embeddings of the student model as metric *BERTScore-MKD*. Nevertheless, the reason why cross-lingual word embedding alignment could be achieved by MKD is still very worthy of in-depth analysis.

3 Experiments

In this section, we evaluate the performance of our metric BERTScore-MKD by correlating its scores with human judgments of translation quality for reference-free MT evaluations, where both segment-level and system-level evaluations are included for full comparisons and are defined as follows.

Segment-level evaluation (the input is a source sentence and a system translation sentence): The metric BERTScore-MKD chooses the outputs of the last layer in the model pmmb-v2 as the cross-lingual word embedding function, and takes the $F1$ score (without token importance weighting) in Eq. 3 as its value.

System-level evaluation (the input is a set of source sentences and the corresponding system translation sentences): The mean value of BERTScore-MKD on each pair of the sentences is used as its score for system-level evaluation.

It should be pointed out that the above definitions are for reference-free MT evaluations, and reference-based MT evaluation is implemented by just replacing source sentences with reference sentences.

3.1 Datasets

The source language sentences, and their system and reference translations are collected from the WMT17-19 news translation shared tasks [8,22,23], which contain predictions of 166 translation systems across 16 language pairs in WMT17, 149 translation systems across 14 language pairs in WMT18, and 233 translation systems across 18 language pairs in WMT19. Each language pair in WMT17-19 has about 3,000 source sentences, and each is associated with one reference translation and with the automatic translations generated by participating systems. In this paper, all the into-English language pairs in WMT17-19 are chosen for reference-free MT evaluation.

3.2 Baselines

In this paper, a range of reference-free metrics are chosen to compare with our metric BERTScore-MKD: LASIM and LP [24], UNI and UNI+ [8], YiSi-2 [11], CLP-UMD [15] and SentSim [17]. To the best of our knowledge, the above metrics could cover most of the current SOTA metrics for reference-free MT evaluation. In addition, BERTScore that uses the multilingual pretrained model XML-R[3] is denoted as BERTScore+XLM-R[4] and is selected to directly compare the cross-lingual word embedding alignment effect with our metric BERTScore-MKD; and reference-based baseline metrics BLEU and sentBLEU [8] are selected as references. It should be pointed out that only the results of the metrics BERTScore-MKD and BERTScore+XLM-R are calculated in this paper, and the results of the other metrics are from their respective papers.

3.3 Results

Evaluation Measures. Pearson correlation (r) and Kendall's Tau correlation (τ) [8] are used as measures for metric evaluations, and are defined as follows:

$$r = \frac{\sum_{i=1}^{n}(H_i - \overline{H})(M_i - \overline{M})}{\sqrt{\sum_{i=1}^{n}(H_i - \overline{H})^2} \cdot \sqrt{\sum_{i=1}^{n}(M_i - \overline{M})^2}}, \tag{9}$$

$$\tau = \frac{|Concordant| - |Discordant|}{|Concordant| + |Discordant|}. \tag{10}$$

---

[3] https://huggingface.co/xlm-roberta-base.

[4] The 9th layer of XLM-R is chosen for the cross-lingual word embeddings and $F1$ score is used as its metric score according to the recommendations in [3].

Table 1. Segment-level metric results (Pearson correlation) for the into-English language pairs of WMT17. Best results excluding sentBLEU are in bold.

Metrics	cs-en	de-en	fi-en	lv-en	ru-en	tr-en	zh-en	Avg
sentBLEU	0.435	0.432	0.571	0.404	0.484	0.538	0.512	0.481
SentSim	**0.499**	**0.523**	0.578	0.574	0.551	0.569	**0.600**	0.556
CLP-UMD	0.494	0.462	**0.647**	**0.664**	0.511	0.560	0.528	0.552
BERTScore+XML-R	0.319	0.409	0.414	0.402	0.337	0.382	0.510	0.396
BERTScore-MKD	**0.499**	0.475	0.644	0.584	**0.597**	**0.579**	0.565	**0.563**

Table 2. Segment-level metric results (Kendall's Tau correlation) for the into-English language pairs of WMT19. Best results excluding sentBLEU are in bold.

Metrics	de-en	fi-en	gu-en	kk-en	lt-en	ru-en	zh-en	Avg
sentBLEU	0.056	0.233	0.188	0.377	0.262	0.125	0.323	0.223
LASIM	−0.024	-	-	-	-	0.022	-	-
LP	−0.096	-	-	-	-	−0.035	-	-
UNI	0.022	0.202	-	-	-	0.084	-	-
UNI+	0.015	0.211	-	-	-	**0.089**	-	-
YiSi-2	0.068	0.126	−0.001	0.096	0.075	0.053	**0.253**	0.096
BERTScore+XLM-R	0.084	0.185	0.149	0.176	0.144	0.057	0.157	0.136
BERTScore-MKD	**0.093**	**0.234**	**0.171**	**0.310**	**0.211**	**0.089**	0.208	**0.188**

In Eq. 9, H_i are human assessment scores of all systems (or sentence pairs) in a given translation direction, M_i are the corresponding scores predicted by a given metric, and $\overline{H}$ and $\overline{M}$ are their mean values respectively. In Eq. 10, *Concordant* is the set of all human comparisons for which a given metric suggests the same order, and *Discordant* is the set of all human comparisons with which a given metric disagrees. It should be pointed out that the measure r could be used for both system-level and segment-level evaluations, while the measure τ is mainly for segment-level evaluation.

Segment-Level Results. Table 1 and Table 2 show the comparison results of the metrics for the reference-free segment-level evaluations on the into-English language pairs of WMT17 and WMT19 respectively.

From the comparison results of BERTScore+XLM-R and BERTScore-MKD in Table 1 and Table 2, it could be seen that BERTScore-MKD has significantly better results on all the into-English language pairs of WMT17 (avg. 0.396 → 0.563) and WMT19 (avg. 0.136 → 0.188), which indicates the cross-lingual word embeddings by MKD have much better alignment effects because only the word embeddings are different for the two metrics.

Table 3. System-level metric results (Pearson correlation) for the into-English language pairs of WMT17. Best results excluding BLEU are in bold.

Metrics	cs-en	de-en	fi-en	lv-en	ru-en	tr-en	zh-en	Avg
BLEU	0.971	0.923	0.903	0.979	0.912	0.976	0.864	0.933
CLP-UMD	**0.984**	0.904	0.861	**0.968**	0.850	0.922	0.817	0.901
BERTScore+XLM-R	0.750	0.692	0.653	0.650	0.332	0.689	0.635	0.629
BERTScore-MKD	0.953	**0.974**	**0.958**	0.871	**0.976**	**0.950**	**0.913**	**0.942**

Table 4. System-level metric results (Pearson correlation) for the into-English language pairs of WMT18. Best results excluding BLEU are in bold.

Metrics	cs-en	de-en	et-en	fi-en	ru-en	tr-en	zh-en	Avg
BLEU	0.970	0.971	0.986	0.973	0.979	0.657	0.978	0.931
CLP-UMD	**0.979**	**0.967**	**0.979**	0.947	0.942	0.673	**0.954**	0.919
BERTScore+XLM-R	−0.528	0.958	0.908	**0.957**	0.905	0.489	0.770	0.637
BERTScore-MKD	0.948	0.963	0.936	0.952	**0.978**	**0.939**	0.925	**0.949**

Table 5. System-level metric results (Pearson correlation) for the into-English language pairs of WMT19. Best results excluding BLEU are in bold.

Metrics	de-en	fi-en	gu-en	kk-en	lt-en	ru-en	zh-en	Avg
BLEU	0.849	0.982	0.834	0.946	0.961	0.879	0.899	0.907
LASIM	0.247	-	-	-	-	0.310	-	-
LP	0.474	-	-	-	-	0.488	-	-
UNI	0.846	0.930	-	-	-	0.805	-	-
UNI+	**0.850**	0.924	-	-	-	0.808	-	-
YiSi-2	0.796	0.642	**0.566**	0.324	0.442	0.339	0.940	0.578
CLP-UMD	0.625	0.890	−0.060	**0.993**	0.851	**0.928**	**0.968**	0.742
BERTScore+XLM-R	0.785	0.866	−0.007	0.117	0.657	−0.372	0.728	0.396
BERTScore-MKD	0.823	**0.956**	0.420	0.828	**0.946**	0.747	0.924	**0.806**

And when being compared with the current SOTA metrics involved in this paper, our metric BERTScore-MKD gets the best average scores and ranks first on the all language pairs except zh-en of WMT19 and 3 language pairs (cs-en, ru-en and tr-en) of WMT17. Moreover, as the sentence embeddings of SBERT are adopted in SentSim [17], and BERTScore-MKD uses the word embeddings distilled from SBERT, it could be seen from Table 1 that using word embeddings has better performance than using sentence embeddings (avg. 0.563 *vs.* 0.556), which means using the cross-lingual word embeddings by MKD is a better choice for reference-free MT evaluation.

System-Level Results. Tables 3, 4 and 5 illustrate the comparison results of the metrics for the reference-free system-level evaluations on the into-English language pairs of WMT17, WMT18 and WMT19 respectively.

From the experimental results in Tables 3, 4 and 5, it could be seen again that BERTScore-MKD has significantly better results than BERTScore+XLM-R on all the into-English language pairs of WMT17-19 (avg. 0.629 → 0.942, 0.637 → 0.949, 0.396 → 0.806) except fi-en of WMT18 (0.952 vs. 0.957), and gets the best average scores on the into-English language pairs of WMT17-19 when the current SOTA metrics are chosen for comparison. Moreover, the reference-free metric BERTScore-MKD even gets better results than the reference-based metric BLEU on WMT17 and WMT18 (avg. 0.942 vs. 0.933, 0.949 vs. 0.931).

Therefore, from the segment-level and system-level experimental results in Tables 1, 2, 3, 4 and 5, it could be seen that BERTScore-MKD is very competitive for reference-free MT evaluation when the current SOTA metrics that we know are chosen for comparison. And in Sect. 3.5 we will show that BERTScore-MKD is also suitable for reference-based MT evaluation.

3.4 Effects of Embedding Layers

Since BERTScore is sensitive to the layer of the model selected to generate the contextual token embeddings [3], we investigate which layer of the model pmmb-v2 is the best choice for BERTScore-MKD as a *reference-free* metric through experimental comparisons on the into-English language pairs of WMT19.

BERTScore+XLM-R is chosen for comparison, and the mean values on the into-English language pairs of WMT19 for segment-level and system-level evaluations are illustrated in Fig. 3.

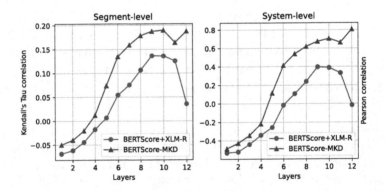

Fig. 3. Mean measure values of BERTScore-MKD and BERTScore+XLM-R with different layers of word embeddings for segment-level and system-level reference-free MT evaluations on the into-English language pairs of WMT19

From Fig. 3, it could be clearly seen that the last layer is the best choice for MKD-BERTScore on both segment-level and system-level evaluations, which

Table 6. System-level reference-based metric results (Pearson correlation) for the into-English language pairs of WMT19. Best results are in bold.

Metrics	de-en	fi-en	gu-en	kk-en	lt-en	ru-en	zh-en	Avg
BLEU	0.849	0.982	0.834	0.946	0.961	0.879	0.899	0.907
BERTScore+XLM-R	0.932	0.981	**0.919**	**0.998**	**0.992**	0.912	0.962	0.957
BERTScore-MKD^{9th}	0.931	**0.994**	0.897	0.970	0.991	0.971	0.964	**0.960**
BERTScore-MKD^{last}	**0.934**	0.990	0.801	0.943	0.981	**0.974**	**0.968**	0.941

Table 7. System-level reference-based metric results (Pearson correlation) for the from-English language pairs of WMT19. Best results are in bold.

Metrics	en-cs	en-de	en-fi	en-gu	en-kk	en-lt	en-ru	en-zh	Avg
BLEU	0.897	0.921	0.969	0.737	0.852	**0.989**	0.986	0.901	0.907
BERTScore+XLM-R	**0.979**	**0.990**	**0.980**	**0.922**	**0.983**	0.978	0.985	**0.929**	**0.968**
BERTScore-MKD^{9th}	0.966	0.986	0.956	0.899	0.980	0.938	**0.991**	0.871	0.948
BERTScore-MKD^{last}	0.942	0.982	0.928	0.889	0.972	0.876	0.985	0.814	0.924

is consistent with our analysis. And it is interesting to find that the best layers of BERTScore+XLM-R for reference-free and reference-based evaluations are almost the same (9th). Meanwhile, it could be also found that our metric BERTScore-MKD outperforms BERTScore+XLM-R on every layer for both segment-level and system-level reference-free MT evaluations.

3.5 As Reference-Based Metric

In this section we investigate the performance of BERTScore-MKD as a reference-based metric, where source sentences in the input are replaced with reference sentences. As the system translations and the reference sentences are in the same language, there is no need for cross-lingual alignment. Therefore, besides the last layer, BERTScore-MKD also uses the outputs of the 9th layers (recommended in [3]) in the model pmmb-v2 as the contextual word embedding function.

Table 6 and Table 7 report the results of BERTScore-MKD as a reference-base metric for system-level evaluations on the into-English and from-English language pairs of WMT19, and the metrics BLEU and BERTScore+XLM-R are chosen for comparison.

From the comparison results in Table 6 and Table 7, it could be seen that both BERTScore+XLM-R and BERTScore-MKD are clearly better than the classical metric BLEU, and our metric BERTScore-MKD is almost the same with the current SOTA metric BERTScore+XLM-R. Meanwhile, the 9th layer is slightly better than the last layer for BERTScore-MKD. In summary, BERTScore-MKD shows its effectiveness and robustness as a reference-base metric.

4   Conclusion

In this paper, it is found out that the cross-lingual word embedding alignment could be achieved implicitly through multilingual knowledge distillation (MKD) for sentence embedding alignment. With the framework of BERTScore, a reference-free metric BERTScore-MKD is proposed by incorporating MKD into MT evaluation. As shown in the performance test of BERTScore-MKD on the into-English language pairs of WMT17-19 for both segment-level and system level evaluations, the reference-free metric BERTScore-MKD is very competitive (best mean scores on WMT17-19 and better than BLEU on WMT17-18) with the current SOTA metrics that we know. Furthermore, the comparison results on WMT19 show the effectiveness and robustness of BERTScore-MKD as a reference-base metric. Although we have found that MKD could achieve the alignment of cross-lingual word embeddings and the last layer of the distilled student model is the best choice for reference-free MT evaluation, the reason why MKD could achieve the alignment is still worthy of further study.

References

1. Papineni, K., Roukos, S., Ward, T., Zhu, W.J.: Bleu: a method for automatic evaluation of machine translation. In: Proceedings of the 40th Annual Meeting of the Association for Computational Linguistics, Philadelphia, Pennsylvania, USA, pp. 311–318. Association for Computational Linguistics, July 2002
2. Lavie, A., Agarwal, A.: METEOR: an automatic metric for MT evaluation with high levels of correlation with human judgments. In: Proceedings of the Second Workshop on Statistical Machine Translation, Prague, Czech Republic, pp. 228–231. Association for Computational Linguistics, June 2007
3. Zhang, T., Kishore, V., Wu, F., Weinberger, K.Q., Artzi, Y.: BERTScore: evaluating text generation with BERT. In: 8th International Conference on Learning Representations, Addis Ababa, Ethiopia, 26–30 April 2020. OpenReview.net (2020)
4. Sellam, T., Das, D., Parikh, A.: BLEURT: learning robust metrics for text generation. In: Proceedings of the 58th Annual Meeting of the Association for Computational Linguistics, pp. 7881–7892, July 2020
5. Zaidan, O.F., Callison-Burch, C.: Crowdsourcing translation: professional quality from non-professionals. In: Proceedings of the 49th Annual Meeting of the Association for Computational Linguistics: Human Language Technologies, Portland, Oregon, USA, pp. 1220–1229. Association for Computational Linguistics, June 2011
6. Devlin, J., Chang, M.W., Lee, K., Toutanova, K.: BERT: pre-training of deep bidirectional transformers for language understanding. In: Proceedings of the 2019 Conference of the North American Chapter of the Association for Computational Linguistics: Human Language Technologies, Minneapolis, Minnesota, pp. 4171–4186. Association for Computational Linguistics, June 2019
7. Conneau, A., et al.: Unsupervised cross-lingual representation learning at scale. In: ACL 2020, 5–10 July 2020, pp. 8440–8451. Association for Computational Linguistics (2020)

8. Ma, Q., Wei, J., Bojar, O., Graham, Y.: Results of the WMT19 metrics shared task: segment-level and strong MT systems pose big challenges. In: Proceedings of the Fourth Conference on Machine Translation, Florence, Italy. Shared Task Papers, vol. 2, pp. 62–90. Association for Computational Linguistics, August 2019
9. Popović, M., Vilar, D., Avramidis, E., Burchardt, A.: Evaluation without references: IBM1 scores as evaluation metrics. In: Proceedings of the Sixth Workshop on Statistical Machine Translation, Edinburgh, Scotland, pp. 99–103, July 2011
10. Specia, L., Shah, K., de Souza, J.G., Cohn, T.: QuEst - a translation quality estimation framework. In: Proceedings of the 51st Annual Meeting of the Association for Computational Linguistics: System Demonstrations, Sofia, Bulgaria, pp. 79–84. Association for Computational Linguistics, August 2013
11. Lo, C.k.: YiSi - a unified semantic MT quality evaluation and estimation metric for languages with different levels of available resources. In: Proceedings of the Fourth Conference on Machine Translation (Volume 2: Shared Task Papers, Day 1), Florence, Italy, pp. 507–513. Association for Computational Linguistics, August 2019
12. Thompson, B., Post, M.: Automatic machine translation evaluation in many languages via zero-shot paraphrasing. In: Proceedings of the 2020 Conference on Empirical Methods in Natural Language Processing (EMNLP), pp. 90–121. Association for Computational Linguistics, November 2020
13. Rei, R., et al.: Are references really needed? Unbabel-IST 2021 submission for the metrics shared task. In: Proceedings of the Sixth Conference on Machine Translation, pp. 1030–1040, November 2021
14. Rei, R., Stewart, C., Farinha, A.C., Lavie, A.: COMET: a neural framework for MT evaluation. In: Proceedings of the 2020 Conference on Empirical Methods in Natural Language Processing (EMNLP), pp. 2685–2702, November 2020
15. Zhao, W., Glavaš, G., Peyrard, M., Gao, Y., West, R., Eger, S.: On the limitations of cross-lingual encoders as exposed by reference-free machine translation evaluation. In: Proceedings of the 58th Annual Meeting of the Association for Computational Linguistics. pp. 1656–1671, July 2020
16. Radford, A., Narasimhan, K., Salimans, T., Sutskever, I.: Improving language understanding by generative pre-training (2018)
17. Song, Y., Zhao, J., Specia, L.: SentSim: crosslingual semantic evaluation of machine translation. In: Proceedings of the 2021 Conference of the North American Chapter of the Association for Computational Linguistics: Human Language Technologies, pp. 3143–3156, June 2021
18. Wan, Y., et al.: UniTE: unified translation evaluation. In: Proceedings of the 60th Annual Meeting of the Association for Computational Linguistics (Volume 1: Long Papers), Dublin, Ireland, pp. 8117–8127. Association for Computational Linguistics, May 2022
19. Reimers, N., Gurevych, I.: Making monolingual sentence embeddings multilingual using knowledge distillation. In: Proceedings of the 2020 Conference on Empirical Methods in Natural Language Processing (EMNLP), pp. 4512–4525. Association for Computational Linguistics, November 2020
20. Reimers, N., Gurevych, I.: Sentence-BERT: sentence embeddings using Siamese BERT-networks. In: Proceedings of the 2019 Conference on Empirical Methods in Natural Language Processing, Hong Kong, China, pp. 3982–3992. Association for Computational Linguistics, November 2019
21. van der Maaten, L., Hinton, G.: Visualizing data using t-SNE. J. Mach. Learn. Res. **9**, 2579–2605 (2008)

22. Bojar, O., Graham, Y., Kamran, A.: Results of the WMT17 metrics shared task. In: Proceedings of the Second Conference on Machine Translation, Copenhagen, Denmark, pp. 489–513. Association for Computational Linguistics, September 2017

23. Ma, Q., Bojar, O., Graham, Y.: Results of the WMT18 metrics shared task: both characters and embeddings achieve good performance. In: Proceedings of the Third Conference on Machine Translation: Shared Task Papers, Belgium, Brussels, pp. 671–688. Association for Computational Linguistics, October 2018

24. Yankovskaya, E., Tättar, A., Fishel, M.: Quality estimation and translation metrics via pre-trained word and sentence embeddings. In: Proceedings of the Fourth Conference on Machine Translation (Volume 3: Shared Task Papers, Day 2), Florence, Italy, pp. 101–105. Association for Computational Linguistics, August 2019

Regularizing Deep Text Models by Encouraging Competition

Jiaran Li$^{(\boxtimes)}$ ⓘ, Richong Zhang ⓘ, and Yuan Tian ⓘ

Beihang University, 37 Xueyuan Road, Haidian District, Beijing, China
{lijr1993,zhangrichong,tianyuan}@buaa.edu.cn

Abstract. The difficulty in acquiring a large amount of labelled training data and the demand of complex neural network models in text learning make developing effective regularization techniques an important research topic. In this paper, we present a novel regularization scheme for supervised text learning, Competitive Word Dropout, or CWD. Experiments on three different natural language learning tasks demonstrate that CWD outperforms significantly the standard regularization schemes such as weight decay and dropout. The CWD scheme has another unique advantage, namely that it can be interpreted semantically.

Keywords: Text learning · Regularization · Word embedding · Word dropout · Deep learning

1 Introduction

Deep learning has reshaped the research frontier of natural language processing. Over the past decade, numerous neural network models have been proposed for learning text and language data and exciting successes have been reported.

In supervised text learning, it is now a common practice that a sentence or a text is encoded in a distributed representation, namely, as a vector that contains features relevant to the learning target. The encoding usually starts with representing words as word-embedding vectors and treating the input sentence as a sequence of such vectors. The sequence is then processed by a neural network, usually built with recurrent neural net (e.g., LSTM or GRU) or CNN, to generate the encoding vector of the sentence. A loss function is then defined for the encoding vector based on the learning target, and the learning is performed by minimizing the loss function over the network parameters.

Despite the great successes in such practice, supervised text learning using neural networks is significantly challenged by several interacting factors. First, it is very expensive to obtain the labelled text data for training purpose, and as a consequence, text learning often suffers from inadequate training examples. On the other hand, most training data involve a large word vocabulary, which further emphasizes the insufficiency of training data. Additionally, feature extraction from text is arguably an extremely complex problem. This often requires high-capacity network models, in which a large number of parameters need to be

M. Sun et al. (Eds.): CCKS 2022, CCIS 1669, pp. 161–173, 2022.
https://doi.org/10.1007/978-981-19-7596-7_13

learned. These facts, interacting with each other, make the networks prone to over-fitting and unable to generalize. As a consequence, effective regularization techniques are highly desirable in text learning.

A number of regularization techniques are well known in the deep learning literature. They include, for example, dropout, weight decay, and penalizing other forms of weight norm. A recently proposed adversarial training technique [3] has also been applied for regularizing text learning models [7]. Unlike weight decay and droupout, adversarial training, when applied to text learning models, is data-dependent. Besides using the original word embeddings, perturbed word embeddings are also used to train the model. In a sense, such a technique may also be regarded as a data-augmentation scheme for text learning. Despite its demonstrated effectiveness in [7], regularizing text-learning models appears highly under-instigated and we believe that there is plenty of room for developing improved techniques. In particular, the working of adversarial training can not be interpreted semantically, since the perturbed word embeddings no longer represent valid words. Thus what the technique does to a model can only be explained mathematically rather than semantically.

Inspired by the great needs of regularization techniques for text learning as well as their semantic interpretability, this paper proposes a new regularization scheme, which we call Competitive Word Dropout, or CWD in short.

To illustrate the key idea of CWD, let us consider a question-answering task as an example. In this task, we need to train a model capable of predicting which one of several given sentences contains the answer to a given question. Table 1 is an example of a training instance (where A1 is given as the correct answer). Usually models for such a task computes a score measuring the match of each candidate sentence to the question. Through the training process, the scoring function is learned to distinguish the correct answers from the wrong one. When CWD is applied to such a model, it makes uses of the model increasing capability of detecting semantic matches, and automatically (soft-)deletes, *from each wrong answer*, some words that match the question poorly. In the example in Table 1, A2 is the wrong answer, and CWD may delete the words "Toronto", "is", "the", and "largest" from it, since they do not match well the question. When these words exist in A2, they serve as "noise" for scoring A2. Deleting these words thus makes A2 scored higher under the current scoring function. Then the wrong answers become harder to distinguish from the correct one. This impose more pressure on training, and the model must learn to further increase the score of the correct answer in order to compete against the increased score of the wrong answer. In the above example, the model must learn to further distinguish the phrase"national capital of Canada" and the phrase "Canadian city" in their fitness as the correct answer. This serves to further constrain the model's parameter space and hence regularize the model.

We note that not only applicable in question-answering settings, the same idea is in fact applicable to a wide class of supervised text learning models.

In this paper, we formally develop the CWD regularization scheme, and demonstrate its use in three different supervised learning tasks: question-

Table 1. A question-answering example

	What is the capital city of Canada?
A1:	**Ottawa is the national capital of Canada**
A2:	~~Ottawa is the largest~~ Canadian city

answering, text classification, and semantic relatedness prediction. Through experiments, we show that CWD significantly outperform the standard regularization techniques such as weight decay and dropout. The performance of CWD appear to level with adversarial training applied to the word embeddings. Comparing with adversarial training, however, CWD has better interpretability.

2   Related Works

In deep learning, a popular regularization scheme to improve the generalization of neural network is dropout [14]. By randomly assigning masks on input or hidden layers in the neural network during its training, dropout can effectively alleviate the occurrence of overfitting. A complete theoretical treatment of the link is built between Gaussian Process and dropout in [2], which can obtain model uncertainty from existing deep leanring models.

Some researchers have found that some architectures of neural network are particularly sensitive to the perturbation, even when the perturbation is so small that human eyes can hardly tell the difference between the original sample and the disturbed one. Adversarial training [3] was proposed to solve this problem. By training the model to mix some slight disturbances in the input data, adversarial training makes the neural network adapt to this change, so as to improve generalization performance and make the model robust against adversarial examples.

Several representative approaches for generating adversarial examples are proposed afterwards, such as FGSM [3], and CPPN EA [8]. [22] systematically analyzed the method of generating adversarial samples and classifies adversarial attack methods in different dimensions, summarized and compared some recent methods of generating adversarial examples and finally discussed three major challenges (transferability, existence of adversarial examples and robustness evaluation) in adversarial examples and the potential solutions.

An adversarial training method that was proposed to prevent existing adversarial attacks [1] was later shown to be vulnerable to some new attacks, which means that the adversarial robustness is necessary to be improved. A min-max optimization framework was utilized in [5] and it made use of the Projected Gradient Descent (PGD) method to generate adversarial examples and then eventually achieved good performance in adversarial robustness. It is proved in [19] that the adversarial robustness and the generalization ability of the model (accuracy) may be essentially contradictory and there is a trade-off between them, which means that the accuracy will drop after adversarial training.

3   Encoding and Scoring in Text Learning

A supervised text learning problem can be formulated generically as follows. Each training example contains a pair $(x; y)$, where x is a single or a set of text documents or sentences and y is a supervising signal. The objective of learning is to leverage the training set $\{(x_i; y_i) : i = 1, 2, \ldots, N\}$ and obtain a predictor of y for a given x not in the training set.

When neural networks are used for text learning, we note that popular modelling strategies often implicitly treat each x as two components $(u, \mathcal{T})$, where we call u the *input* and $\mathcal{T}$ the set of *targets*. Such a treatment is largely reflected by a generic component in those models where u is first *encoded* using a neural network, and then *scored* based on each target t in $\mathcal{T}$. We call such a component an *encoding-scoring branch*. Specifically, an encoding-scoring branch is a composition of an encoding function ENC with learnable parameter φ and a scoring function SCORE with learnable parameter θ. The function ENC encodes the input sentence (or document) u to a vector $\bar{u}$ by

$$\bar{u} := \mathrm{ENC}(u; \varphi). \tag{1}$$

Here u is represented as a sequence of word-embedding vectors, each in some space $\mathbb{R}^{K_W}$, and the encoding $\bar{u}$ is a vector in some space $\mathbb{R}^{K_E}$. The function SCORE maps the encoding $\bar{u}$ and a target $t \in \mathcal{T}$ to a scalar score

$$s = \mathrm{SCORE}(\bar{u}, t; \theta). \tag{2}$$

We note that the objective of SCORE is to evaluate how well the encoding fits the target t.

Example 1 (Text Classification). *In an M-class text classification problem, each training example is specified by a input text u, and a supervising signal y, which is the correct text label taking values in $\mathcal{T} = \{1, 2, \ldots, M\}$. In this case $\mathcal{T}$ is also taken as the set of targets. Such a setting is reflected by the models with architecture shown in Fig. 1(a).*

Example 2 (Question Answering). *In a form of question-answering problem, each training example is specified by a question q text, a list of answer texts $a^{(1)}, a^{(2)}, \ldots, a^{(M)}$, and the index y of the correct answer. Here the correct answer refers to the text that contains the answer to question. In this case, we may take the input u as $a^{(1)}, a^{(2)}, \ldots, a^{(M)}$, the set $\mathcal{T}$ of targets as the singleton set $\{q\}$. The model architecture reflecting such a setting is shown in Fig. 1(b).*

It is remarkable that all these model architectures contains several encoding-scoring branches. Such branches exist widely in many supervised text learning models. In some cases, these branches are parallel and have different inputs (e.g. Fig. 1(b)), and in some other case, these branches may have the same input (e.g. Fig. 1(a)). Even in the latter case, it is also possible to duplicate the input-encoder and convert the model to contain parallel encoding-scoring branches, namely, converting the structure in Fig. 1(a) to the one in Fig. 1(c).

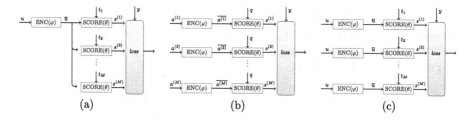

Fig. 1. Popular model architectures. (a) Architecture for text classification and sentence similarity. (b) Architecture for question answering. (c) Re-expressing (a) as parallel encoding-scoring branches.

For the ease of reference, an encoder-scoring branch will be called a *positive* branch if its input u matches its target t. For example, in text classification models, the positive branch is the one in which the target t is the correct label. In question-answering models as shown in Fig. 1(b), the positive branch is the one in which the input is the correct answer. An encoder-scoring branch that is not positive will be called *negative*. We note that whether a branch is positive or negative is known for the training examples.

4 Competitive Word Dropout

The Competitive Word Dropout (CWD) scheme is a regularization technique we propose to train a deep neural network model in supervised text learning. Briefly, the technique is to modify the network at the training time, where each negative encoding-scoring branch is related by a CWD module. At the heart of the CWD module is a "word-neglecting" component, which is denoted by $\mathcal{D}$ throughout the paper. In this section, we will first describe this word-neglecting component, and then discuss its design rationale and where it is situated in the overall CWD structure. We will conclude the section with a description of how CWD is used.

4.1 The Word-Neglecting Component $\mathcal{D}$

The word-neglecting component $\mathcal{D}$ takes u and the target t as input and outputs a modified version u_- of u, namely, a sequence of modified word-embedding vectors in $\mathbb{R}^{K_{\mathrm{W}}}$, and the sequence u_- has the same length as u. That is,

$$u_- := \mathcal{D}(u, t; \varphi, \theta). \tag{3}$$

Suppose that the sentence u is a sequence of L words and is represented as $(w_1, w_2, \ldots, w_L)$, where w_l is the word embedding vector for the lth word in the sentence. We note that u is also treated as a $K_{\mathrm{W}} \times L$ matrix.

For each $j = 1, 2, \ldots, L$, let d_j be a length-L one-hot vector representing integer j. That is, d_j is a binary vector where the only the jth element $d_j[j]$ is 1 and all other elements are 0.

Let $\overline{\text{UNK}}$ be a vector in the word-embedding space $\mathbb{R}^{K_W}$, which represents the embedding of an "unknown" or "meaningless" word. Further let $\overline{\text{UNK}}^L$ denote the $K_W \times L$ matrix in which each column is $\overline{\text{UNK}}$.

For each $j = 1, 2, \ldots, L$, let

$$u_{-j} := u \cdot \text{Diag}(d_j) + \overline{\text{UNK}}^L \cdot (\mathbf{I} - \text{Diag}(d_j)) \tag{4}$$

where $\mathbf{I}$ refers to the $L \times L$ identity matrix. We note that u_{-j} is essentially the matrix u with the jth column set to $\overline{\text{UNK}}$, namely, the jth word of u is "neglected".

For each $j = 1, 2, \ldots, L$, let

$$s_j := \text{SCORE}\left(\text{ENC}\left(u_{-j}; \varphi\right), t; \theta\right) \tag{5}$$

$$\widehat{d_j} := \text{sigmoid}\left(\alpha \cdot (s_j - s_0 - b)\right) \cdot d_j \tag{6}$$

where α and β are hyper-parameters and $\widehat{d_j}$ is also an L-vector. Define

$$\hat{d} := \sum_{j=1}^{J} \widehat{d_j} \tag{7}$$

and let

$$u_- := u \cdot \left(\mathbf{I} - \text{Diag}(\hat{d})\right) + \overline{\text{UNK}}^L \cdot \text{Diag}(\hat{d}). \tag{8}$$

At this end, the $\mathcal{D}$, or Eq. (3), is completely specified via Eqs. (4) to (8).

4.2   Property of $\mathcal{D}$

We now show that the component $\mathcal{D}$ in fact implements a "soft" version of a word dropout algorithm (Algorithm 1).

It can be seen that the key function of NEGLECT is to remove some useless words with respect to the target t. Specifically, NEGLECT first tests whether replacing a word of u at each location j with the "unknown" word will lead to a significant increased score of encoding (namely, the score increased by a margin larger than b). When this is the case, the word is replaced with the "unknown" word.

Lemma 1. *For the same u and t, the output of $\mathcal{D}$ approaches that of function NEGLECT in Algorithm 1, as $\alpha \to \infty$.*

To see why this lemma holds, let $\text{STEP}(x)$ denote the function that evaluates to 0 when $x < 0$ and to 1 otherwise. Then it can be verified that $\text{sigmoid}(\alpha \cdot x) \to \text{STEP}(x)$ as $\alpha \to \infty$. The lemma then follows. By this lemma, we see that the component $\mathcal{D}$ is a softened version of the NEGLECT function.

Algorithm 1. Hard Word-Neglecting Algorithm

Require: ENC with parameter φ
Require: SCORE with parameter θ
Require: REPLACE, where REPLACE(A, i, v) replaces the ith column of matrix A with column vector v and returns the resulting matrix.

```
1: function NEGLECT(u, t)
2:     s₀ ← SCORE (ENC (u; φ) , t; θ)
3:     u₋ ← u
4:     for j ← 1 to L do
5:         u₋ⱼ ← REPLACE(u, dⱼ, UNK)
6:         sⱼ ← SCORE (ENC (u₋ⱼ; φ) , t; θ)
7:         if sⱼ − s₀ > b then
8:             u₋ ← REPLACE(u₋, dⱼ, UNK)
9:         end if
10:     end for
11:     return u₋
12: end function
```

1: **function** NEGLECT(u, t)
2: $\quad s_0 \leftarrow$ SCORE $(\text{ENC}(u; \varphi), t; \theta)$
3: $\quad u_- \leftarrow u$
4: $\quad$ **for** $j \leftarrow 1$ to L **do**
5: $\qquad u_{-j} \leftarrow$ REPLACE$(u, d_j, \overline{\text{UNK}})$
6: $\qquad s_j \leftarrow$ SCORE $(\text{ENC}(u_{-j}; \varphi), t; \theta)$
7: $\qquad$ **if** $s_j - s_0 > b$ **then**
8: $\qquad\quad u_- \leftarrow$ REPLACE$(u_-, d_j, \overline{\text{UNK}})$
9: $\qquad$ **end if**
10: $\quad$ **end for**
11: $\quad$ **return** u_-
12: **end function**

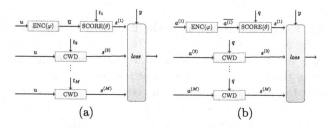

(a)   (b)

Fig. 2. Application of CWD to models (a) and (b) in Fig. 1

4.3   Using CWD

For any model that can be expressed as M parallel encoding-scoring branches followed by loss computation, namely, the structure in Fig. 1(b) and (c), CWD can be applied as follows: Replace each *negative* encoding-scoring branch by its corresponding CWD module, which concatenates the word-neglecting component $\mathcal{D}$, the encoding component ENC and scoring component SCORE. The parameters (φ, θ) are shared across $\mathcal{D}$, ENC and SCORE. Figures 2(a) and (b) show respectively the architectures of the models (a) and (b) in Fig. 1 after CWD is applied.

When CWD is applied to a network, the component $\mathcal{D}$ identifies the useless or noisy words in the negative branches and drop them out (softly). This raises the score of each negative branch to a higher value s_-, making these scores more competitive to the score s_0 of the positive branch. Note that the training of the network aims at forcing the score s_0 of the positive branch to stay at a sufficient contrast above the scores of the negative branches. This in term causes the model to further shape its encoding and scoring functions and squeeze out its

Table 2. Dataset

Dataset	#Train	#Valid	#Test
WikiQA	8627	1130	2351
SST-1	8544	1101	2210
SICK	4500	500	4927

dependency on the non-essential features. We note that a model being sensitive to non-essential features is a manifest of over-fitting. When the score given by the model is made less dependent on the presence of such non-essential information, the model is expected to generalize better. This has been the rationale in the design of the CWD scheme.

5   Experiments

5.1   Tasks

Question Answering. The task is in the form as stated in Example 2. The WikiQA [20] dataset is used in this task. The dataset contains 3,047 questions from Bing query log. Each question is associated with one wikipedia page, where each sentence in the summary paragraph of the page is chosen as a candidate answer. Among the candidate answers, the correct answer is marked according to labels given by crowd workers. In total, 1,473 questions are labeled and exact one correct answers is identified. The standard Mean Reciprocal Rank (MRR) and Mean Average Precision (MAP) are used as the performance metrics in this task.

Sentiment Analysis. The task is defined as in Example 1. The SST-1 [13] dataset is used in this task, in which each sentence is to be classified into one of the 5 sentiment classes. The dataset contains 11,855 sentences. Each sentence is associated with a label, i.e. very positive, positive, neural, negative and very negative. The model performance in this task is measured by the prediction accuracy.

Semantic Relatedness Prediction. The SICK [6] dataset is used in this task. Each training example consists of a pair (a, b) of sentences, together with a supervising signal y indicating the semantic relatedness of the sentence. It contains 9,927 sentence pairs together with their respective average user assessment score. To evaluate the model performance for this task, we used the standard Pearson Correlation and the Spearman Correlation coefficients between the predicted user assessment scores and the true user assessment scores.

The numbers of training, validation and testing exampels in each of the used datasets are given in Table 2.

5.2 Models and Regularization Schemes

For each task, we choose the popular CNN and Bidirectional LSTM ("LSTM") as the baseline, and evaluate the performances of various regularization schemes on baselines. The studied regularization schemes include weight decay ("WD"), dropout ("DROP"), word dropout ("wDROP"), adversarial training ("ADV") and CWD. We note that the difference between DROP and wDROP is that in DROP, some randomly selected dimensions of a word embedding vector in u are dropped, whereas in wDROP, some randomly selected word embedding vectors in u are dropped in their entirety.

The word embedding vectors are taken from GloVe [10] with dimension 300. For CNN we choose filter sizes of 3, 4, and 5, and model contains 50 filters at each size. For LSTM the state dimension is taken as 150 for WikiQA and SICK and 300 for SST-1.

5.3 Experimental Results

Performances. Tables 3, 4 and 5 show the performances of CNN and LSTM models and their regularized versions on the three tasks. The hyper-parameter settings of the compared regularization schemes (i.e. dropout probabilities for DROP and wDROP, weighting factors for WD) are also provided in the tables (in the brackets). Also given in the tables are the state-of-art performances for these tasks.

From these results, it is apparent that in these studied tasks, CWD and ADV provides the greatest performance gain over the baseline model. The performance improvements brought by CWD and ADV are in general significantly greater than those provided by other regularization schemes. For example, the best performing regularization scheme in Table 3 results in a performance gain of no more than 1–1.5% over the baseline CNN and LSTM models, whereas CWD brings a performance gain of 2.5% over the baseline LSTM and of more than 4% over the baseline CNN. In semantic analysis, CWD shows a performance gain of 3% over the baselines, whereas other schemes only shows a gain of about 1%. It can also be seen that the performance of ADV levels with that of CWD, where in some cases ADV performs slightly better and in other cases, the observation reverts.

Although the baseline models are quite basic, when trained with the CWD regularization scheme, they appear to perform quite close to the best possible performances known for these tasks. For example, in the semantic analysis task, CWD-regularized LSTM model presents an accuracy of 0.5109, very close to the best known performance of 0.517.

Training Behaviours. Figure 3 shows the performances of the compared schemes over training iterations, where the performances on both the training set and the testing set are plotted. On CNN, the training performances of all regularization schemes reaches a plateau in about 2 epochs, where CWD appears

Table 3. Model performances in question answering.

Model	MRR	MAP
CNN	0.6671	0.6519
CNN+WD(1e–4)	0.6716	0.6582
CNN+DROP(0.05)	0.6702	0.6557
CNN+wDROP(0.05)	0.6658	0.6506
CNN+wDROP(0.15)	0.6385	0.6218
CNN+ADV	**0.7200**	**0.7075**
CNN+CWD	**0.7113**	**0.6978**
LSTM	0.7001	0.6863
LSTM+WD(5e–4)	0.7026	0.6874
LSTM+DROP(0.2)	0.7135	0.6998
LSTM+wDROP(0.15)	0.7122	0.6960
LSTM+ADV	**0.7081**	**0.6957**
LSTM+CWD	**0.7257**	**0.7109**
CNN_{WO+SO} [9]	0.7391	0.7224
Multihop-Seq-LSTM [18]	0.738	0.722
MVFNN [11]	**0.7576**	**0.7462**

Table 4. Model performances in sentiment analysis

Model	Accuracy
CNN	0.4702
CNN+WD(5e–4)	0.4801
CNN+DROP(0.2)	0.4814
CNN+wDROP(0.05)	0.4774
CNN+ADV	**0.5014**
CNN+CWD	**0.5014**
LSTM	0.4805
LSTM+WD(1e–4)	0.4910
LSTM+DROP(0.05)	0.4923
LSTM+wDROP(0.01)	0.4860
LSTM+ADV	**0.5100**
LSTM+CWD	**0.5109**
Paragraph Vector [4]	0.487
DSA [21]	0.506
DiSAN [12]	**0.517**

Table 5. Model performances in semantic relatedness prediction

Model	Pearson	Spearman
CNN	0.8536	0.7950
CNN+WD(1e–5)	0.8653	0.8069
CNN+DROP(0.05)	0.8622	0.8157
CNN+wDROP(0.01)	0.8418	0.7922
CNN+ADV	**0.8732**	**0.8263**
CNN+CWD	**0.8721**	**0.8144**
LSTM	0.8609	0.7994
LSTM+WD(5e–5)	0.8671	0.8147
LSTM+DROP(0.15)	0.8595	0.8000
LSTM+wDROP(0.01)	0.8624	0.7989
LSTM+ADV	**0.8727**	**0.8276**
LSTM+CWD	**0.8670**	**0.8112**
Tree-LSTM [15]	0.868	–
large RNN-CNN [16]	0.8698	–
Multi-view [17]	**0.8785**	–

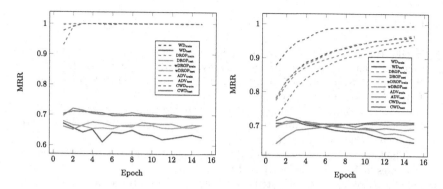

Fig. 3. Training/testing performances vs training iterations for compared regularization schemes in question answering. Left: CNN. Right: LSTM

to grow the fastest. More interesting results are revealed when these regularization schemes apply to the LSTM baseline. Specifically, except for CWD and ADV, the testing performances of all other schemes start to decay after certain epochs, exhibiting signs of over-fitting. It is worth noting that the training performance of CWD again grows fastest in this case, consistent with its behaviour on CNN. Additionally, the training performances of CWD stay at a much higher level than other schemes, particularly ADV. This suggests that CWD operates with very different principle from ADV and other schemes. That is, to achieve regularization, CWD sacrifices much less its fit to the training data. The fact that this is not observed on the CNN baseline suggesting that this might be a model-dependent phenomenon. Further understanding of such behaviours of CWD is certainly of great curiosity.

6   Conclusion

Perhaps a common wisdom, the student who is trained on harder questions does better in exams. CWD does exactly that. Selectively dropping out noisy words in the negative encoding-scoring branches increases the score of those branches. This pressures the model to train harder so as for the positive branch to maintain a competitive score and translates to additional constraints on the model's parameter space, hence serving to regularize the model.

Acknowledgments. This work was supported in part by the National Key R&D Program of China under Grant 2021ZD0110700, in part by the Fundamental Research Funds for the Central Universities, in part by the State Key Laboratory of Software Development Environment.

References

1. Biggio, B., et al.: Evasion attacks against machine learning at test time. In: Blockeel, H., Kersting, K., Nijssen, S., Železný, F. (eds.) ECML PKDD 2013. LNCS (LNAI), vol. 8190, pp. 387–402. Springer, Heidelberg (2013). https://doi.org/10.1007/978-3-642-40994-3_25
2. Gal, Y., Ghahramani, Z.: Dropout as a bayesian approximation: representing model uncertainty in deep learning. In: International Conference on Machine Learning, pp. 1050–1059. PMLR (2016)
3. Goodfellow, I.J., Shlens, J., Szegedy, C.: Explaining and harnessing adversarial examples. arXiv preprint. arXiv:1412.6572 (2014)
4. Le, Q., Mikolov, T.: Distributed representations of sentences and documents. In: International Conference on Machine Learning, pp. 1188–1196. PMLR (2014)
5. Madry, A., Makelov, A., Schmidt, L., Tsipras, D., Vladu, A.: Towards deep learning models resistant to adversarial attacks. arXiv preprint. arXiv:1706.06083 (2017)
6. Marelli, M., Menini, S., Baroni, M., Bentivogli, L., Bernardi, R., Zamparelli, R.: A sick cure for the evaluation of compositional distributional semantic models. In: Proceedings of the 9th International Conference on Language Resources and Evaluation (LREC'14), pp. 216–223 (2014)
7. Miyato, T., Dai, A.M., Goodfellow, I.: Adversarial training methods for semi-supervised text classification. arXiv preprint. arXiv:1605.07725 (2016)
8. Nguyen, A., Yosinski, J., Clune, J.: Deep neural networks are easily fooled: high confidence predictions for unrecognizable images. In: Proceedings of the IEEE Conference on Computer Vision and Pattern Recognition, pp. 427–436 (2015)
9. Nicosia, M., Moschitti, A.: Semantic linking in convolutional neural networks for answer sentence selection. In: Proceedings of the 2018 Conference on Empirical Methods in Natural Language Processing, pp. 1070–1076 (2018)
10. Pennington, J., Socher, R., Manning, C.D.: Glove: global vectors for word representation. In: Proceedings of the 2014 Conference on Empirical Methods in Natural Language Processing (EMNLP), pp. 1532–1543 (2014)
11. Sha, L., Zhang, X., Qian, F., Chang, B., Sui, Z.: A multi-view fusion neural network for answer selection. In: 32nd AAAI Conference on Artificial Intelligence (2018)
12. Shen, T., Zhou, T., Long, G., Jiang, J., Pan, S., Zhang, C.: Disan: directional self-attention network for rnn/cnn-free language understanding. In: Proceedings of the AAAI Conference on Artificial Intelligence, vol. 32 (2018)
13. Socher, R., et al.: Recursive deep models for semantic compositionality over a sentiment treebank. In: Proceedings of the 2013 Conference on Empirical Methods in Natural Language Processing, pp. 1631–1642 (2013)
14. Srivastava, N., Hinton, G., Krizhevsky, A., Sutskever, I., Salakhutdinov, R.: Dropout: a simple way to prevent neural networks from overfitting. J. Mach. Learn. Res. 15(1), 1929–1958 (2014)
15. Tai, K.S., Socher, R., Manning, C.D.: Improved semantic representations from tree-structured long short-term memory networks. arXiv preprint. arXiv:1503.00075 (2015)
16. Tang, S., Jin, H., Fang, C., Wang, Z., de Sa, V.R.: Speeding up context-based sentence representation learning with non-autoregressive convolutional decoding. arXiv preprint. arXiv:1710.10380 (2017)
17. Tang, S., de Sa, V.R.: Multi-view sentence representation learning. arXiv preprint. arXiv:1805.07443 (2018)

18. Tran, N.K., Niedereée, C.: Multihop attention networks for question answer matching. In: The 41st International ACM SIGIR Conference on Research & Development in Information Retrieval, pp. 325–334 (2018)

19. Tsipras, D., Santurkar, S., Engstrom, L., Turner, A., Madry, A.: Robustness may be at odds with accuracy. arXiv preprint. arXiv:1805.12152 (2018)

20. Yang, Y., Yih, W.t., Meek, C.: Wikiqa: a challenge dataset for open-domain question answering. In: Proceedings of the 2015 Conference on Empirical Methods in Natural Language Processing, pp. 2013–2018 (2015)

21. Yoon, D., Lee, D., Lee, S.: Dynamic self-attention: computing attention over words dynamically for sentence embedding. arXiv preprint. arXiv:1808.07383 (2018)

22. Yuan, X., He, P., Zhu, Q., Li, X.: Adversarial examples: attacks and defenses for deep learning. IEEE Trans. Neural Netw. Learn. Syst. **30**(9), 2805–2824 (2019)

A Survey on Table Question Answering: Recent Advances

Nengzheng Jin[1], Joanna Siebert[1], Dongfang Li[1], and Qingcai Chen[1,2(✉)]

[1] Harbin Institute of Technology (Shenzhen), Shenzhen, China
qingcai.chen@hit.edu.cn
[2] Peng Cheng Laboratory, Shenzhen, China

Abstract. Table Question Answering (Table QA) refers to providing precise answers from tables to answer a user's question. In recent years, there have been a lot of works on table QA, but there is a lack of comprehensive surveys on this research topic. Hence, we aim to provide an overview of available datasets and representative methods in table QA. We classify existing methods for table QA into five categories according to their techniques, which include semantic-parsing-based, generative, extractive, matching-based, and retriever-reader-based methods. Moreover, because table QA is still a challenging task for existing methods, we also identify and outline several key challenges and discuss the potential future directions of table QA.

Keywords: Natural language processing · Table QA · Semantic parsing

1 Introduction

Tables, which are an effective way to store and present data, are pervasive in various real-world scenarios, for example, financial reports and scientific papers. To leverage valuable information in tables, recent studies have applied **table question answering** as one important technique [30,35,51]. Given the user's

Question: What was the reported mainline RPM for American Airlines in 2017?

Table 1.	Year Ended December 31.		
	2017	2016	2015
Mainline			
Revenue passenger miles (millions)[(a)]	**201,351**	199,014	199,467
Available seat miles (millions)[(b)]	243,806	241,734	239,375
Passenger load factor (percent)[(c)]	82.6	82.3	83.3

Fig. 1. An illustration example of table QA (tailored from [23]). The bold number (201,351) is the target answer.

M. Sun et al. (Eds.): CCKS 2022, CCIS 1669, pp. 174–186, 2022.
https://doi.org/10.1007/978-981-19-7596-7_14

question, table QA aims to provide precise answers through table understanding and reasoning. For example, Fig. 1 illustrates the question answering over the tables from airline industry.

Generally speaking, table QA tasks can be traced back to querying relational databases with natural language, in which the tables are relatively structured. In this case, table QA task is solved by using a semantic parser that transforms natural language into a structured query (e.g., SQL), then executing it to retrieve answers [11,49]. For the tables that do not come from a database (non-database tables, e.g., web tables, spreadsheet tables), researchers also treat semantic parsing as an important method [27,35]. However, for tables with surrounding text, some methods directly extract [13,18,51] or generate answers [7,31] from the tables and their surrounding text without generating a structured query. For open-domain table QA, a retriever is needed to retrieve the related tables from a large corpus; then a reader is used to produce the answers from the retrieved tables [5,17].

Despite plenty of studies being conducted on table QA, there is a lack of systematic survey of this research field. In contrast, for entirely structured data (e.g., knowledge base), [14] provides a detailed survey of knowledge base question answering (KBQA). For unstructured text, [1] discusses the existing approaches and challenges of text-based question answering. Hence, our survey aims to provide a relatively thorough introduction to related datasets, existing methods and challenges of table QA, to help researchers grasp the recent advancements.

The main contributions of our survey are as follows: (1) we present most of the available datasets of table QA and create a mapping between each dataset and existing methods, to show which methods can be applied on a given dataset. (2) We summarize five kinds of table QA methods and make a relatively thorough introduction of each one. (3) We identify and discuss two main challenges of table encoding and table reasoning, which might be helpful for future research.

The remainder of the paper is organized as follows: In Sect. 2, we introduce the preliminary knowledge of table QA. In Sect. 3, we provide an overview of the available datasets. After that, we introduce semantic-parsing-based methods individually in Sect. 4 because they are a big group, and introduce the rest of methods in Sect. 5. Finally, in Sect. 6, we discuss several key challenges and potential future directions to explore.

2   Background

This section provides preliminary information for an in-depth understanding of table QA, including the composition of tables, definitions of semantic parsing and table question answering.

2.1   The Composition of Tables

A table can be seen as a grid of cells arranged in rows and columns [48]. Tables that come from database are relatively structured and consist of several columns (i.e., attributes). However, there are additional elements in web tables [48], including page title, caption, headers, and so forth. Considering that tabular data is usually surrounded by textual annotations in table QA, we refer two additional elements called pre-annotation and post-annotation as supplement parts of a table. Specifically, pre/post-annotation refers to the related sentences that appear before or after a table.

2.2 Semantic Parsing

Semantic parsing refers to transforming the natural language utterance into a logical form that can be executed by machines. One of classical semantic parsing tasks is text2sql, which converts the natural language utterances into structured query language (SQL). For instance, the question "What's the lowest pick in round 1?" should be transformed into "SELECT MIN(Pick) FROM mytable WHERE Rnd = 1;".

2.3 Table Question Answering

In this subsection, we disentangle the relationship between KBQA, text-based QA and table QA, and introduce two classifications of table QA.

Three QA tasks aim to provide answers to a user's question. The main difference is their reference source. KBQA is conducted over knowledge base, which is regarded as a kind of structured knowledge, text-based QA is conducted over unstructured text, and table QA is conducted over non-database tables which are regarded as semi-structured knowledge [35], as well as over database tables which are relatively structured. We introduce two classifications of table QA below.

Open-Domain vs. Closed-Domain. This classification is for web tables. Open-domain table QA answers the question based on large-scale table documents. In contrast, closed-domain table QA answers the question based on a limited number of tables (usually one table).

Free-Form vs. Non-free-form. This classification is based on the form of the answers. Give the user's question, free-form table QA requires generating dialog-like answers from the tables [31]. However, non-free-form table QA aims to provide a factual answer, which usually consists of a few words.

3 Overview of Datasets

The research on table QA has been increasing over the past few years due to the availability of large datasets. In this survey, we present an overview of these table QA datasets. As shown in Table 1, most of the datasets are closed-domain, and their question type is factoid[1].

---

[1] We extend the question type with free form and multiple choice, which originally includes factoid, list, definition and complex.

Table 1. An overview of table QA datasets. The representative methods without marks (e.g. †✭✦) can be used on the datasets aligned in the same horizontal zone, and the methods with marks are currently adopted on the datasets with the same mark.

Dataset		Closed-Domain	Question type	Representative methods
Table-Only	WTQ✭ [35]	Yes	Factoid	Semantic-parsing-based
	SQA✦✭ [20]	Yes	Factoid	[10–12, 16, 19, 20, 27, 33, 35]
	WikiSQL✭ [49]	Yes	Factoid	[37, 40, 41, 43, 45, 49]
	Spider [46]	Yes	Factoid	Generative method✦ [30]
	HiTab [8]	Yes	Factoid	Matching-based method† [15]
	AIT-QA†✭ [23]	Yes	Factoid	Extractive method✭ [18]
Non-table-only	FeTaQA [31]	Yes	Free form	Generative method [31]
	FinQA [7]	Yes	Factoid	Semantic parsing-based [7]
	TAT-QA [51]	Yes	Factoid	Extractive methods
	HybridQA [6]	Yes	Factoid	[6, 13, 51]
	TabMCQ [22]	Yes	Multiple choice	Matching-based methods
	GeoTSQA [26]	Yes	Multiple choice	[22, 26]
	OTTQA [5]	No	Factoid	Retriever-reader-based
	NQ-tables [17]	No	Factoid	methods [5, 17, 25, 34, 50]

Table-Only Datasets contain database tables or non-database tables without pre/post-annotation. These datasets contain different kinds of supervision for model training. Some datasets, such as WikiSQL [49] and Spider [46], provide logical form annotations as supervision. However, others provide the final answers as supervision, for example, WTQ [35] and SQA [8]. Most of the table-only datasets consist of relational tables with regular structure except HiTab [8] and AITQA [23], whose tables have hierarchical structure and a number of merged cells.

Non-table-only Datasets include samples that consist of a table and its pre/post-annotation. Among these datasets, OTTQA [5] and NQ-tables [17], which are used for open-domain table QA, are constructed from existing closed-domain datasets. TAT-QA [51] and FinQA [7] are extracted from financial reports with a large number of tables. Moreover, researchers propose TabMCQ [22] and GeoTSQA [26] datasets that contain multiple choice questions. Generally, non-table-only datasets require modelling over tables and text, which have been a popular and challenging research topic in recent years.

4   Semantic-Parsing-Based Methods

In table QA tasks, the semantic-parsing-based methods first transform the question into a logical form (e.g., SQL), and then execute the logical form on tables to retrieve the final answer. These methods can be categorized into weakly-supervised and fully-supervised methods. In the weakly supervised setting, given the question q and table t, the semantic parser for table QA is to generate the logical form y with weak supervision of the final answer z. In this setting, no gold logical forms are provided. However, in the fully-supervised setting, logical forms that execute to the correct answers will be provided as stronger supervision. We depict two of these methods in Fig. 2 and discuss them in more detail below.

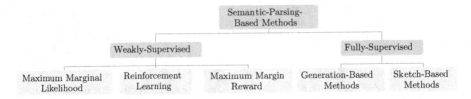

Fig. 2. The overview of semantic-parsing-based methods for table QA

4.1 Weakly-Supervised Table Semantic Parsing

In earlier research, weakly-supervised semantic parsing for table QA was based on hand-crafted features and grammar rules. For instance, Floating Parser [35] builds logical forms by applying predefined deduction rules recursively; it uses beam search to contain a limited number of partial logical forms at each recursion and prunes invalid partial logical forms with type constraints. The final logical form will be executed on related tables to obtain the answers.

However, the Floating Parser is domain-specific and only a few of learnable parameters of it can be adjusted. Hence, Yin et al. [43] propose a more powerful semantic parser, Neural Enquirer. They use a query encoder and table encoder to encode the question and table, respectively. Then, an executor implemented with DNN generates the partial logical form, and final result will be generated by the final layer. Similarly, Neelakantan et al. [32] provide an approach based on Neural Programmer [33]. Neural Programmer takes the hidden states of question RNN and history RNN as input and selects an operation and column that are related to the final answers. In practice, [32,33] find it difficult to train the model under weak supervision. Hence, some learning strategies [20,24,49] are proposed to tackle the problem, which can be categorized into *maximum marginal likelihood, reinforcement learning,* and *maximum margin reward.*

Maximum Marginal Likelihood (MML). The MML strategy in a weakly-supervised setting is to optimize the objective function $\log p(z_i|x_i, t_i)$, which represents the probability of generating the correct answer z_i by using candidate logical forms Y, based on question x_i and table t_i.

$$J_{MML} = \log p(z_i \mid x_i, t_i) = \log \sum_{y \in Y} p(z_i \mid y, t_i) p(y \mid x_i, t_i) \tag{1}$$

The MML algorithm is usually adapted with an **encoder-decoder neural network**, where the encoder encodes the questions and tables, and the decoder generates the logical forms step by step [24,39]. Based on this, Dasigi et al. [10]

extends MML training with a coverage-augmented loss function. The usage of coverage-augmented training and searching provides extra guidance to search for more consistent logical forms under binary supervision signals, which leads to better performance. Recently, Min et al. [28] have proposed a variation of MML (called HardEM) that simplifies the sum operation in the MML objective with a max operation and that outperforms previous methods in several QA tasks.

Reinforcement Learning (RL). In this learning strategy, semantic parsing for table QA is accomplished by an agent that takes a sequence of actions based on a certain policy. In practice, the policy is initialized as stochastic and trained with the goal of maximizing the expected reward. The expected reward for the sample (x_i, z_i, t_i) is shown in Eq. 2.

$$J_{RL} = \sum_{y \in Y} p(y \mid x_i, t_i) R(y, z_i) \qquad (2)$$

Zhong et al. [49] are the first to apply policy gradient, an important method of reinforcement learning, on the WikiSQL-weak dataset. It adopts the attentional sequence to sequence neural semantic parser [11] and augment this model with a pointer network to enable copying the input symbol as a part of the output. To further improve the performance, Misra et al. [29] adopt policy shaping that refers to introducing prior knowledge into a policy. They propose two kinds of prior knowledge-$match(x, y)$ and $co\_occur(y, x)$, which help to select the logical form with the higher probability of being correct. Additionally, the semantic parser MAPO [27] utilizes memory buffer to store the logical forms (trajectories) with high rewards for stabilizing and accelerating the model training.

Maximum Margin Reward (MMR). The MMR strategy maximizes a margin objective, which only update the score of the highest scoring logical form and the logical form that violates the margin constraint the most. Iyyer et al. [20] use this learning strategy in DynSP model [20], which achieves better performance against previous methods on SQA dataset.

4.2 Fully-Supervised Table Semantic Parsing

We have discussed the weakly supervised semantic parsing in the above subsections. However, there are also a number of methods requiring a fully supervised setting to achieve better performance for real-world applications. In the question answering task over database tables (e.g., WikiSQL), fully supervised semantic parsing can be roughly categorized into generation-based methods and sketch-based methods.

Generation-Based Methods. Generation-based methods usually adopt a sequence-to-sequence (Seq2Seq) framework, where an encoder is used to encode the question and optional table, and the decoder generates the logical form autoregressively [11,49]. Based on this framework, Sun et al. [37] leverage the structure of a table and syntax of SQL language for better SQL generation. To further constrain the decoder, Yin et al. [44] utilize a grammar model to evaluate the generation at each timestep and exclude those invalid candidates based on grammar rules. Similarly, Wang et al. [40] detect and exclude faulty programs by conditioning on the execution of partially generated program. Besides, Cho et al. [9] replace SQL annotations in WikiSQL dataset with special logical forms that annotate operand information, and improve the robustness of the semantic parser by supervising attention weights through the operand information and using cascade selective unit at each decoding step. Recently, some researchers (e.g., [4,38]) have proposed schema linking that links the mentions in questions to the schema content; they use relation-aware Transformer or graph neural network (GNN) as the encoder to model the links, which is proved to be an effective method.

Sketch-Based Methods. Sketch-based models decompose the target SQL query into several modules. Through performing classification for each module, complete SQL is then recomposed based on the classification results. For example, SQLNet [41] formulates the SQL sketch as "SELECT $AGG $COLUMN WHERE $COLUMN $OP $VALUE (AND $COLUMN $OP $VALUE)" and predicts the value for each $ variable through classification. Following this, Type-SQL [45] leverages the type information of the question entities based on external knowledge base to better understand the rare entities. Further, some researchers [16,19] have adopted pre-trained model as an encoder to better understand the question for the classification, which significantly enhances the performance. In another type of sketch-based method, the Coarse-to-Fine model [12] uses two-stage decoding. Unlike SQLNet [41], the sketch in the Coarse-to-Fine model are not statically predefined but generated by an decoder. Based on the sketch, the complete SQL is then generated through the second decoder.

5   Non-semantic-Parsing-Based Methods

5.1   Generative Methods

Notice that there are a number of semantic-parsing-based methods adopting generative models, for example, Seq2Seq neural network [11,40,49]. The main difference between generative methods and Seq2Seq semantic-parsing-based methods is that the former does not generate the logical form, but instead generates the answer directly. Hence, compared with Seq2Seq semantic-parsing-based methods that can handle both database tables and non-database tables, generative methods mainly focus on question answering over non-database tables.

For free-form table QA, a generative model becomes necessary to generate free-form answers. [31] is the first to conduct free-form question answering over tables. It adopts an end-to-end pre-trained model to encode the question and linearized tables, as well as to generate free-form answers. Generative models can also be used for non-free-form table QA. Müller et al. [30] propose a graph-based generative model for SQA task [20]; they transform tables into graphs by representing the columns, rows and cells as nodes, introducing cell-column and cell-row relation. Then, the graphs are encoded using a graph neural network, and the answers are generated by a Transformer-based decoder. However, the graph-based generative model [30] is only feasible for table-only tasks because it dose not model the pre/post-annotation of the tables. Hence, Zayats et al. [47] extend this method to hybrid question answering tasks. Because it technically belongs to extractive methods, we present this method in the following subsection.

5.2   Extractive Methods

Rather than generating the answer through a decoder, extractive methods directly select or extract the token spans from the linearized table as candidate answers or evidences. For example, Herzig et al. [18] use a pre-trained encoder to represent tables and select table cells with the highest probability as answers. Zhu et al. [51] also follow the same paradigm to extract evidences from tables; then, they retrieve answers by simple reasoning over the evidences.

In this kind of methods, the semantic representations of table cells become important because the model needs to understand which table cells are relevant to the question. To avoid incorporating irrelevant information into the table cell representations, several structure-aware approaches have been proposed by researchers. The simplest way to incorporate structural information into table cell representations is by adding hand-crafted features. For example, TAPAS [18] uses row/column embedding as an additional input of Transformer to indicate the position of a table cell, which implicitly models the table structure. But this setting does not models the relation between tables cells, which is achieved by the following methods.

Attention Mask. This type of methods model the table structure through attention mask that selectively masking the irrelevant token in self-attention layer of Transformer. Eisenschlos et al. [13] propose a multi-view attention mechanism that splits attention heads into row heads and column heads, where each row/column head only incorporates the information of cells from the same row/column and information from the question into current token. Further, they reorder the input sequence for row heads and column heads separately and apply a windowed attention mechanism. This technique turns quadratic time complexity into a linear one, leading to better structure-aware table representations and smaller time complexity simultaneously.

Attention Bias. Another way to represent the table structure is to inject attention bias into the attention layer of Transformer. For example, Zayats et al. [47] propose an extractive model based on the Transformer-based GNN model [30]. The "GNN model" is implemented by introducing attention bias when calculating the attention weight. Furthermore, they enrich the table representations with the embedding of the relevant text, leading to more precise and richer table cell representations. Similarly, TableFormer [42], a variation of Transformer, also proposes 13 table-text attention biases in the self-attention layer (e.g., *same row*, *cell to column header*). Through pre-training, this model achieves remarkable performance on several benchmarks.

5.3 Matching-Based Methods

Matching-based models usually process the question and each fragment of the table (e.g., row, cell) individually, and predict the matching score between them. The final answer is retrieved by simple reasoning on the most relevant fragments. For example, Sun et al. [36] formulate the table QA task as a joint entity and relation matching problem. They first transform the question and each row of the table into chains, which are two-node graphs. Then, this model matches the question chain to all candidate column chains through snippets matching and deep chain inference, hence retrieving top-K candidate chains for final answer generation. Similarly, in a multiple-choice table QA task, Jauhar et al. [22] match each question-choice pair (also referred to QA pair) to the rows of the table and return the highest matching score as the confidence of the QA pair. In a similar way, the RCI model [15] predicts a matching score between a row/column and question. Then, the confidence of a table cell as being the correct answer can be calculated by combining the matching score of its row and column.

5.4 Retriever-Reader-Based Methods

The methods discussed in the above subsections are used for closed-domain table QA. In this subsection, we discuss the retriever-reader architecture that is usually adopted for **open-domain table QA**, which provides answers by retrieval and reading. The retrieval model is in charge of retrieving the related documents containing tables from a large corpus, and the reader is used to produce the answers from the retrieved table documents. The retriever can be further categorized into *sparse retriever*, *dense retriever*, and *iterative retriever*. The sparse/dense retriever uses sparse/dense representations for the question and candidate documents and then performs matching between them. The iterative retriever tries to retrieve the relevant documents in multiple steps, which appends the reliable retrieval from the previous step for the next step of retrieval. As for the reader, it can be further classified into *generative reader* and *extractive reader*, which adopt the generative method and extractive method discussed in Subsects. 5.1 and 5.2, respectively. We depict an overview of these categories in Fig. 3 and present the representative works below.

Extractive Reader. Chen et al. [5] propose the fusion retriever (a dense retriever) and cross-block reader for OTT-QA task. The fusion retriever first pre-aligns the table segments to their related passages by entity linking and groups them into a *fused block*. Then, it retrieves the top K fused blocks for

Fig. 3. The category of retriever and reader

cross-block reading that uses the long range Transformer [2]. Moreover, Zhong et al. [50] also train a chain extractor as the auxiliary model for RoBERTa-based dense retriever and Longformer-based [3] extractive reader. The chain extractor extracts possible reasoning chains from the table; then the reasoning chains are flattened and appended to the retrieved tables as the input of the reader, which leads to better answer selection. Instead of using general pre-trained models, Herzig et al. [17] adopt a table-oriented pre-trained model, TAPAS [18], as both the dense retriever and extractive reader to achieve better performance.

Generative Reader. Li et al. [25] adopt a sparse retriever using BM25 to retrieve tables or text, in which the tables are flattened into passages by concatenating the cell values of each row. After retrieving the top-K candidate tables or passages, a generative dual reader-parser that is based on FiD model [21] is used to generate the answer directly or produce an SQL query. The FiD model is a Seq2Seq transformer that takes the question and top-K candidates as input and fuses them in decoder for answer or logical form generation (referred to as Fusion in Decoder, FiD). Whether the output will be a final answer or SQL query is decided by the FiD model automatically based on the input question and its context. UniK-QA [34] also adopts a FiD model as the reader but takes a BERT-based dense retriever. Moreover, it adapts the model to multiple knowledge sources, including text, tables, and knowledge base, by flattening the (semi-)structured data.

The open-domain table QA task is a new challenge that has appeared in recent years. Most works [18,25,34] simply flatten the tables and adapt methods used in open-domain text-based QA for this task. However, this may lead to the loss of important information in the (semi-)structured data [34]. Hence, the encoding methods of tables can be further explored in the open-domain setting.

6   Challenges and Future Directions

This paper presents an overview of existing datasets and five different methods for table QA. Some methods have revealed desirable performance on relatively easier benchmarks. However, there are still several key challenges for future work, especially in table QA for non-database tables. In this survey, we share our thoughts on some of the main challenges in table QA.

Numerical Representation for Table QA. Numerical values are the common content of table cells, especially for spreadsheet tables. Dedicated numerical representation might be a key factor for non-database table QA. For example, Zhu et al. [51] report that about 55% of errors in the RoBERTa-based model (called TAGOP) are caused by incorrect evidence extraction, most of them arising because of premature numerical representation. Hence, it is an interesting challenge to incorporate better numerical representations into table QA models.

Complex Reasoning in Non-database Table QA. For database tables, researchers have developed semantic parsing-based methods for complex reasoning. However, most existing methods for non-database table QA only support simple reasoning. For example, TAGOP [51] only support one-step operation, FinQANet [7] supports nested operations but limited to four basic arithmetics. Hence, future works include how to design a more general logical form that could support complex reasoning on most non-database table QA tasks.

References

1. Abbasiantaeb, Z., Momtazi, S.: Text-based question answering from information retrieval and deep neural network perspectives: a survey. Wiley Interdiscip. Rev. Data Min. Knowl. Disc. **11**(6), e1412 (2021)
2. Ainslie, J., et al.: Encoding long and structured inputs in transformers. In: EMNLP (2020)
3. Beltagy, I., Peters, M.E., Cohan, A.: Longformer: the long-document transformer. arXiv:2004.05150 (2020)
4. Cao, R., Chen, L., Chen, Z., Zhao, Y., Zhu, S., Yu, K.: LGESQL: line graph enhanced text-to-SQL model with mixed local and non-local relations. In: ACL (2021)
5. Chen, W., Chang, M.W., Schlinger, E., Wang, W.Y., Cohen, W.W.: Open question answering over tables and text. arXiv:2010.10439 (2021)
6. Chen, W., Zha, H., Chen, Z., Xiong, W., Wang, H., Wang, W.Y.: HybridQA: a dataset of multi-hop question answering over tabular and textual data. In: FINDINGS (2020)
7. Chen, Z., et al.: FinQA: a dataset of numerical reasoning over financial data. arXiv:2109.00122 (2021)
8. Cheng, Z., et al.: HiTab: a hierarchical table dataset for question answering and natural language generation. arXiv:2108.06712 (2021)
9. Cho, M., Amplayo, R.K., Hwang, S.W., Park, J.: Adversarial TableQA: attention supervision for question answering on tables. In: PMLR (2018)
10. Dasigi, P., Gardner, M., Murty, S., Zettlemoyer, L., Hovy, E.H.: Iterative search for weakly supervised semantic parsing. In: NAACL (2019)
11. Dong, L., Lapata, M.: Language to logical form with neural attention. arXiv:1601.01280 (2016)
12. Dong, L., Lapata, M.: Coarse-to-fine decoding for neural semantic parsing. In: ACL (2018)
13. Eisenschlos, J.M., Gor, M., Müller, T., Cohen, W.W.: MATE: multi-view attention for table transformer efficiency. In: EMNLP (2021)
14. Fu, B., Qiu, Y., Tang, C., Li, Y., Yu, H., Sun, J.: A survey on complex question answering over knowledge base: recent advances and challenges. arXiv:2007.13069 (2020)
15. Glass, M.R., et al.: Capturing row and column semantics in transformer based question answering over tables. In: NAACL (2021)
16. He, P., Mao, Y., Chakrabarti, K., Chen, W.: X-SQL: reinforce schema representation with context. arXiv:1908.08113 (2019)
17. Herzig, J., Müller, T., Krichene, S., Eisenschlos, J.M.: Open domain question answering over tables via dense retrieval. arXiv:2103.12011 (2021)
18. Herzig, J., Nowak, P.K., Müller, T., Piccinno, F., Eisenschlos, J.M.: TAPAS: weakly supervised table parsing via pre-training. arXiv:2004.02349 (2020)
19. Hwang, W., Yim, J.Y., Park, S., Seo, M.: A comprehensive exploration on WikiSQL with table-aware word contextualization. arXiv:1902.01069 (2019)

20. Iyyer, M., tau Yih, W., Chang, M.W.: Search-based neural structured learning for sequential question answering. In: ACL (2017)
21. Izacard, G., Grave, E.: Leveraging passage retrieval with generative models for open domain question answering. In: EACL (2021)
22. Jauhar, S.K., Turney, P.D., Hovy, E.H.: TabMCQ: a dataset of general knowledge tables and multiple-choice questions. arXiv:1602.03960 (2016)
23. Katsis, Y., et al.: AIT-QA: question answering dataset over complex tables in the airline industry. arXiv:2106.12944 (2021)
24. Krishnamurthy, J., Dasigi, P., Gardner, M.: Neural semantic parsing with type constraints for semi-structured tables. In: EMNLP (2017)
25. Li, A.H., Ng, P., Xu, P., Zhu, H., Wang, Z., Xiang, B.: Dual reader-parser on hybrid textual and tabular evidence for open domain question answering. In: ACL (2021)
26. Li, X., Sun, Y., Cheng, G.: TSQA: tabular scenario based question answering. In: AAAI (2021)
27. Liang, C., Norouzi, M., Berant, J., Le, Q.V., Lao, N.: Memory augmented policy optimization for program synthesis and semantic parsing. In: NeurIPS (2018)
28. Min, S., Chen, D., Hajishirzi, H., Zettlemoyer, L.: A discrete hard EM approach for weakly supervised question answering. In: EMNLP (2019)
29. Misra, D.K., Chang, M.W., He, X., Yih, W.T.: Policy shaping and generalized update equations for semantic parsing from denotations. In: EMNLP (2018)
30. Müller, T., Piccinno, F., Nicosia, M., Shaw, P., Altun, Y.: Answering conversational questions on structured data without logical forms. arXiv:1908.11787 (2019)
31. Nan, L., et al.: FeTaQA: free-form table question answering. Trans. Assoc. Comput. Linguist. 10, 35–49 (2022)
32. Neelakantan, A., Le, Q.V., Abadi, M., McCallum, A., Amodei, D.: Learning a natural language interface with neural programmer. arXiv:1611.08945 (2017)
33. Neelakantan, A., Le, Q.V., Sutskever, I.: Neural programmer: inducing latent programs with gradient descent. CoRR abs/1511.04834 (2016)
34. Oguz, B., et al.: UniK-QA: unified representations of structured and unstructured knowledge for open-domain question answering. arXiv preprint arXiv:2012.14610 (2020)
35. Pasupat, P., Liang, P.: Compositional semantic parsing on semi-structured tables. In: ACL (2015)
36. Sun, H., Ma, H., He, X., tau Yih, W., Su, Y., Yan, X.: Table cell search for question answering. In: WWW (2016)
37. Sun, Y., et al.: Semantic parsing with syntax- and table-aware SQL generation. arXiv:1804.08338 (2018)
38. Wang, B., Shin, R., Liu, X., Polozov, O., Richardson, M.: Rat-SQL: relation-aware schema encoding and linking for text-to-SQL parsers. In: ACL (2020)
39. Wang, B., Titov, I., Lapata, M.: Learning semantic parsers from denotations with latent structured alignments and abstract programs. In: EMNLP (2019)
40. Wang, C., et al.: Robust text-to-SQL generation with execution-guided decoding. arXiv:1807.03100 (2018)
41. Xu, X., Liu, C., Song, D.X.: SQLNet: generating structured queries from natural language without reinforcement learning. arXiv:1711.04436 (2017)
42. Yang, J., Gupta, A., Upadhyay, S., He, L., Goel, R., Paul, S.: Tableformer: robust transformer modeling for table-text encoding. arXiv:2203.00274 (2022)
43. Yin, P., Lu, Z., Li, H., Kao, B.: Neural enquirer: learning to query tables with natural language. In: IJCAI (2016)
44. Yin, P., Neubig, G.: A syntactic neural model for general-purpose code generation. arXiv preprint arXiv:1704.01696 (2017)

45. Yu, T., Li, Z., Zhang, Z., Zhang, R., Radev, D.R.: TypeSQL: knowledge-based type-aware neural text-to-SQL generation. In: NAACL (2018)
46. Yu, T., et al.: Spider: a large-scale human-labeled dataset for complex and cross-domain semantic parsing and text-to-SQL task. In: EMNLP (2018)
47. Zayats, V., Toutanova, K., Ostendorf, M.: Representations for question answering from documents with tables and text. In: EACL (2021)
48. Zhang, S., Balog, K.: Web table extraction, retrieval, and augmentation. ACM Trans. Intell. Syst. Technol. (TIST) **11**, 1–35 (2020)
49. Zhong, V., Xiong, C., Socher, R.: Seq2SQL: generating structured queries from natural language using reinforcement learning. arXiv:1709.00103 (2017)
50. Zhong, W., et al.: Reasoning over hybrid chain for table-and-text open domain QA. arXiv:2201.05880 (2022)
51. Zhu, F., et al.: TAT-QA: a question answering benchmark on a hybrid of tabular and textual content in finance. In: ACL (2021)

Knowledge Graph Applications

Knowledge-Aware Topological Networks for Recommendation

Jian Pan[1,2], Zhao Zhang[3(✉)], Fuzhen Zhuang[4,5], Jingyuan Yang[6],
and Zhiping Shi[1(✉)]

[1] Capital Normal University, Beijing 100048, China
`panjian2@sgepri.sgcc.com.cn, shizp@cnu.edu.cn`
[2] NARI Group Corporation (State Grid Electric Power Research Institute),
Nanjing 211106, China
[3] Institute of Computing Technology, Chinese Academy of Sciences,
Beijing 100190, China
`zhangzhao2017@ict.ac.cn`
[4] Institute of Artificial Intelligence, Beihang University, Beijing 100191, China
`zhuangfuzhen@buaa.edu.cn`
[5] SKLSDE, School of Computer Science, Beihang University,
Beijing 100191, China
[6] School of Business, George Mason University, Fairfax, VA 22030, USA
`jyang53@gmu.edu`

Abstract. Knowledge graphs (KGs) play a critical role in recommender systems, aiming to provide diverse, accurate, and explainable recommendations to users. Enhanced with KGs, recommender systems are able to leverage valuable auxiliary information, which is beneficial to predict new user-item interactions. Specifically, the connectivity between relations and entities in a KG can reveal the structural and semantic information, as well as help to provide inferences for user choices. However, the information of the holistic topological structure in KGs has not been fully taken into account in most existing studies. To this end, we propose the *Knowledge-aware Topological Recurrent Network* (KTRN), an end-to-end network for recommendation with recurrent neural network and knowledge graph embedding. To simultaneously discover sequential dependencies and semantic information in a KG, we consider both relevant paths and triplets. Moreover, we focus on the importance of relation-entity pairs in learning representations, rather than treating relations and entities as independent units. We conduct experiments on three public datasets about movie, book, and music recommendation scenarios, and extensive experimental results show that our method outperforms benchmark approaches.

Keywords: Recommendation system · Knowledge graph · Representation learning

1 Introduction

Recommender systems (RS) have been actively studied in the past decade in both industry and academia. The success of RS makes it prevalent in many

M. Sun et al. (Eds.): CCKS 2022, CCIS 1669, pp. 189–201, 2022.
https://doi.org/10.1007/978-981-19-7596-7_15

aspects of web applications, since it is indispensable when providing suitable contents/services to users. To infer users' preferences, various side information [2, 5], has been adopted to advance RS, such as context information [3], images [13] and social networks [10]. A few recent studies [3,9] not only simply used isolated attributes but also linked up with items by relations, which form a heterogeneous information network called knowledge graph (KG).

Existing KG enhanced recommender systems utilize knowledge graph embedding (KGE) or meta-path to facilitate recommendation. Despite the wide recognition of the advantage of applying KGs to RS in the existing literature, we identify two key challenges that may hinder KG from reaching its full potentials. First, the facts are defined as triplets (e_h, r, e_t) in a KG, e_h and e_t represent entities, r is the relation between e_h and e_t. One entity can be involved in multiple triplets, serving as the bridge connecting two triplets and propagating information. Taking $[(e_1, r_1, e_2), (e_2, r_2, e_3)]$ as an example, e_1 can transmit information to e_3 over a path which is made up of r_1, e_2 and r_2. However, most existing works did not explicitly model the sequential dependency such as $e_1 \rightarrow r_1 \rightarrow e_2 \rightarrow r_2 \rightarrow e_3$. Thus, the information of connectivity within KG was not captured. Second, entities and relations affect each other. The same entity with different relations have diverse meanings, also the same relation may be involved with different entities. Yet existing works tend to neglect the contextual information and to regard entities and relations as independent units. In other words, the difference of the combinations between relations and entities has not been taken into account. Therefore, it is vital to distinguish different combinations of entities and relations to generate appropriate representations of entities and relations.

The aforementioned challenges call for a more efficient and comprehensive approach to make the most of KGs for recommendations. In this paper, our objective is to automatically and integrally capture both sequential dependencies and semantic information by the connections between relations and entities. Inspired by recurrent neural network (RNN) and word2vec [4], we propose *Knowledge-aware Topological Recurrent Network* (KTRN) for recommender systems. Similar to the CBOW model, we believe that the central entity can be represented by neighboring entities. The key idea is to utilize LSTM, one of the RNN models, to aggregate the latent representations of neighboring entities as auxiliary data to calculate the representation of the central entity, simultaneously paying attention to the indivisibility of relation and entity as a pair. Such a design has two advantages: (1) through the special learning of latent representations of neighboring entities, the local topological structure is successfully captured and stored in each entity; (2) the representations of entities are dependent on sequential dependencies and specific users, which characterizes sufficient information of KG, difference of relation-entity sequences, and users' personalized interests. Empirically, we apply KTRN to three real-world datasets of MovieLens-1M (movie), Book-Crossing (book), and Last.FM (music). The experimental results show that our model outperforms baselines on datasets from different domains.

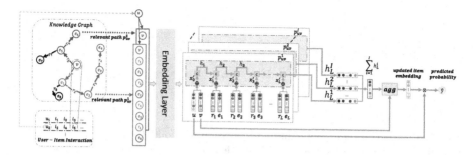

Fig. 1. The overall framework of the KTRN. It takes one user and one item as input, and outputs the predicted probability that the user will click the item.

Below, we highlight the key contributions in this paper as follows:

- We develop an end-to-end network for recommendation named *Knowledge-aware Topological Recurrent Network* (KTRN). Specifically, it utilizes recurrent neural network to model sequential dependencies, and incorporates knowledge graph embedding to capture the information of the topological structure in KG.
- By combining entities and relations into pairs, our proposed model can learn the reasonable representations of entities and provide personalized entity representation.
- We conduct experiments on three real-world datasets, and experimental results prove the effectiveness of our framework in accurate recommendation.

2   Methodology

In this section, we discuss the framework of Knowledge-aware Topological Recurrent Network (KTRN). As shown in Fig. 1, the overall framework of KTRN consists of two main components: (1) topological graph network, which parameterizes each node as a vector by preserving the topological structure of the KG; (2) personalized entity embedding based on sequential relation-entity pairs.

2.1   Background and Preliminary

First, we present the background and preliminaries of this study in two folds: item recommendation and knowledge graphs.

Given users U and items V, the purpose of the item recommendation is to identify items which each user is most likely to interact based on historical information. A user expresses his or her preferences by purchasing or scoring items, then a matrix can represent these interaction information. With m users $U = \{u_1, ..., u_m\}$ and n items $V = \{v_1, ..., v_n\}$, we define the user implicit feedback matrix $Y = \{y_{uv} \mid u \in U, v \in V\}$, which $y_{uv} = 1$ indicates that user u had interacted with item v; otherwise $y_{uv} = 0$.

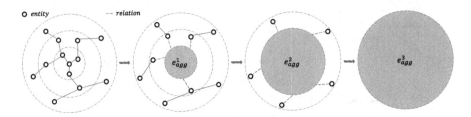

Fig. 2. An illustration of hierarchical aggregation methods. Green dotted lines represent the broken connections when e_{agg}^i is calculated. e_{agg}^i is the representation of the central entity and its neighbors. (Color figure online)

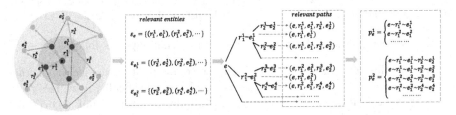

Fig. 3. The left subfigure shows the two-hop neighboring entities (blue entities) of the red entity e in a KG. Dotted lines represent the information learned by KGE. The mid subfigure shows relevant paths constructed according to the left subfigure. The right subfigure shows relevant entities with different entities. (Color figure online)

Additionally, a knowledge graph G is a heterogeneous information graph composed of entities e and relations r as nodes and edges, respectively. We can use many (*entity, relation, entity*) as triplets (h, r, t) to represent the facts in the knowledge graph [11]. Here $h \in E$, $r \in R$, and $t \in E$ denote the head, relation, and tail of a triplet, respectively. E and R denote the set of entities and relations in the KG.

2.2   Topological Graph Network

A knowledge graph usually contains fruitful facts and connections among entities. The connections between relations and entities within a KG also play a pivotal role, no matter such connections are within triplets or among a path consisting of multiple triplets. But existing methods can not fully model the sequential dependency, such as the *hierarchical aggregation method*, which aggregates neighboring entities iteratively as the central entity embedding or a substitute of the user embedding. The hierarchical aggregation methods typically separate a KG into individual layers, breaking the connections between layers when aggregating entities of a certain layer as shown in Fig. 2.

To characterize valuable sequential dependencies and connectivity in KG, in KTRN, we first define the set of relevant information for the given entity e. Considering a candidate entity e, the definition of relevant relation-entity pair for entity e is as follows:

Definition 1 (relevant relation-entity pair). *Given a knowledge graph G, the set of relevant relation-entity pairs for entity e is defined as:*

$$\varepsilon_e = \{(r,t) \mid (h,r,t) \in G \text{ and } h \text{ is } e\} \tag{1}$$

Relevant relation-entity pairs ε_e can be regarded as natural extensions of an item's local information concerning the KG. Given the definition of relevant relation-entity pairs, we then define the relevant path set of entity e. For the given entity e, we can find out the relevant relation-entity pairs by ε_e, then iteratively getting next-hop relations and entities by the relevant relation-entity pairs. Finally our model links these entities with corresponding relations to model sequential dependencies as shown in Fig. 3. A relevant path is defined as follows:

Definition 2 (relevant path). *The k-hop relevant path is defined as the set of knowledge triples starting from ε_e:*

$$p_e^k = \left\{ p_e^{k-1} \sim r \sim t \mid (r,t) \in \varepsilon_{[p_e^{k-1}]_{-1}} \right\}, \tag{2}$$

where $\sim$ is the operation of adding an element at the end of the sequence and $p_e^0 = \{e\}$. $[p_e^{k-1}]_{-1}$ is the last element of p_e^{k-1}. The pattern of p_e^k explicitly preserves the sequential dependencies among entity e and its neighboring entities.

After constructing the relevant paths, we can employ RNN models to explore the sequential dependency of a relevant path and generate a latent representation that encodes holistic semantics of this path into the last state. We choose LSTM among various RNN methods finally, since LSTM is capable of memorizing long-term dependency in a sequence. Such an ability is crucial to retain the topological information of KG.

Assuming a relevant path $[e, r_1, e_2, \cdots, r_{L-1}, e_L]$, LSTM is used to generate the latent vector of the sequential holistic semantic. At the $(l-1)$-th path-step, the LSTM layer outputs a hidden state vector h_{l-1}. We use LSTM to learn the representation of the path. Noted that, the dimension of the mapping coefficient matrices in LSTM is $\mathbb{R}^{d \times d}$, $e \in \mathbb{R}^d$ and $r \in \mathbb{R}^d$ are entity embedding and relation embedding respectively. Taking advantages of the memory state, the last state h_L is capable of storaging the sequential representation of the whole path. We take h_L as the latent vector to supplement the first entity e.

The final step is to aggregate the entity e and the latent vectors h_L of its multi-hop neighboring entities into a single vector. We implement four types of aggregators $agg : \mathbb{R}^d \times \mathbb{R}^d \to \mathbb{R}^d$:

- *Add aggregator* takes the summation of two representation vectors as the final vector:

$$agg_{add} = e + \sum_{i=1}^{I} h_L^i \tag{3}$$

- *Sum aggregator* takes the summation of two representation vectors, followed by a nonlinear transformation:

$$agg_{sum} = tanh(W \cdot (e + \sum_{i=1}^{I} h_L^i) + b). \tag{4}$$

- *Concat aggregator* concatenates the two representation vectors first before applying nonlinear transformation:

$$agg_{concat} = tanh(W \cdot concat(e, \sum_{i=1}^{I} h_L^i) + b). \tag{5}$$

- *Bi aggregator* takes bidirectional LSTM to learn h_L, so we get forward output $[h_L^i]^+$ and reverse output $[h_L^i]^-$:

$$agg_{bi} = tanh(W \cdot concat(e, \sum_{i=1}^{I} [h_L^i]^+, \sum_{i=1}^{I} [h_L^i]^-) + b), \tag{6}$$

where I is the number of relevant paths, h_L^i is the last state of the LSTM which takes the i-th relevant path as input. $[h_L^i]^+, [h_L^i]^-$ are the last state of bidirectional LSTM.

KG is a kind of heterogeneous information network that leads to serious 1-to-N, N-to-1, and N-to-N issues. Therefore, to alleviate the issues mentioned above, TransH [11] defines relation hyperplanes that projects head entity h and tail entity t to the hyperplane of relation r. If (h, r, t) exists in KG, the translation between head entity and tail entity is valid. It defines a score function for a triplet as follows:

$$f(e_h, r, e_t) = \left\| e_h^\perp + r - e_t^\perp \right\| \tag{7}$$

Triplets with lower scores indicate higher plausibility. e_h and e_t are projected into the relation hyperplane as vectors $e_h^\perp$ and $e_t^\perp$.

Finally, the training of TransH encourages the discrimination between positive triplets and negative ones using margin-based ranking loss:

$$L_{kge} = \sum_{(e_h, r, e_t) \in G} \sum_{(e_h', r, e_t') \in G^-} [f(e_h, r, e_t) + \gamma - f(e_h', r, e_t')]_+ \tag{8}$$

where $[\cdot]_+ := max(0, \cdot)$, G^- contains incorrect triplets constructed by replacing head entity or tail entity in a true triplet randomly, and γ controls the margin between positive and negative triplets.

Incorporating KGE makes the topological graph network learn the semantic meaning of triplets, simultaneously it supplements the connection among relevant paths to a certain degree. Such supplements make local structure more complete, so as to achieve the goal of a better use of KG.

2.3   Personalized Relation-Aware Entity Embedding

Personalized relation-aware entity embedding emphasizes the integration of user information and sequential relation-entity pairs. User information plays a personalized role and relation-entity pairs make representation learning more reasonable.

As we discussed earlier in Sect. 2.2, the first category of entity embedding is *hierarchical aggregation method*. And the second category is *collaborative knowledge graph method* [7], which combines user-item interactions and knowledge graph as a unified graph called Collaborative Knowledge Graph (CKG). These methods first define each user-item interaction as a triplet $(u, Interact, v)$ and incorporate these triplets into a KG.

In general, both of the two methods mentioned above neglect sequential dependency in KG and the importance of aggregation weights. Entities among KG can transmit information to each other. Such information must associate with the sequential dependencies of entities and relations. For example, there are two paths consisting of the same start and end as follows:

- c_1 : *Far Away* $\xrightarrow{isIncluded}$ *Remini* $\xrightarrow{isAuthorof^{-1}}$ *YuChing Fei* $\xrightarrow{isSingerof}$ *Yi Jian Mei*
- c_2 : *Far Away* $\xrightarrow{isSingerof^{-1}}$ *Jay Chou* $\xrightarrow{isFriendof}$ *YuChing Fei* $\xrightarrow{isSingerof}$ *Yi Jian Mei*

There are two types of recommendation modes c_1 and c_2 when recommending the same song *Yi Jian Mei* depending on *Far Away*. c_1 recommends *Yi Jian Mei* for music appreciation while c_2 leans towards social attributes. One of the reasons for such a difference is the various sequences, so it is crucial to attach importance to the sequential dependencies within a KG. Due to the operation, *hierarchical aggregation method* and *collaborative knowledge graph method* cut off entities' connectivity. It is hard for them to discover multi-hop consequent sequential dependency explicitly.

The aggregation weight is also an important part of representation learning, we consider relation and entity as a whole, such a relation-entity pair embodies the difference between various combinations of relations and entities. No longer learning a weight for a single relation or entity, the same relation with different entities should have different weights, and different relations with the same entity should also be so. While personalized entity embedding retains the sequences in the KG, it also emphasizes the importance of relation-entity pairs, and finally learns a personalized latent vectors for neighboring entities.

With the idea of relation-entity pairs, we extend the topological graph network module by combining relations and entities. Moreover, for the personalized embedding, user information and user-item interactions are also necessary. For a given user-item interaction (u, v), we concatenate them as a vector for the first input x_0 of LSTM. $u \in \mathbb{R}^d$ and $v \in \mathbb{R}^d$ are user embedding and item embedding respectively. In this way, the model starts with the user and the user's previous behavior. Furthermore, the cell state vector saves user interaction information, thereby exerting influence on every input relation-entity pair. For the same entity, it will own personalized embedding due to different users.

Therefore, we concatenate the embedding of current relation r_{l-1} and entity e_{l-1} as the input vector. The relevant path defined as sequence $p_e : [e, r_1, e_1, \cdots, r_{L-1}, e_{L-1}, r_L, e_L]$ should be changed to $p_{uv} : [u \oplus v, r_1 \oplus e_1, \cdots, r_{L-1} \oplus e_{L-1}, r_L \oplus e_L]$, where e is the corresponding entity of v in the KG,

$\oplus$ is the concatenation operation. As a result, the state of LSTM observes fruitful information, including personalized information, the historical behavior, the relatedness of entities and relations, and the sequential contextual information.

At the $(l-1)$-th path-step $(l > 0)$, the LSTM layer outputs a hidden state vector h'_{l-1}, preserving the sequential dependency of $[u \oplus v, r_1 \oplus e_1 \cdots, r_{l-1} \oplus e_{l-1}]$. The hidden state of the l-th path-step is calculated by h'_{l-1} and x'_l, x'_l is the l-th element in p_{uv}. Noted that, the dimension of the mapping coefficient matrices are $\mathbb{R}^{2d \times d}$ due to the new input. We can obtain the final state h'_L that is the latent vector of the last element in a path. We use the result of the aggregation method agg as the final representation of the item v. Finally, we conduct inner product with the representations of user u and item v, so as to predict the probability:

$$\hat{y}(u,v) = \sigma \left(u^T \cdot agg \left(v, h'_L \right) \right) \qquad (9)$$

To optimize the recommendation model, we have the following loss function:

$$L_{rs} = \sum_{(u,v) \in Y} - \left(y_{uv} \log \left(\hat{y} \right) + (1 - y_{uv}) \log \left(1 - \hat{y} \right) \right), \qquad (10)$$

we combine Eqs. (8) and (10) jointly as the complete loss function of KTRN, which is shown as follows:

$$L_{KTRN} = L_{rs} + \lambda L_{kge} + \mu \|\Theta\|_2^2. \qquad (11)$$

λ and μ are hyper-parameters. The last term is the L2-regularizer, and hyper-parameter μ on Θ is conducted to prevent overfitting.

3   Experiments

3.1   Datasets

We use the following three publicly available datasets in our experiments:

- **MovieLens-1M**[1] collects nearly one million scoring data on the Movie-Lens website. It is the most commonly used dataset for movie recommendation.
- **Book-Crossing**[2] consists of approximately 1 million explicit ratings in the Book-Crossing community.
- **Last.FM**[3] contains musician listening information from a set of 2 thousand users from Last.FM online music platform.

We followed KGCN [6] to transform them into implicit feedback. Microsoft Satori[4] is used to construct the KG for each dataset. Three datasets are presented in Table 1 for basic statistics.

---

[1] https://grouplens.org/datasets/movielens/1m/.
[2] http://www2.informatik.uni-freiburg.de/~cziegler/BX/.
[3] https://grouplens.org/datasets/hetrec-2011/.
[4] https://searchengineland.com/library/bing/bing-satori.

Table 1. Basic statistics and hyper-parameter settings for the three datasets (K: neighbor sampling size, d: dimension of embedding, H: depth of receptive field, λ: learning rate, L_2: L_2 regularizer weight, B: batch size)

Datasets	Users	Items	Interactions	KG triplets	Hyper-parameters
MovieLen-1M	6,036	2,347	753,772	20,195	$d = 8$, $H = 2$, $\lambda = 0.02$, $L_2 = 0.01$, $B = 1024$, $K = 4$
Book-Crossing	17,860	14,910	139,746	19,793	$d = 6$, $H = 1$, $\lambda = 0.02$, $L_2 = 0.003$, $B = 512$, $K = 16$
Last.FM	1,872	3,846	42,346	15,518	$d = 8$, $H = 1$, $\lambda = 0.02$, $L_2 = 0.05$, $B = 1024$, $K = 8$

Table 2. The results of AUC and Accuracy in CTR prediction.

Model	MovieLens-1M		Book-Crossing		Last.FM	
	ACC	AUC	ACC	AUC	ACC	AUC
PER	0.662	0.705	0.576	0.613	0.576	0.633
CKE	0.735	0.796	0.630	0.671	0.674	0.764
KGCN	0.786	0.865	0.628	0.685	0.711	0.780
Wide&Deep	0.815	0.890	0.629	0.701	0.672	0.761
KGAT	0.824	0.895	0.631	0.704	0.686	0.771
KGIN	0.831	0.906	0.639	0.707	0.699	0.785
KTRN-add	0.835	0.911	0.636	0.702	0.711	0.782
KTRN-sum	0.840	0.917	0.642	0.705	0.711	0.792
KTRN-bi	0.833	0.910	0.635	0.701	0.713	0.783
KTRN-concat	**0.845**	**0.920**	**0.647**	**0.712**	**0.715**	**0.793**
KTRN-w/o r	0.829	0.910	0.634	0.702	0.710	0.779

3.2 Baselines

We compare our proposed KTRN with the following baselines.

- **PER** [12]: a classic KG-enhanced recommendation method, which represents the connectivity between users and items based on manually designed meta-paths in KG.
- **CKE** [13]: a KG-based recommendation model, which extracts structural, textual, and visual knowledge to facilitate recommendation.
- **KGCN** [6]: a state-of-the-art KG-enhanced recommendation method, which calculates weights for neighboring entities and aggregates them as the representation of the central entity.
- **Wide&Deep** [1]: a deep recommendation model combining a linear module with a deep neural network module.
- **KGAT** [8]: a strong KG-enhanced recommendation model which explores high-order connectivity with semantic relations for recommendation.

– **KGIN** [9]: a recent KG-enhanced recommendation model which uncovers user-item relationships at the granularity of intents.

3.3 Experiments Setup

Table 1 shows hyper-parameter settings in KTRN. We optimize ACC on the validation set to get the best setting of hyperparameters. We split each dataset into a ratio of 6 : 2 : 2 as training, evaluation, and test set, respectively. The reported performance is the average of 3 times repeated test experiments. We evaluate our model in two experiment scenarios: (1) We use ACC and AUC to evaluate the model in click-through rate (CTR) prediction. (2) We choose $Recall@K$ and $Precision@K$ to evaluate the recommended sets in top-K recommendation. Finally, we test the trained model on the test set.

3.4 Results

Overall Comparison. The results of all methods in CTR prediction are presented in Table 2. We add a variant named KTRN-w/o r to verify the impact of relation-entity pair. Particularly, we disable the relation as the part of the input of LSTM in KTRN-w/o r. Figure 4 and Fig. 5 show the performance of top-K recommendation. We have the following observations:

– In CTR prediction, our proposed method performs the best compared with the baseline methods on the three datasets. The result shows that only the structural information or the paths can not explore the KG sufficiently. It is observed that the improvement of KTRN on the movie dataset is higher than that on book and music datasets. Since the movie dataset is denser than the other two, this result demonstrates that KTRN can make better use of the wealth of information to benefit recommendations in the scenario with more information.
– PER performs worst among all baselines on movie, book, and music recommendation. In fact, manually designed meta-path can not explore the KG effectively and sufficiently, the designed path has a fixed length and poor scalability.
– The two KG-aware baselines KGCN and CKE perform worse than the KG-free baseline Wide&Deep, we can conclude that inappropriate embedding methods cannot make full use of the KG. While our model is better than Wide&Deep, it indicates that topological graph network is a more suitable method.
– On MovieLens-1M, all models perform much better due to the relatively sufficient training data. Obviously, the improvement by utilizing KG is larger on the dense dataset of MovieLens-1M than that on the sparse datasets of Book-Crossing and Last.FM. For this result, more connections within KG may own more real topological structure.

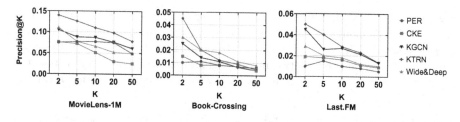

Fig. 4. The results of *Precision@K* in top-*K* recommendation.

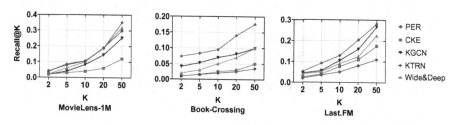

Fig. 5. The results of *Recall@K* in top-*K* recommendation.

Comparison with KTRN Variants. The performance of KTRN variants is shown in Table 2. The four (*add, sum, concat, bi*) different aggregation have been introduced in Sect. 2.2. From the results, we find that:

- KTRN performs best compared with all baselines, while there is a slight difference between their performances: KTRN-concat achieves the best performance in general. The reason may lie in that the concat aggregator concatenates the neighborhood representation and the central entity as an input of fully-connected layer, thus the fitting capacity of the neural network is most effectively utilized.
- KTRN-add and KTRN-bi do not achieve satisfactory performance. This demonstrates that methods that are too simple or too complex will not capture users' personalized preferences and semantic information of the KG well. A naive aggregator may not exploit enough information, while too much noise is mixed in a complex aggregator.

Impact of the LSTM Layer. Compared with KGCN, our proposed method incorporates LSTM to learn the representations of neighboring entities, and achieves better performance. In KGCN, the inner product function is used to compute the weight of neighboring entities. The weights are used to calculate the representations of neighboring entities. In spite of this, KGCN still sees relations as isolated individuals rather than as important roles linked to entities in a KG.

Intuitively, this is not a good solution that changes such a complex situation to a simple one. Exactly, the LSTM can handle such changing scenarios because of its powerful ability to process sequential data. As shown in Table 2, the performance of all KTRN models is better than KGCN. It denotes that the sequential dependency in a KG is vital to exploit the topological structure. Due to the structure of a KG and our designed operations, the LSTM layer can capture complex connections between relations and entities. The results show that the LSTM layer is able to significantly improve the recommendation results.

Impact of Relation-Entity Pair. To verify the impact of relation-entity pair, we do an ablation study by considering a variant of KTRN. We disable the relation as the part of the input of LSTM, termed KTRN-w/o r. We summarize the experimental results and have the findings: (1) Removing relation component degrades the model's performance. It makes sense since KTRN-w/o r breaks connectivity within relation-entity pairs. The model can not specialize in different combinations of relations and entities. (2) KTRN-w/o r still achieves better performance than KGCN, which indicates the superiority of LSTM on the secondary side.

4   Conclusion

This paper proposed a novel approach called Knowledge-aware Topological Recurrent Network (KTRN) for recommender systems. KTRN applied LSTM to KG to aggregate neighborhood information sequentially, which can learn both structural information and semantic information of the KG. Experimental results on three real-world datasets validated that KTRN consistently outperformed state-of-the-art baselines in movie, book, and music recommendations.

Acknowledgements. The research work is supported by the National Key Research and Development Program of China under Grant No. 2021ZD0113602, the National Natural Science Foundation of China under Grant No. 62176014 and 61977048. Zhao Zhang is supported by the China Postdoctoral Science Foundation under Grant No. 2021M703273.

References

1. Cheng, H., Koc, L.: Wide & deep learning for recommender systems. In: DLRS@RecSys (2016)
2. Liu, Y., et al.: Pre-training graph transformer with multimodal side information for recommendation. In: Proceedings of the 29th ACM International Conference on Multimedia, pp. 2853–2861 (2021)
3. Mezni, H., Benslimane, D., Bellatreche, L.: Context-aware service recommendation based on knowledge graph embedding. IEEE Trans. Knowl. Data Eng. (2021)
4. Mikolov, T., Chen, K., Corrado, G., Dean, J.: Efficient estimation of word representations in vector space. In: ICLR (2013)
5. Qiu, N., Gao, B., Tu, H., Huang, F., Guan, Q., Luo, W.: LDGC-SR: integrating long-range dependencies and global context information for session-based recommendation. Knowl.-Based Syst. 108894 (2022)

6. Wang, H., Zhao, M., Xie, X., Li, W., Guo, M.: Knowledge graph convolutional networks for recommender systems. In: WWW (2019)
7. Wang, X., He, X., Cao, Y., Liu, M., Chua, T.: KGAT: knowledge graph attention network for recommendation. In: SIGKDD (2019)
8. Wang, X., He, X., Cao, Y., Liu, M., Chua, T.S.: KGAT: knowledge graph attention network for recommendation. In: SIGKDD (2019)
9. Wang, X., et al.: Learning intents behind interactions with knowledge graph for recommendation. In: The Web Conference, pp. 878–887 (2021)
10. Wang, Y., Dai, Z., Cao, J., Wu, J., Tao, H., Zhu, G.: Intra-and inter-association attention network-enhanced policy learning for social group recommendation. In: World Wide Web, pp. 1–24 (2022)
11. Wang, Z., Zhang, J., Feng, J., Chen, Z.: Knowledge graph embedding by translating on hyperplanes. In: AAAI (2014)
12. Yu, X., et al.: Personalized entity recommendation: a heterogeneous information network approach. In: WSDM (2014)
13. Zhang, F., Yuan, N.J., Lian, D., Xie, X., Ma, W.: Collaborative knowledge base embedding for recommender systems. In: SIGKDD (2016)

Knowledge Graph Open Resources

IREE: A Fine-Grained Dataset for Chinese Event Extraction in Investment Research

Junxiang Ren[✉], Sibo Wang, Ruilin Song, Yuejiao Wu, Yizhou Gao,
Borong An, Zhen Cheng, and Guoqiang Xu

China Pacific Insurance (Group) Co., Ltd., Shanghai, China
renjunxiang@cpic.com.cn

Abstract. This paper introduces a dataset for event extraction in the
field of investment research. Event extraction is a key area of research
in the field of investment. In recent years, a large number of datasets
for common event extraction as well as financial event extraction have
been released. However, they only cover few event types compared with
real-world business scenarios. Hence, by combining actual requirements
of financial investment risk management with business needs and experience in terms of investment, we construct a dataset for financial event
extraction. The released dataset is the first fine-grained dataset for event
extraction in investment research areas, with 5 main categories and
59 event types totally. The dataset is available on http://openkg.cn/
dataset/iree.

Keywords: Event extraction · Dataset · Investment research

1 Introduction

Event extraction aims to identify all the target event types and roles according
to pre-specified schema from given context. The event type and role decide the
range of extractions. The event types like abnormal fluctuation of stock price
and roles like subject, time as well as numerical values are significant factors in
the field of investment research.

Recently, the focus of event extraction is gradually shifting from event detection, event subject extraction and event argument extraction to full event extraction. Many related competitions have been held and the corresponding open-
source datasets have been released as well. Those well-known Chinese datasets
come from LUGE by Baidu, CCKS held by CIPS, CCF-BDCI held by CCF, etc.
But few event types are involved in these datasets, which is still distinct from
real business scenarios.

Therefore, based on the experience of investment as well as actual demands
of financial transactions in investment research areas, we construct the dataset
for financial event extraction. We conclude contributions of the paper as follows:

All authors contribute equally.

M. Sun et al. (Eds.): CCKS 2022, CCIS 1669, pp. 205–210, 2022.
https://doi.org/10.1007/978-981-19-7596-7_16

- High applicability: The data are all from a real investment decision support system which have been operated over 2 years since 2020, with tens of millions of public sentiment news.
- Wide coverage: The dataset involves 15 industries, 4000 A-share listed companies and 59 event types.
- Strong professionalism: Each piece of data is annotated by 5 financial industry annotators. If the marked results are consistent, it will be reviewed by a senior researcher and then entered into the database.

2   Related Work

The Event extraction datasets for common scenarios are comparatively well-labelled, including ACE2005[1], Rich ERE [1], TAC KBP 2017[2], MAVEN [2], TimeBank[3], MUC[4] and DuEE [3]. Datasets in areas of expertise require the involvement of business experts and are relatively expensive to annotate. For example, CySecED [4] and CASIE [5] focus on cyber security, Commodity News Corpus for Event Extraction [6] is commodity news event extraction and LitBank [7] is document-level news event extraction of fictional novel works. Datasets in the finance scenario include DuEE-fin[5], Document-level event argument extraction in the field of finance[6] and Small-scale financial event extraction and adapting to new types[7], which have narrow event coverage and are coarse-grained.

3   Datasets Construction

3.1   Data Resource

We use the news corpus from the investment decision support system as the source of data. Original corpus contains various mainstream information platforms, traditional media and new media. The corpus contains the industries, the texts and the corresponding risk types. The data are firstly annotated by 5 business experts. Then they are checked by experienced experts.

After discussions with operation specialists, we divide all the news into 5 main categories, including market conduct, financial reports, corporate operations, credit assessment and company reputation. There are 98 kinds of event types originally. With discussion and voting, those that have high similarity, such as the risk types, receipts of court summons and winning or losing the case, are merged. Finally, we get 59 event types which are demonstrated in Fig. 1.

---

[1] https://catalog.ldc.upenn.edu/LDC2006T06.
[2] https://tac.nist.gov/2017/KBP/Event/index.html.
[3] https://catalog.ldc.upenn.edu/LDC2006T08.
[4] https://www-nlpir.nist.gov/related_projects/muc/muc_data/muc_data_index.html.
[5] https://aistudio.baidu.com/aistudio/competition/detail/46.
[6] https://www.biendata.xyz/competition/ccks_2021_task6_1.
[7] https://www.biendata.xyz/competition/ccks_2020_3/.

Level1	Level2	Event Type	Main Argument	Other Argument
市场行为	停牌复牌	停牌	主体，时间	停牌时间
		复牌	主体，时间	
	戴帽	戴帽	主体，时间	
	异常交易	股价异常波动	主体，时间，数值	
	增减持	大股东减持	主体，时间，数值	
	关联交易	关联交易	主体，时间，数值	
	股份解禁	股份解禁	主体，时间，数值	
财报信息	财务指标变动	主营业务收入减少	主体，时间，数值	
		利润增速下滑	主体，时间，数值	
		利润下滑	主体，时间，数值	
		净资产减少	主体，时间，数值	
	业绩预期	业绩暴雷	主体，时间，数值	
		延期披露	主体，时间	
		业绩承诺未达标	主体，时间	
	管理层变动	董监高一主动离职	主体，时间	
		董监高一被迫离职	主体，时间	
公司运营	企业担保	担保风险预警	主体，时间，数值	质押
	并购重组	重大资产重组	主体，时间	
	发行股份	发行股份	主体，时间，数值	
	意外事件	爆炸事故	主体，时间	
		场所失火	主体，时间	
		自然灾害	主体，时间	
	债务	债务重组	主体，时间	债务人
		债务增加	主体，时间，数值	
		债务减少	主体，时间，数值	
	业务重组	业务重组	主体，时间	
	资产管理	资产剥离	主体，时间，数值	受让方
		资产注入	主体，时间	
	公司收购	公司收购	主体，时间	被收购人
	股权	股份回购	主体，时间，数值	回购期限
		股权激励	主体，时间，数值	
	股权质押	股权质押	主体，时间，数值	
	裁员	裁员	主体，时间	
	破产清算	破产清算	主体，时间	申请人
	业务合作	业务合作	主体，时间	被合作方
	引进战略投资	引进战略投资	主体，时间，数值	增资方
	产品创新	产品创新	主体，时间	
	企业转型	企业转型	主体，时间	
	退市	退市	主体，时间	
信用评估	债券违约	债券违约	主体，时间，数值	应付时间
	评级调整	主体评级上调	主体，时间	
		主体评级下调	主体，时间	
		债券评级上调	主体，时间	
		债券评级下调	主体，时间	
公司声誉	违规处罚	利益输送	主体，时间	
		内幕交易	主体，时间	
		行政整改	主体，时间	
		行业整顿	主体，时间	
		通报批评	主体，时间	
		监管处罚	主体，时间	
		停业整顿	主体，时间	
		自查违规	主体，时间	
		资产被查封	主体，时间，数值	
		其他违规行为	主体，时间	
	诉讼纠纷	提起诉讼	主体，时间	
		收到起诉	主体，时间	
	公司丑闻	产品服务负面消息	主体，时间	
		造假欺诈	主体，时间	
		内部丑闻	主体，时间	

Fig. 1. Overview of schema

3.2   Data Annotation

Data Annotation includes originalq texts reading, subject prompting, event type detecting, argument annotating and tag integrating. Event subject is automatically highlighted based on the company knowledge base. Event types detection and argument extraction are based on Label Studio[8]. The details are shown in Fig. 2.

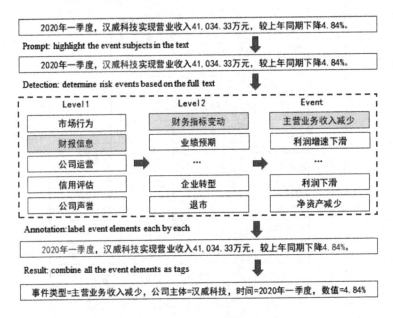

Fig. 2. Detail of data annotation

4   Experiments

We conducted internal evaluations of event detection and argument extraction respectively based on the pipeline.

Event Detection. Event detection is based on whether the event type is correctly detected, with a detection label as 1 and a non-detection label as 0. For event detection, we considered three options: do multi-label binary classification of text with TextCNN based on open-source word vectors; input

---

[8] https://labelstud.io/.

[CLS]*context*[SEP] into BERT and do multi-label binary classification with [CLS] based on open-source language models; combine the event type or description as a prompt with the context, like [CLS]*event_type*[SEP]*context*[SEP], as an input into BERT to do a binary classification with [SEP].

Argument Extraction. Argument extraction only evaluates whether the argument type is correct. The correctly extracted argument types are labeled as 1, while the opposite is labeled as 0. For event argument extraction, we also consider three options: as an entity recognition task, with [CLS]*context*[SEP] as an input into BERT and the entity, event type and argument attributes as outputs; as a reading comprehension task with event type or description as queries, like [CLS]*event_type*[SEP]*context*[SEP], as an input into BERT to get entities and argument attributes of *context*; as an entity recognition task for feature fusion, with [CLS]*context*[SEP] as an input into BERT where *context* is merged with event type vector to output entities and argument attributes of the texts.

$$P = \frac{TP}{TP + FP} \quad R = \frac{TP}{TP + FN} \quad F1 = 2 \cdot \frac{P \cdot R}{P + R} \tag{1}$$

The performances are demonstrated in the tables below (Tables 1 and 2).

Table 1. Event detection

	Micro-F1	Macro-F1
TextCNN	0.6857	0.4952
BERT	0.7091	0.5014
BERT-Prompt	0.6769	0.4663

Table 2. Argument extraction

	Micro-F1	Macro-F1
BERT-NER	0.5085	0.4531
BERT-MRC	0.6336	0.5775
BERT-CasRel	0.6649	0.6139

Because trigger words do not always exist explicitly, it is difficult to detect events through text classification. On the one hand, irrelevant description will affect the representation of the full text. On the other hand, events in terms of investment are very similar in terms of semantics, such as profit transmission and insider trading. The similarity of events also leads to argument extraction errors, which are mainly reflected in semantic roles, including irrelevant argument extraction and argument category errors.

The events can be divided in terms of identification difficulty based on the performance of the model and actual feedback from business, which is shown in Table 3.

Table 3. Difficulty level of event types

Difficulty	Event
Easy	利益输送、业绩承诺未达标、造假欺诈、产品服务负面消息、大股东减持、股份回购、延期披露、债务增加、债务减少、业务合作、股份解禁、债务重组、股权质押、行政整改、退市、内幕交易、监管处罚、股权激励、裁员、主营业务收入减少、利润下滑、董监高—主动离职、董监高—被迫离职、复牌、债券违约、爆炸事故、场所失火、利润增速下滑、主体评级上调、重大资产重组、债券评级上调、主体评级下调、债券评级下调、戴帽、停牌、股价异常波动、自然灾害、资产被查封、内部丑闻
Hard	公司收购、破产清算、关联交易、引进战略投资、提起诉讼、收到起诉、企业转型、发行股份、净资产减少、业绩暴雷、担保风险预警、业务重组、资产剥离、行业整顿、通报批评、自查违规、其他违规行为、产品创新、 资产注入、停业整顿

5　Conclusion

This paper presents a Chinese fine-grained dataset for event type extraction, which provides experience for the construction of the datasets for event extraction in the investment field. Annotators identify the significant financial events that reflect investment risks based on their domain expertise in investment. As the field covers widely and investment risks are subject to policies and regulations, we will make continual update as our follow-up work.

References

1. Song, Z., et al.: From light to rich ERE: annotation of entities, relations, and events. In: Proceedings of the 3rd Workshop on EVENTS at the NAACL-HLT, pp. 89–98 (2015)
2. Wang, X., et al.: MAVEN: a massive general domain event detection dataset. In: Proceedings of EMNLP, pp. 1652–1671 (2020)
3. Li, X., et al.: DuEE: a large-scale dataset for Chinese event extraction in real-world scenarios. In: Zhu, X., Zhang, M., Hong, Yu., He, R. (eds.) NLPCC 2020. LNCS (LNAI), vol. 12431, pp. 534–545. Springer, Cham (2020). https://doi.org/10.1007/978-3-030-60457-8_44
4. Trong, H.M.D., et al.: Introducing a new dataset for event detection in cybersecurity texts. In: Proceedings of the 2020 Conference on Empirical Methods in Natural Language Processing (EMNLP), pp. 5381–5390 (2020)
5. Satyapanich, T., Ferraro, F., Finin, T.: CASIE: extracting cybersecurity event information from text. In: Proceedings of the AAAI Conference on Artificial Intelligence, vol. 34, no. 05, pp. 8749–8757 (2020)
6. Lee, M., et al.: An annotated commodity news corpus for event extraction (2021)
7. Sims, M., Park, J.H., Bamman, D.: Literary event detection. In: Proceedings of the 57th Annual Meeting of the Association for Computational Linguistics, pp. 3623–3634 (2019)

ELETerm: A Chinese Electric Power Term Dataset

Yi Yang, Liangliang Song[✉], Shuyi Zhuang, Shi Chen, and Juan Li

State Grid Jiangsu Electric Power Company Research Institute, Nanjing, China
`songliang1005@163.com`

Abstract. The domain-specific knowledge graph construction and its corresponding applications are gradually attracting the attention of researchers. However, the lack of professional knowledge and term datasets restricts the development of domain-specific knowledge graph. In the electric power field, knowledge graph has been verified effective in electric fault monitoring, power consumer service, and decision-making on dispatching. Although the electric power knowledge graph is of great application prospects, it is difficult for artificial intelligence experts to create professional knowledge and terms for knowledge graph construction. To assist the process of building electric power knowledge graph, we introduce a new Chinese electric term dataset (ELETerm) containing 10,043 terms. We make full use of reliable data resources from State Grid Jiangsu Electric Power Company Research Institute to extract terms. Our approach includes four stages: word extraction, candidate term selection, term expansion, and dataset generation. We give the statistics and analysis of the dataset. The dataset is publicly available under CC BY-SA 4.0 in github.

Keywords: Term dataset · Term extraction · Electric power knowledge

Resource type: Dataset

Github Repository: https://github.com/wuyike2000/ELETerm

1 Introduction

Knowledge Graph [16] has been proven effective in modeling structured information and professional knowledge. In the electric power field, knowledge graph is attracting attention from both academic and electric industries due to its power to break the knowledge isolated island and the corresponding applications [14]. Different from general knowledge graphs, the electric power knowledge graph is highly professional, which means the construction process usually requires large numbers of domain-specific terms.

The definition of the term is a set of expressions used to represent concepts in a specific domain. Unithood and termhood are two basic characteristics of terms. Unithood refers to the possibility that words become a stable structure, and termhood is defined as the degree that a linguistic unit relates to domain-specific concepts [15].

© The Author(s), under exclusive license to Springer Nature Singapore Pte Ltd. 2022
M. Sun et al. (Eds.): CCKS 2022, CCIS 1669, pp. 211–216, 2022.
https://doi.org/10.1007/978-981-19-7596-7_17

To extract such domain-specific terms, lots of existing studies have explored different methods. Some of them [4,13] leverage the experience of experts and semantic rule based methods to design hand-crafted features and extract terms from domain-specific corpus, which requires sufficient labeled data, and large annotation costs. With the great success of deep learning models, some studies [2, 3] attempt to propose a term extraction model using the combination of Bi-directional Long Short-Term Memory (BiLSTM) [5] and Conditional Random Field (CRF) [11].

Although the previous studies have achieved good results, it still has the following problems, especially in the electric power field. Firstly, the existing studies are usually used for method testing, and seldom generating large-scale domain-specific datasets; secondly, in the evaluation phase, it is hard for technologists to judge the correctness of the extracted terms since they are not familiar with domain-specific knowledge.

As a result, a high-quality dataset of electric power terms is still blank, which restricts the construction of professional knowledge graphs and their applications. To address this issue, we introduce ELETerm, a new Chinese term dataset, in which terms are extracted from business documents and professional documents. We first utilize various statistical textual features to extract keywords in documents, and invite experts to select terms from these keywords. Then we adopt the IOB2 format [12] to annotate the extracted terms for discovering more domain-specific terms with the BiLSTM-CRF model. We summarize contributions of this paper as follows:

- We build the first Chinese term dataset ELETerm in the field of electric power. We combine automated techniques and expert experience to extract high-quality terms from real-world electric power relevant documents.
- We publish ELETerm as an open resource. This dataset could help artificial intelligence (AI) experts to develop the electric power knowledge graphs. ELETerm is publicly available under CC BY-SA 4.0 in github.

2   The ELETerm Dataset

2.1   Data Resources

ELETerm is derived from a large scale text corpus composed of 87 business documents and professional documents from State Grid Jiangsu Electric Power Company Research Institute. As shown in Table 1, business documents contain the documents about equipment ledgers, protection setting values, power grid events, protection action information, device alarm information, defect disposal, and etc., which are stored in the provincial D5000 system (a document management system), the operation management system, and the production management system. The professional documents include the documents about substation secondary drawings, regulations, technical standards, work instructions, calibration reports, installation instructions, training courses, and competition question bases.

Table 1. Resources of ELETerm dataset.

Business documents	Equipment ledgers, Protection setting values
	Protection action information
	Device alarm information, Defect disposal
	Power grid events, etc.
Professional knowledge documents	Substation secondary drawings
	Installation instructions, Training courses
	Regulations, Technical standards
	Work instructions, Calibration reports
	Competition question bases

2.2 Data Processing

To construct ELETerm, we propose a electric power term dataset construction approach, which has four stages. As shown in Fig. 1, in **Stage One: Word Extraction**, we extract words from our text corpus; **Stage Two: Candidate Term Selection** is divided into two steps, and we first select keywords by many statistical textual features, then electric power experts select terms among the keywords; as for **Stage Three: Term Expansion**, we adopt the IOB2 format for data annotation, and get terms by the BiLSTM-CRF model; in **Stage Four: Dataset Generation**, we use the terms from the above stages to build ELETerm.

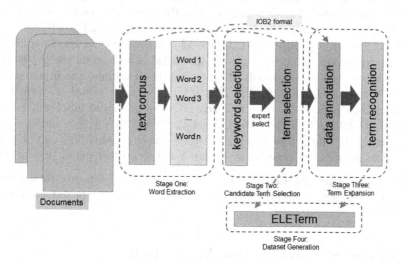

Fig. 1. The overview of the ELETerm dataset construction approach.

Stage One: Word Extraction. We first extract words from text corpus. We employ a classic statistical feature based word extraction method [7] to generate words from text corpus due to its good generalization ability in Chinese word extraction. In this stage, we can extract 32,758 candidate words.

Stage Two: Candidate Term Selection. We propose a term selection approach, including two steps: **1) keyword selection:** we adopt a voting method to select keywords from the extracted candidate words. We first use three methods, including RAKE [10], TextRank [6], YAKE [1], to extract keywords from the candidate words. RAKE and YAKE are statistical textual feature based models for keyword extraction; TextRank is another graph-based ranking model for keyword extraction. Only the candidate words which are determined as keywords by at least two of these three methods will be accepted. We obtain approximately 6,100 keywords after this step; **2) term selection:** we invite electric power experts from State Grid Corporation of China to filter out the keywords (e.g., "人工智能控制 *(artificial intelligence control)*") which are irrelevant to the electric power field. Here, we obtain 4,328 accurate terms.

Stage Three: Term Expansion. While the terms extracted from stage two are of high accuracy, their number is too small. Thus, we propose a term expansion approach, including two steps: **1) data annotation:** we use the extracted terms to annotate the text corpus in the IOB2 format [12]. "B" denotes that the character is the begin of a term; "I" denotes that the character is the intermediate of a term; "O" denotes others which mean that the character does not belong to any term. We first segment the corpus into sentences, and remove the stop words. Then, we take the extracted terms as seeds to annotate the processed sentences. Specially, for each character in a given sentence, if it is the begin of a term, then it will be annotated "B"; if it is the intermediate of a term, then it will be annotated "I"; else it will be annotated "O". **2) term recognition:** We first use the annotated sentences to train a BiLSTM-CRF model [8] which uses the Conditional Random Field (CRF) to output the optimal label sequences in the IOB2 format. The BiLSTM-CRF model is proved to have good performance in term extraction; then, we send the unlabeled sentences as the input to the model, it will output the labels of sentences. For example, the input is "模拟信号的特征在于时间和数值的连续变化 *(The analog signal is characterized by continuous changes in time and value)*". The predicted label will be "*BII-IOOOOOOOOOOOOOOOO*". We will get the term "模拟信号 *(analog signal)*" by selecting the characters which are corresponded to label "B" and "I". After manual verification by experts, we obtain 5,484 terms to expand the dataset.

Stage Four: Dataset Generation. Finally, we use the terms obtained from stage two and stage three to build ELETerm, and this term dataset contains 10,043 terms in total.

3   Datasets Statistics and Application

3.1   Statistics and Analysis

Owing to the different usage between nouns and verbs, we divide terms in ELETerm into two categories, and respectively analyze their words, the result is shown in Table 2.

Table 2. The analysis result of terms in different categories includes the lexicology feature: the average word length (Ave-Len), the statistical feature: the average word frequency in text corpus (Ave-Wfreq), and the dictionary feature: the proportion of words in dictionary of common words (Common-Wrate).

	Noun	Verb
Numb	6,408	3,625
The lexicology feature **Ave-Len**	5.095	3.976
The statistical feature **Ave-Wfreq**	0.078	0.069
The dictionary feature **Common-Wrate**	0.114	0.132

It can be found that the Ave-Len of both nominal and verbal terms in ELETerm is not small. This phenomenon reflects that terms usually are complex due to the extensive use of word nesting. For example, the term "压力传感器 *(pressure sensor)*" contains the shorter term "传感器 *(sensor)*". As for the statistical feature and the dictionary feature, both Ave-Wfreq and Common-Wrate are quite small, which shows that most of the obtained terms are sparse, and it is difficult to be extracted from general corpora and dictionaries.

3.2 Application

We introduce ELETerm to help AI researchers to develop knowledge graphs in the field of electric power without excessive supports of electric power experts. The verbal terms extracted from the text corpus usually is a concrete expression of the relationship in knowledge graphs. Therefore, a simple matching (e.g., automatic lexical comparison or manual judgement) between verbal terms and widely used relationship expressions in knowledge graphs could help the task of relation extraction. Moreover, ontology construction methods [9] can be divided into top-down methods driven by knowledge, the bottom-up methods driven by data, and the combination of both methods. The top-down ontology construction methods often define the classes using manually summarized domain-specific terms, while researchers can directly start to build a electric power ontology through the terms in ELETerm.

4 Conclusion and Future Work

In this paper, we introduce ELETerm, a Chinese domain-specific term dataset in the field of electric power. Based on high-quality resources, we carefully design a extraction approach to obtain a high-quality dataset. The statistics and analysis show the great prospect for ELETerm to further build electric power knowledge construction. The introduction of this dataset can help fill in the blank of the Chinese electric term dataset. As for the future work, we plan to continually expand this dataset and build large-scale electric power knowledge graph.

Acknowledgements. This work was supported by the Science and Technology Project of State Grid Jiangsu Electric Power Co., LTD. under Grant J2021129 Research on the construction technology of relay protection knowledge graph.

References

1. Campos, R., Mangaravite, V., Pasquali, A., Jorge, A.M., Nunes, C., Jatowt, A.: YAKE! collection-independent automatic keyword extractor. In: Pasi, G., Piwowarski, B., Azzopardi, L., Hanbury, A. (eds.) ECIR 2018. LNCS, vol. 10772, pp. 806–810. Springer, Cham (2018). https://doi.org/10.1007/978-3-319-76941-7_80
2. Giannakopoulos, A., Musat, C., Hossmann, A., Baeriswyl, M.: Unsupervised aspect term extraction with B-LSTM & CRF using automatically labelled datasets. arXiv preprint arXiv:1709.05094 (2017)
3. Han, X., Xu, L., Qiao, F.: CNN-BiLSTM-CRF model for term extraction in Chinese corpus. In: Meng, X., Li, R., Wang, K., Niu, B., Wang, X., Zhao, G. (eds.) WISA 2018. LNCS, vol. 11242, pp. 267–274. Springer, Cham (2018). https://doi.org/10.1007/978-3-030-02934-0_25
4. Hippisley, A., Cheng, D., Ahmad, K.: The head-modifier principle and multilingual term extraction. Nat. Lang. Eng. **11**(2), 129–157 (2005)
5. Huang, Z., Xu, W., Yu, K.: Bidirectional LSTM-CRF models for sequence tagging. arXiv preprint arXiv:1508.01991 (2015)
6. Li, W., Zhao, J.: TextRank algorithm by exploiting Wikipedia for short text keywords extraction. In: 2016 3rd International Conference on Information Science and Control Engineering (ICISCE), pp. 683–686. IEEE (2016)
7. Luo, S., Sun, M.: Two-character Chinese word extraction based on hybrid of internal and contextual measures. In: Proceedings of the Second SIGHAN Workshop on Chinese Language Processing, pp. 24–30 (2003)
8. Ma, J., Zhang, Y., Yao, S., Zhang, B., Guo, C.: Terminology extraction for new energy vehicle based on BiLSTM_Attention_CRF model. Appl. Res. Comput. **36**(05), 1385–9 (2019)
9. Noy, N.F., McGuinness, D.L., et al.: Ontology development 101: a guide to creating your first ontology (2001)
10. Rose, S., Engel, D., Cramer, N., Cowley, W.: Automatic keyword extraction from individual documents. Text Min. Appl. Theory **1**, 1–20 (2010)
11. Tseng, H., Chang, P.C., Andrew, G., Jurafsky, D., Manning, C.D.: A conditional random field word segmenter for SIGHAN bakeoff 2005. In: Proceedings of the Fourth SIGHAN Workshop on Chinese Language Processing (2005)
12. Vanegas, J.A., Matos, S., González, F., Oliveira, J.L.: An overview of biomolecular event extraction from scientific documents. Comput. Math. Methods Med. **2015** (2015)
13. Vu, T., Aw, A., Zhang, M.: Term extraction through unithood and termhood unification. In: Proceedings of the Third International Joint Conference on Natural Language Processing, vol. II (2008)
14. Wang, J., Wang, X., Ma, C., Kou, L.: A survey on the development status and application prospects of knowledge graph in smart grids. IET Gener. Transm. Distrib. **15**(3), 383–407 (2021)
15. Wong, W.: Determination of unithood and termhood for term recognition. In: Handbook of Research on Text and Web Mining Technologies, pp. 500–529 (2009)
16. Wu, T., Qi, G., Li, C., Wang, M.: A survey of techniques for constructing Chinese knowledge graphs and their applications. Sustainability **10**(9), 3245 (2018)

Author Index

Printed in the United States
by Baker & Taylor Publisher Services